Small Time Operator

HOW TO START YOUR OWN SMALL BUSINESS, KEEP YOUR BOOKS,
PAY YOUR TAXES, & STAY OUT OF TROUBLE

A Guide and Workbook
by Bernard Kamoroff, C.P.A.

Small-Time Operator discusses common types of laws and regulations affecting small businesses, including a general discussion of federal income tax laws. The information presented herein is meant to serve as a general guideline only. The information given is not intended to substitute for legal advice and cannot be considered as making it unnecessary to obtain such advice. In all situations involving local, state or federal law, obtain specific information from the appropriate government agency or from a competent person.

The word, once printed, cannot be altered. The laws, however, change all the time. Use the information in **Small-Time Operator** with this in mind.

You can keep this book up to date. This edition of **Small-Time Operator** is current as of the date shown below. Every January, we publish a one-page Update Sheet for **Small-Time Operator**, listing changes in tax laws and other government regulations, referenced to the corresponding pages in the book. If you would like a copy of the Update Sheet, send a self-addressed, stamped No. 10 envelope and $1.00 to **Small-Time Operator Update,** Box 640, Laytonville, CA 95454.

Published by
BELL SPRINGS PUBLISHING
Box 640 Bell Springs Road
Laytonville, California 95454
(707) 984-6746

17th Edition, 43rd printing, 1992
Printed in the United States of America
Library of Congress Catalog Number: 92-070267

ISBN: 0-917510-10-0

"**Small-Time Operator**" is a trademark of Bell Springs Publishing.

PRINTED ON RECYCLED PAPER

Many thanks to Jim Hayes for your original idea. To Jim Robertson for your encouragement and for suggesting the title. To Robert Greenway for helping to launch the company. To the business people who allowed me to interview them: Joe Campbell, Lara Stonebraker, Charles Dorton, Jan Lowe, Kathy Ward Eisman, Bob Mathews, Pat Ellington, Mike Simon, Nick Mein, Mike Snead, Mike Madson and Key Dickason. To the people who generously shared their expertise: Paul Paul and Mary Lai (insurance), Dave Raub and Tony Mancuso (corporations), Joe Sachs (SBA), Larry Jacobs (taxes), John Bobbitt (marketing), Lance Hoffman, Don McCunn and Leigh Robinson (computers). To my tireless editor Andy Blasky: this book would not be half as well written without him. To my photographers Kinu Haas and John Brenneman, my illustrators Bruce McCloskey, Kitty and Bill Emerson, and my dad David Kamoroff for drafting the ledgers. To the people who helped design and produce the book and get it out there: Hal Hershey, Sharon Miley, Dick Ellington, J'Ann Forgue, John Weed, Sharon Kamoroff, Peter and Paul deFremery, Cynthia Frank, John Fremont, Linda Gatter, Chuck Hathaway and Tommy Kay. To the people who had faith in me and supported the project when it was just a manuscript and a dream: Lance and Kathy Hoffman, Beth Hackenbruch, Jerry Eisman, Richard Benson and Paul and Laura Klipfel. To my long lost friend H. Berry. And especially to the sweet Yodelady. This book is dedicated to John Muir, The Mechanic.

In this world a man must either
be anvil or hammer.

—Longfellow

BE YOUR OWN BOSS

You can be your own boss. All it really requires is a good idea, some hard work, and a little knowledge. "A little knowledge" is what this book is all about. *Small-Time Operator* will show you how to start and operate your own small business.

Small-Time Operator is a technical manual, a step-by-step guide to help you set up the "machinery" of your business—the "business end" of your business—and keep it lubricated and well maintained. It is written in everyday English so anyone can understand it. You will not need a business education or an accounting dictionary to grasp the concepts or do the work. *Small-Time Operator* is also a workbook that includes bookkeeping instructions and a sample set of ledgers, especially designed for small businesses.

Many people think that businessmen and businesswomen all come out of business school, kind of like Chevys coming out of a G.M. assembly plant. This just isn't true. I know many people in business who had no formal business education and little or no experience. They are people just like you and me who got tired of the nine-to-five life, tired of working for someone else, and who decided to go into business for themselves. They have done it, and so can you.

Business, to many inexperienced people, is a mystifying and often maligned world. You mention the word, and they start thinking about giant corporations and oil monopolies. Businessmen, business suits, big business. The words conjure up images of subways and elevators crowded with men, all dressing alike, all talking alike, all thinking alike. To most people, business means *big business,* the world of the office and the corporation.

But there is such a thing as a small business, and the difference between big business and small business is more than just size. Men and women involved in big business work for someone or some company. They are employees. They have a job and they do it (or else they get fired). A small business, one that you yourself run, is completely different. You are your own boss. You are the person who is going to make the business work if it's going to work at all.

Small-Time Operator comes out of my experience during the past fifteen years as a financial advisor and tax accountant for small businesses, businesses started from scratch by inexperienced people, and from operating two of my own small businesses. I've learned from successes and I've learned from mistakes—my own and others'. Now I hope to teach you what I've learned.

Small-Time Operator will show you things to do and things not to do. But like any book, it can't do more than that. You've got to go ahead and do it yourself. Bilbo Baggins said, "One should always begin at the beginning." That's where you are now. Other people—many others—now run their own small businesses. You can too.

The journey of a thousand miles begins with a single step.
—*Lao Tzu*

Contents

Section One
GETTING STARTED

Trying seems to be a start for getting things done
You get to know the right way by doing it wrong
And when you cross a bridge over shallow water
Does it always mean you're afraid to get wet
When you ought to?

—Barbara Pack

A Small-Time Operator: A True Story

When I first met Joe several years ago, he was working as a switchman for Southern Pacific. He liked working on the railroad—didn't love it, but it was a job.

Joe's hobby and one of his great pleasures in life was electronics. He especially enjoyed assembling electrical gadgets from kits, repairing old radios, playing with anything that had wires and resistors. In the process of building and experimenting, Joe also acquired a good theoretical and technical knowledge of radio and electronics. It was not long before he'd built himself a few test meters and started repairing the neighbors' TV's and radios. He used to offer to fix my stereo for free, just to get the experience.

Gradually, Joe's hobby developed into a business. He moved slowly at first, a step at a time. He set up a small test bench in the spare bedroom and began taking in paying business on evenings and weekends. Joe was a good repairman, he didn't charge very much, and he gave his customers fast service. And Joe's business grew. He soon found himself with more business than he could handle in his spare time. He started working less hours for the railroad, then quit altogether and set up a small repair shop of his own.

Joe is a success, but not just because he makes his own living. Joe has shaped his life around his interests. He enjoys his work, and his customers recognize and appreciate the personal interest he takes in what he's doing. Joe "made it" because he worked hard to develop his interests and because he had the ambition to learn his trade. It *never* just comes naturally. Prior experience? He had none. A business background? None. Money? He saved a few hundred dollars to spend on test gear and parts, not much more.

The most important lesson to learn from Joe, I feel, is that you can start out easily and simply. You don't have to make the Big Plunge, selling everything you own and going into debt. Start slowly, try it out and learn as you go. You'll get there.

Things worked well for Joe. But if they had not—if he really did not have it in him to be in business for himself, or if he just picked the wrong thing at the wrong time—he could easily have stopped anywhere along the way with little or no loss. And maybe try it again sometime.

What Kind of Business?

Joe's repair shop is an example of what is commonly called a "service" business. He *does* something for his customers and they pay him for his services. You can also support yourself by *selling* something ("sales") or by *making* something ("manufacturing"). Many businesses combine several of these aspects, such as manufacturing and sales, or sales and service.

A *service* business is the easiest to set up. It requires the smallest initial investment and the simplest bookkeeping. It is also the easiest kind of business to operate out of your own home. On the other hand, you will have to be reasonably competent at the service you render. More than any other business, service will require some experience. The owner of a service business is also more likely to be subject to state licenses and regulations (discussed in this section of the book).

If you do something well—fixing things, painting or decorating, writing or editing, cutting hair—these are all possibilities for your own service business. And if you are good at something, you might consider teaching those skills to others. Be imaginative. Don't ignore your own resources.

A *sales* business can take many different forms: retail, wholesale, storefront, mail order, door-to-door. Your own sales business allows you to select and handle merchandise that reflects your own interests and tastes and your personal estimate of the needs of your community. Most sales businesses will require inventory (stock on hand) which means a bigger investment than a service business. You are also more likely to need a storefront to display your goods. You will have to keep inventory records. Bookkeeping is a little more complex. Sales businesses, however, offer more flexibility than service. Service people are often limited by their training and experience. With sales, as your interests change and as the fashions change, it is easy for your sales business to change with them.

Manufacturing, for most small businesses, means crafts—leather, clothing, pottery, jewelry and furniture to name a very few. Crafts offer, probably more than any other business, an opportunity for the craftsperson to do what he or she enjoys for its own pleasure, and get paid for it, too.

A crafts business, on the other hand, is probably the most risky business of all. You will need money to invest in your materials and your tools. Again, you have to be good at what you're doing. Nobody wants an ugly necklace or a chair that falls apart. And more than with a simple sales or service business, you will have more work finding a steady and reliable market for your product. But if you have imagination and talent, you might discover that what you think of as your hobby can become your source of income.

Mike Madsen owns Mike Madsen Leather, Oakland, California: "Look around, figure out what you want to do, and then try to sum up your business in one sentence or a paragraph at the most. No more than that or you haven't done it. And then concentrate on doing just that. Realize that business is just like life in a lot of ways, and you take things step by step. You don't become a big business overnight. You build it little by little every day you walk into the building. You get started through your own will and determination and have a little fun at it.

"You can learn an awful lot by observation. Anyone in a small business should try to visit other people who are in similar businesses. When I was in Argentina I went to seven leather factories. They're very willing to show you something when you're not in direct competition, and they're kind of pleased to show off their business. But if you and I lived in the same city, you might be less willing to show your manufacturing process to a future competitor.

"Small business is the backbone of this country. Big businesses provide main-line products, but it's the small business that provides all the little things that make your life interesting. I think it's also the kind of people who are in small business, those of a pioneering spirit. We built a country on pioneering spirit. That's just what being in a small business is, being a pioneer."

Can You Do It?

You don't have to be an expert in the line of business that you're thinking of going into, but you do have to be willing to learn. There are people who actually try to start a certain business because it's a "sure thing," a "guaranteed" big seller, and they know absolutely nothing about the field. Some of these people are, of course, real hustlers, selling refrigerators to Eskimos and all that. Not my favorite kind of people. But there are also a lot of honest dopes in this group. They think that a little money and some good intentions are all they need to get started. And most of them soon wind up with neither their money nor any intention of ever being in business again.

I've known a lot of people in business—some who made it, some who didn't. And while nobody has a guaranteed secret for success in business, I believe that there are a few basic characteristics that you've got to have or be willing to develop if you're going to start a business, *any* business.

The first and most important characteristic, I feel, is a clear head and the ability to organize your mind and your life. The "absent-minded professor" may be a genius, but he will never keep a business together. In running a small business, you are going to have to deal with many different people, keep schedules, meet deadlines, organize paperwork, pay bills, and the list goes on. It's all part of every business. So if balancing your checkbook is too much for you, or you just burned up your car engine because you forgot to check the oil, maybe you're not cut out for business. The work in a small business is rarely complicated, but it has to be done and done on time. Remember, this is going to be *your* business. It's all up to you.

A second important characteristic is the ability to read carefully. Most of your business transactions will be handled on paper, and if you don't pay attention to what you're doing, you could miss out. You may receive special orders for your product. You will be billed by your suppliers in all kinds of

---

Find a need and fill it.
    —*lettered on a concrete truck in Oakland, CA.*

ways, sometimes offering discounts if you are prompt in paying. You will have to fill out a lot of government forms. Government agencies can't exist without forms, and the instructions for these forms are sometimes tricky. If you mess up, these agencies have the most aggravating way of casually telling you that you're going to have to do it all over again.

A third important trait is, if not a "head for numbers," at least a lack of fear of numbers. Tax accountants get rich off of people who look at a column of six numbers and panic. It doesn't have to be that way. The math involved in running a small business is mostly simple arithmetic—addition, subtraction, some multiplication.

Is all of this too much for you? Still feel you have a good product or a good service to sell but, Oh! all this paperwork…. If you are alone in your venture, short of hiring a bookkeeper or finding a partner, there is no alternative. You're gonna have to learn to do it. Very often, however, the future business owner with no business moxie is blessed with a wife or husband who has all those fine traits and is just itchin' to be part of it all.

Beyond the numbers, if you plan to operate a retail store, a service business, or any other business where you will be in regular contact with the public, you should be a person who likes to deal with people. Are you friendly and outgoing, pleased to talk about your products—and the weather, the ball scores, and the latest neighborhood gossip? Do you like selling, solving people's problems, listening to complaints, answering the same questions over and over again? Do you look forward to running a store five, six or even seven days a week, keeping regular hours, stocking shelves, doing repetitive tasks every day?

There are many fine people, potentially excellent business people, who are not the outgoing type, who would never survive behind the counter, and who certainly shouldn't be running a retail operation. And fortunately, there are many businesses that don't require these personality traits. Mail-order businesses, manufacturing businesses, some service businesses, businesses where you don't face the public every day, businesses where you know all your customers, businesses where you do custom work for only a few people—these businesses do not rely so much on your personality, and they won't require that you constantly act and dress a certain way.

Mike Madsen, Mike Madsen Leather: "You talk to people who are outside of business, they don't understand it. You talk to somebody who's on a fixed income or working on a salary or an educator or a student, they don't understand what being in business is. They're not risk takers. They're not striving to make a whole number of things work simultaneously. They go to work in the morning or go to school and have a prescribed routine and they get off at five o'clock, and they go home and their business is done. But if you're in business for yourself, you don't turn off the switch when you go home. You're constantly thinking about it.

Your Idea—and the Market

Every person who has ever started a business, I imagine, thought he had a good idea. It's the smart person, and the rare person, who tries to find out the most important thing: do other people think it's a good idea? The majority of new businesses fail because the majority of new business owners never looked past their own desires and dreams, gave no real forethought to their ventures—no "market research," which is just a fancy term for "look before you leap."

Do people really want what you have to sell? Can you find these people and convince them that they should buy from you instead of from someone else—someone else who may have a better product, a better price, a better location, a good reputation?

No matter how good your business idea is, you still must have a market—someone who is willing to buy your product or pay for your services. Talk to your friends; they're consumers. How many of them would buy what you have to sell? Then look around your community. Does your product or service fit the social, economic and ethnic make-up of the area? Will your product appeal to these people? And can they afford it? How many other businesses in the area are doing the same thing? What would it be like to compete with them? Don't be afraid to talk with your future competition. You will learn a lot from them, not only about the business but also about your chances for success. A new business always starts at a disadvantage. Try not to duplicate services already available in your area unless you have good reason to believe that you can attract customers away from existing businesses.

DESIGNER PRETZELS
THEY COST MORE BUT
AREN'T YOU WORTH IT!

P. Steiner

Mike Simon, owner of Metric Motors, Palm Springs, California: "There are some people who want to work for themselves, and they're not going to be happy working for anybody else. And then other people don't like the responsibility. They want to go in and work their nine to five and not have to worry about it when they go home. It takes a certain kind of person to do your own business, to accept the responsibilities of it and be thinking abut it all the time. The first two years I worked, I worked seven days a week from seven o'clock in the morning until seven o'clock at night. And now I take Sundays off. But I wouldn't have it any other way. I could have made a lot more money the other way, working for somebody else, but I'm happy with the way it is. And I think later in the future it will be to my advantage. As for the guy who's working nine to five, I'll be better off than he is. Of course, he thinks he's better off than I am."

Business Location

Your choice of location will be one of the most important decisions you will make when going into business, so consider it carefully.

For retail stores, retail service businesses, restaurants, and other businesses where customers come to you, location is critical. A bad neighborhood, a street that's hard to find, a location away from other shops, a location where it's difficult to park, a store too far away from the kind of customer you seek—any of these factors can easily lead to business failure, quickly. Do not underestimate the importance of location. Do not settle for a poor location. Do not compromise.

Many people want to locate in their own neighborhood, but is it a good business area? How many people shop in your neighborhood? Is there adequate parking? Is there already a similar business in the area?

Before you rent a storefront, find out why it's vacant in the first place. Try to locate the former tenant and ask him why he moved. Talk to other shopkeepers in the area and learn as much as you can about the area and its shoppers. A nearby supermarket or discount store is usually a plus because it will draw a lot of people to your area. Be wary if there are several unoccupied buildings for rent. Besides being a general sign of a poor business area, vacant buildings make poor neighbors. Shoppers tend to stay away from them—and from you. Spend a full day or two observing the area. A steady stream of pedestrians passing by your door is the biggest single help a little store can get.

For businesses that don't rely on customers coming to the door—manufacturers, wholesalers, crafts workshops, mail-order operators, many service businesses—location is no longer of critical concern. You can find a place suitable to your own needs: close to home, inexpensive, close proximity to your suppliers and the services you require, easy access for deliveries and pick-ups.

In many cities, small businesses are finding excellent facilities in old and formerly run-down warehouse and industrial areas of town. Real estate developers are buying old, abandoned commercial buildings, fixing them up, cutting them up into smaller offices, shops, and warehouse spaces; and renting at prices much, much lower than you'll find in busy shopping areas.

A different approach to this new wave of busi-

If you can't do it excellently, don't do it at all. Because if it's not excellent it won't be profitable or fun, and if you're not in business for fun or profit, what the hell are you doing here?

—*Robert Townsend from Up the Organization*

ness redevelopment are the "business incubators" popping up in many cities. Incubators provide, in addition to a location, pooled support services such as secretaries, management counselors, exhibit and conference rooms, shared truck docks, and other amenities. As the term implies, incubators are often first-step locations for new businesses. After a few years, you no longer need nor care to pay for their assistance or other support services. You are ready to be totally on your own. You've been hatched, so to speak.

Most incubators are privately owned, profit-making ventures; but some are publicly funded and supported. The U.S. Small Business Administration (the SBA) works with a lot of public and private business incubators across the country. If you are interested, contact a local SBA office for a list of incubators in your area.

No matter where you finally decide to locate, before you sign a rental agreement, be sure the building is right for you. Is it large enough, or is it perhaps too large? Will it require extensive remodeling? Can you afford it? Can you get a suitable lease? Without a lease, the landlord can—with little or no notice—evict you or arbitrarily raise the rent to any amount he pleases. Have the store examined by the local building inspector and, if you plan to serve food, by the health inspector. You don't want to learn after you've moved in that you must spend a thousand bucks to bring the premises up to code.

How about locating your business at home? Many businesses are perfectly suited to being run out of the home; and many, of course, are not. There is a long chapter in the Appendix on Home Based Businesses.

"As far as I'm concerned, location is everything." Lara Stonebraker, Cunningham's Coffee in Oakland, California: "That can make or break a business. If you don't already have an established reputation, nobody will go looking for you in some obscure place. So you have to be where there is a lot of foot traffic, and you have to be located next to some other significant business that already has a clientele you can draw on.

"The corner is obviously the best choice, and you usually have to pay more rent for it. The middle of the block is less desirable because there isn't the visibility that a corner affords and there's not as much parking. Parking can be a great problem. I've known

a lot of very fine businesses to fail because people would just get exasperated not being able to find a parking space and never go in them.

"One of the things we did at every location we looked at was spend a day just sitting around, hanging around, and watching the traffic flow, the patterns of the way people walk, where they stopped, and how many people came in and out of different stores in order to assess the desirability of that location.

"When you negotiate your lease you want to be careful not to do it before you talk to the building inspector and the health inspector and find out what the building codes and health codes are for your particular business. We made the mistake of seeing them after we signed the lease and then discovered that we had to put in just a load of improvements that rightfully should not have been our responsibility. That was a tremendous amount of money which will just be lost. They don't check old businesses, but they check every new one. You apply for a permit; you have to get a business license, then they know what kind of business it is and they send out their people. If you're doing any kind of reconstruction inside and any electrical work, the plumber has to get a permit, the electrician has to get a permit—you can't get away from it. And they'll come around every six months to check and see that everything is up to code if you're handling food."

Joe Campbell owns Resistance Repair, a stereo repair shop in Berkeley, California. He recently moved his shop *away from* a high foot traffic area into a more remote section of town:

"In a service business, especially a technical service business, customers don't have the slightest idea how to determine even the most rudimentary things about their equipment. If it doesn't work, they don't have the means of determining what is wrong. So you get an incredible amount of people who come in and just bullshit with you about some problem which is extremely minor and usually is a hookup problem. They've just got it hooked up wrong, which means they didn't read their instruction book. But it's very hard to convince them of that, and they all want detailed explanations.

"If you're in a high foot traffic area, you get the guy who's going to the restaurant next door for lunch, and as he walks out he thinks, 'Ah, there's a stereo repair shop. I'll stop in here and ask this guy about my problem...' and he comes in and there's twenty minutes gone. And the next guy comes in and there's fifteen minutes gone. You get all the people in town who have wires that need to be soldered. You get people who come in and say, 'I need your recommendation of the fifteen best stereos you can buy, and why.' Just enormous energy sinks and time sinks. Those people do not spend money. The kind of people who spend money are the people who walk in the door with stereos under their arms, and say, 'Fix this mother, it doesn't work, and call me when it's ready.'

"My traffic was never off the street. It was from referrals from other stereo shops. I took around cards and there was such a big demand for a reasonable, good repair shop that they'd send people by. You don't need those twerks who walk in off the street. You need the people who have the confidence in you and, by reputation, know that they can dump it in your hands. Now, when somebody walks through that door they've either got a stereo under their arm or they're there to pick one up. If they're there to pick it up, that means when they leave you're going to have money in the cash register. If they're coming in the door with one, that means two weeks later you're going to have money in the cash register. Those are the only two reasons you want that front door to open."

Another Roadside Attraction: A Business in the Country

Perhaps you're thinking about moving out of the city altogether to set up a small business in the country. Many people try to open shops out there in the sticks, and a very large percentage of these rural shops fail. The reason is solely this: there's not enough people and there's not enough money in rural communities to support anything but the most basic businesses. The typical small town has a grocery, general store or hardware store, feed store, tavern and gas station. If the population is more than a few thousand, there may be a clothing store, a restaurant, a video store and a beauty parlor. Not much else.

A hanging plant store is not going to survive in West Pork Chop, Oklahoma. Nor will a gourmet coffee and tea shop, an art gallery or a leather crafts workshop. The business just isn't there. Service businesses—repair shops, trades—have the best chance of survival in a rural area. But even these will probably have to compete with established locals who already know everyone in town and have all the business.

If you are interested in setting up a country store, first take a drive through some small towns and see what's there. If you do come across a shop of the sort you have in mind, stop in and find out how they're doing, how long they've been there, and—if they'll tell you—any of their "secrets of success." When you have a particular area in mind, get to know the area and its inhabitants first before you try to set up a business. Ideally, you should live there a while, and then try to judge what product or service the people need. Most country people are not wealthy; they don't spend money on things they have no use for.

Before You Act

Let's say you've decided on an idea for a new business. Now comes the most important step:

Ponder
   Think
      Relax

Let the idea simmer for a week or two and see how it feels then. Picture yourself as the owner-operator of the business you have in mind. Does it still sound like a good idea? This new business is going to take a lot of your time and energy. Above all else, it's got to feel right.

Lara Stonebraker, Cunningham's Coffee: "If you don't enjoy what you're doing, it's going to be very obvious to the customers. It will be obvious in your attitude. I find it very exciting, and I also find it a great challenge to try to make the business profitable. That's why I look at all the angles to decrease my expenses and bring in more income. I want to prove that I can do it. I don't just want a mediocre business, I want a booming business."

You can make a thing—a book or a house or a camera—in such a way that it commands respect. I hate to think that the only people who care about the way things are made are a couple of oddball craftsmen out in the woods. The culture needs the attitude of making things with purpose, attention to detail and a certain kind of love
—*James Robertson, publisher & book crafter*

Financing: How Much Do You Need?

How much money you need depends a lot on the type of business you are starting and the type of person you are. If you are willing to work hard, to make a few sacrifices, to live on canned beans for a while, you can start a successful business for little or no investment.

Every service business I know started with almost no money. I started my accounting practice with a $30 adding machine and 500 business cards. My friend Joe Campbell started Resistance Repair with $500 worth of test equipment. Another friend's computer programming service was started with $50 in supplies. Self-employed carpenters, mechanics and repair people often start with their box of tools, period.

If you start a crafts business, you will need, besides your tools, raw materials to make your product. But you do not have to stock a large supply of inventory, and if you hunt around you can always find good deals on remnants and close-out materials. All of the craft business owners interviewed for this book started their businesses with less than $1000 initial investment.

A retail store requires a good stock of inventory, which will cost at least a few thousand dollars, often a good deal more. A retail business can sometimes save on initial inventory costs by taking goods on consignment, as in a custom dress shop, or by having only samples on hand and taking orders for the goods.

Mike Simon, owner of Metric Motors (a repair shop): "I started with basically nothing and built from that. I had a box of hand tools, and my partner had some heavy equipment, jacks and things like that, nothing very impressive. If I had to have a tool, I'd buy it and then I'd have it. I'd just keep going like that. I guess I have about $3,000 worth of equipment now. A lot of garage owners buy $20,000 worth of equipment right at the start and don't have the clientele to pay it off. I'd say starting out small would be a very smart thing to do. Find some place that's not expensive to rent, like this place. Don't put a lot of money into tools or inventory, and try to keep your costs down to a minimum until you can build your business up."

Lara Stonebraker's coffee shop (a retail store):

"The worst thing you can do is start a retail business on a shoestring. If you're under-capitalized in the beginning, your store will not be impressive when you open because it will be empty. There's nothing worse than walking into an empty store. It's just bound to fail because it embarrasses people. If you don't have your shelves just crammed with stuff, and if you don't have an attractive, prosperous looking store, you might as well forget it. And you really ought to have not only enough money to open the doors, but enough money to run the business for the first six months, because you'll be running it at a loss for sure."

Jan Lowe, former owner of the Midnight Sewing Machine, Mendocino, California (clothing store): "One of our biggest problems was that we started with zero capital. We had 37 cents to our name after we bought the shop. You can't really expect to start it out that way. You gotta have some kind of backing. I don't know what amount it would take, but I know 37 cents didn't make it."

Key Dickason is the former co-owner of Xanadu Computer Service: "We got the business on a no-cash deal. We just took over their accounts, and the only thing the prior owner wanted was that we continue the employees on. We didn't have to pay anything. We just took the equipment and the accounts and the employees."

Mike Snead, manager/operator of Ms. Perc Leather, San Francisco: "Starting on a shoestring is a very viable concept. It's possible to start with nothing and build something up, but it involves a lot of sacrifices. It did for us."

Pat Ellington, Kipple Antiques, Berkeley, California: "We started this business on $1,400 cash and a lot of work, a lot of energy. When my partner first approached me with the idea for the business, she asked, 'What do you think it will take—how much money?' I sat down and figured out cost sheets, budgets, projections. And the very best I could come up with for six months' operation was $15,000, which appalled her. But that was reasonable. It was as cheap as I could get it, because you've got to assume you're going to lose your shirt the first six months."

Start-Up Capital:
Financing A New Business

There are three typical financing arrangements for new businesses: (1) Self-financing—you put up your own money. (2) Debt financing—you borrow money from a bank, an individual, the Small Business Administration (the SBA) or some other source. (3) Equity financing—you take on a partner or a stockholder—an individual who acquires an ownership interest in your business in exchange for start-up money.

Self-Financing

Just about every new business is at least partly self-financed, and many are 100% self-financed. A lot of new business owners simply cannot find anyone to loan them money or to invest in their untested and obviously risky ventures. Just as often, however, new business owners do not want the risk and pressure of having to pay off a loan, and do not want to worry about—or share the profits with—a partner or co-owner.

Debt Financing (Loans)

When someone lends you money, you promise to pay it back, usually with interest. Most business loans are also personal loans; you, the owner of the business, personally guarantee the loan, and you must repay the loan whether your business succeeds or not, out of your personal non-business assets if necessary. This is quite different from "equity financing" where you acquire a partner or an investor who only gets paid back if the business succeeds.

Most loans to new businesses come from relatives, friends, and acquaintances in the community. Conventional bank loans are very difficult to get for first-time business people. People who know you, and possibly people they know, are much more likely to help finance your venture than an extra-cautious, policy-laden bank. You just have to ask around. Quite often, someone you know or someone you can be introduced to has some extra money, and might be willing to take a chance on your business if they like you and your idea and the terms of the financing. There are no real standards when it comes to this kind of informal financing. People lending you money will most likely want a better interest rate than they will get at a bank. Often they already have a good idea of the rate they would like to get. The repayment terms are entirely between you and the lender.

Private loans should be in writing and should include the names and addresses of the lender and borrower, the amount of the loan, the date the loan was given, the interest rate, and the pay-back terms. Most loans are paid back over a period of months or years, with equal periodic payments. Some loans are repaid all at once at the end of the loan period. Again, the terms are entirely up to the lender and borrower. You may also want a clause in the agreement allowing you to pay off the loan early without penalty if you, the borrower, so desire.

The loan agreement should be prepared in duplicate, a copy for the lender and a copy for the borrower, and both parties should sign and date both copies. If the agreement is kept simple, you can write it up yourself. No need for careful legal wording or lawyers. If the agreement gets complicated, with late-payment penalties, collateral, provisions for death of one of the parties, etc., you will probably want professional help drafting the agreement. You should find out if your state requires a notary's endorsement, filing or registering the loan papers, or other requirements. Your state's Secretary of State office, the county clerk, or the city hall clerk can probably give you information.

When the loan is finally paid off, it is a good idea to have the lender write "Paid in full" on your copy, and sign and date it. If the loan is filed with the state or county, the final pay-off should also be recorded.

Bank Loans

Bank loans are hard to get. The banks are less willing than ever to take chances on new and untested businesses and new and untested entrepreneurs. Bankers, it seems, forget quickly how they managed to get rich in the first place—by taking chances on ventures just like yours.

The door is not completely closed. Banks still make some small business loans, and a bank just may make one to you. Banks generally will lend up to 50% of the required starting capital if they can be convinced that your business has a good potential for success, that you are competent and reliable, and that you have a good plan for repayment of the loan.

Not all banks are alike, so try several. A young and progressive bank is more likely to be interested in you and your needs than staid old First Conservative, Est. 1833. The physical appearance of the bank and the character of the bank's advertising may give you some indication of its progressiveness.

When you meet a banker, sell yourself. Openly discuss your plans and difficulties with him (or her). Come well prepared. Bring a personal resume, which should include your general and educational background and your prior experience. Bring a personal financial statement and a statement projecting income and expenses of your business for the first six months or year. The chapters "Profit And Loss Analysis" and "Cash Flow" in the bookkeeping section will help you to prepare this projection.

If you have done business with or obtained a loan from a particular bank, that bank is a good place to start. When a bank knows you, knows something of your willingness and capability to repay a loan, it will be more willing to give serious consideration to your ideas. If you have collateral, security to give the bank in exchange for a loan, you are yet another step closer to cash-in-hand. If you own your own home (if there is a mortgage on your home, you still "own" it) and are willing to mortgage it further, a bank may very likely loan you money on it.

But stop! Are you ready to risk your home or other valuables on your new business venture? When you borrow money for your business, you are *personally* liable to pay it back. If the business fails, you will be required to repay the loan from your personal funds. In taking out a loan, you are making a big personal commitment. Be sure you are not getting yourself in over your head.

Banks, when granting loans, will usually require you to take out property and liability insurance on your business and a personal life insurance policy naming the bank as beneficiary.

Other Possible Loan Sources

If you own a life insurance policy and have been making payments for at least a few years, you can probably borrow on the "cash value" of your policy. Most long-term life insurance policies acquire a cash value within a few years. That is, the policy is worth money to you. If you were to cash in your policy, you would receive that money—sort of a refund. As long as you keep the policy, you cannot get the money, but you can borrow as much as your cash value from the insurance company. The insurance policy remains effective during the loan. Interest rates on insurance policy loans are substantially lower than bank interest rates (after all, you're borrowing your own money). Your insurance agent can give you all the details.

The company that sells you your equipment may also "loan" you money in the form of credit. Most manufacturers have financing plans allowing you to buy your equipment on the installment basis. Commercial finance companies also offer short-term loans for purchase of equipment.

Your wholesalers or suppliers may also extend short-term credit. But if you are new to the world of business, you may have difficulty proving your credit worthiness. You may have to operate C.O.D. with your suppliers until you are a little better established.

Small Business Administration Loans

I blow hot and cold on government agencies and on the reliability and consistency of government policy. Too much depends on politics and the whims of whoever is in power this year.

With that little bit of a warning, you may want to investigate, and you may even get your money from, the United States Small Business Administration (SBA). The SBA has a variety of loan programs for new and expanding "small" businesses. But watch out here: by government definition, a "small" business is one with as much as $22 million in yearly sales and as many as 1,500 employees! So there are a lot of big businesses in these small business programs.

The loan program most applicable to new businesses is one the SBA calls the 7(a) Program, also known as the Loan Guarantee Plan. Under this program, a commercial bank loans you money and the SBA guarantees up to 80% of the loan.

The maximum loan under the 7(a) Program is $750,000 with up to a fifteen year payback period. Maximum interest is 2-3/4% above the prime rate. The banks set the actual terms and interest rates.

The only direct SBA loans available to small businesses (money loaned directly by the SBA) are made through the 7(a)11 Program. These loans are available only to handicapped people, Viet Nam era veterans, and businesses located in special areas designated by the Department of Commerce as "labor surplus areas," which are usually large cities where a factory or a major employer has recently shut down. The maximum SBA direct loan is $150,000, and the interest rate is below prime.

The SBA will make loans for up to 70% of your starting capital (as opposed to a 50% bank maximum). You will be expected to have some of your own capital invested in your business.

Another SBA loan program, the "Local Development Company Program" (also known as the 502, 503 and 504 Program) makes loans to businesses in certain economically depressed cities and rural areas, but only if the loans are used primarily to create jobs. The requirements and limits are different from other SBA programs.

SBA loans are only available to people who have been unsuccessful in obtaining financing through the private sector. In other words, first the bank has to turn you down. Then the government may step in. To get an SBA loan, you will have to convince them that you have the ability to operate a business successfully and that the loan can be repaid from the earnings of your business.

The SBA makes or guarantees only about 25,000 loans per year, and only about 30% of the available loan funds go to new businesses. The bulk of the money is lent to existing and expanding small businesses.

SBA loans also come with strings attached. The agency has a set of operating guidelines you must follow, which limits your freedom and flexibility somewhat. The SBA will periodically audit your books, which can be both a help and a nuisance.

SBA-backed loans are also available from Community Development Corporations (CDC's), which are usually non-profit, community-based organizations; and from Small Business Investment Companies (SBIC's) and Minority Enterprise Small Business Investment Companies (MESBIC's), which are licensed by the SBA. These organizations, in addition to giving loans, sometimes actually invest in small businesses (acquire an ownership interest) and are discussed in more detail in the Venture Capital chapter.

Lastly, there are a few SBA-sponsored loans made not by the SBA, but by a few large (and generous) corporations. Your local SBA office will know if any are available in your area.

There are over 100 SBA field offices in the country. Contact the one closest to you or write Small Business Administration, Washington, D.C. 20416.

Pat Ellington, Kipple Antiques: "There's no point in even going to a bank and talking to them unless you can say 'Well, we've been operating now for two years, and we've established a certain track record, and we want to expand. We've got our books, our balance sheets, and we've got good references, some people do extend us credit.' I know that from my own credit experience. If you go there armed with a certain amount of paperwork, a certain kind of history, you'll have fewer problems dealing with them.

"I have mixed feelings about SBA loans. Sometimes they can be gotten easily, but it's sort of like by magic. And other times, no matter what you give them, no matter what sound business approach you give them, they're deaf to you. Officers in the SBA say how far you get there really depends on who you know. That's kind of discouraging. It's like grantsmanship. There's a whole lot to applying, and if you don't have the art, you don't get the grant."

Loans To Yourself

For tax and bookkeeping purposes, there is no such thing as a loan to yourself (except for corporations). Any of your own money that you put into your business is considered personal funds. It is not taxable income, the repayment is not a tax deduction, you cannot pay yourself interest on the funds. As far as the IRS is concerned, loaning your own business money is the same as taking money out of your right pocket and putting it in your left pocket. The reasoning behind this law will make a little more sense after you read the next chapter, "Sole Proprietorship". Partners in partnerships come under the same law.

A special note, for corporations: Corporations are different. If you incorporate your business, you can loan your business money and treat it as a regular loan. But you must be careful here. Most states require corporations to have some amount of equity capital—money that actually belongs to the corporation, money that you (the owner) invest in the corporation. Before you "loan" money to your corporation, with a formal loan agreement and interest payments, make you sure you aren't going to run afoul of state or IRS requirements for minimum capitalization. You should talk to a good accountant.

Equity Financing

"Equity" means ownership. "Equity financing" is money put up by the owner or owners of the business. Self-financing is, in fact, equity financing, even though I gave it a separate category in this chapter.

When most people think of equity financing, they think of an investor who buys into your business—as a partner in a partnership with you, or as a shareholder who owns part of the stock in your corporation. The investor is taking a risk on your business, just as you are. Like the typical lender, the typical investor is usually a friend, acquaintance or relative. Unlike a lender, however, the investor gets his money back only if the business succeeds. The owner of the business is usually not obligated to repay the investor out of personal non-business funds.

What percentage of profits goes to the investor and what percentage to the business owner is something to be negotiated. A 50-50 split is the most common. I've known investors to accept as little as 30-35% of the profits; some may want a much bigger return. Investments can be for a specified, limited time or for the life of the business.

Investments can be set up in a variety of ways, depending on how much the investor will or will not participate in the actual running of the business, how much liability exposure the investor wants, and how the business and the investment are legally structured. The investor might become a full partner in a regular partnership, a limited partner in a limited partnership (discussed below), a stockholder in a corporation, or perhaps some other arrangement. Most states have laws regulating investments and how to set them up legally. You will need some professional advice from a good tax accountant or lawyer.

Limited Partnerships

Limited partners are not partners in the usual sense of the word. They are investors only. Their liability is limited to the amount of their investment. They are legally prohibited from participating in the management and operation of the business. Don't confuse a limited partner with a regular business partner who invests money in the business. Limited partnerships are very different from regular (general) partnerships. Limited partnerships are subject to much greater government scrutiny than general partnerships. Most states require limited partnerships to be registered with the county or the state. The Internal Revenue Service has special income tax rules for limited partnerships, not covered in *Small Time Operator*.

Venture Capital

Venture capitalists are a different breed of investor than limited partners. Limited partners are usually friends and relatives. Venture capitalists are usually wealthy and make their living as investors. Venture capitalists love to play with their money. They love new ideas and new products. They love to gamble, looking for the big payoff. And they invariably love to stick their noses in your business affairs. They are not restricted from management the way limited partners are. When you get financing from a venture capitalist you will be taking on a partner who not only wants a percent of the profits but may even want ownership control (51% interest) of your business.

Venture capitalists come in all guises. The majority of them are individuals and privately owned corporations. You may be able to locate one of these people through referral (talk to other business people) or in the Yellow Pages.

A new breed of venture capitalist is the Community Development Corporation (CDC), which combines public interest with private business investment. Many CDC's are non-profit, community sponsored and community operated organizations and many receive government grants. Their goal, in addition to making money on their investments, is to encourage small-scale local enterprises and to expand local job markets. To locate a CDC, contact a regional Community Action Agency, SBA office or state office of community affairs.

Venture capital is also available from Small Business Investment Companies (SBIC's) and Minority Enterprise Small Business Investment Companies (MESBIC's). SBIC's are licensed by the Small Business Administration but they are privately organized and privately managed firms; they set their own policies and make their own investment decisions. The SBA often makes loans to SBIC's so they can turn around and invest the money in your business. The Small Business Administration publishes a National Directory of SBIC's. Write the SBA, Washington, D.C., 20416.

Herbert Heaton, a well known business counselor, once described venture capital financing as "selling out before starting." Bill Friday, author of

Successful Management For One to Ten Employee Businesses put it this way: "At best you will be taking on backseat drivers, and at worst you will get pushed to the back seat with an investor doing the driving." Caveat emptor.

Legal Structure

Every new business must decide if it will start as a sole proprietorship, partnership or corporation. Most new one-person and husband-and-wife businesses start as sole proprietorships, simply because a sole proprietorship is the quickest, easiest and least expensive form of business to start.

If you don't incorporate and if you don't have a partner (other than your spouse), you are *automatically* a sole proprietor. The simple act of starting a business legally makes you a sole proprietor. The fact that you have or have not filed any forms, gotten any permits or licenses, notified any government agency or filed a tax return is not material.

If you have one or more partners (other than your spouse) and if you don't incorporate, you have legally started a partnership. It's automatic, just like the sole proprietorship. Partnerships are covered in detail in the Growing Up section.

A husband and wife who start an unincorporated business together can be either a sole proprietorship or a partnership. It's their choice. Generally, unless a husband and wife prepare a partnership agreement and file a partnership tax return, the business is considered to be a sole proprietorship owned by one spouse. Even though both spouses are working in the business, even though both spouses may actually own the business, if they set up a sole proprietorship, they must pick one spouse to be the "official" owner of the business. The Husband and Wife chapter in the Appendix explains these options in detail.

To become a corporation, nothing is automatic. You must file incorporation papers with your state department of corporations, prepare articles of incorporation and corporate bylaws, issue state-approved stock certificates, and pay filing and registration fees and prepaid "franchise" taxes (minimum corporate income taxes). Corporations are covered in detail in the Growing Up section.

A business can start as a sole proprietorship or a partnership and incorporate at any later date. In fact, most small corporations started as unincorporated businesses and incorporated at a later date, after they were successful and found a real need to incorporate.

Sole Proprietorship: The Traditional One Person Business

A one-person business that has not incorporated is known as a sole proprietorship. There are over 20 million small businesses in this country, and most of them are sole proprietorships. This form of business has flourished over the years because of the opportunities it offers to be boss, run the business, make the decisions and keep the profits. A sole proprietorship is the easiest form of business to start up. Despite all the regulations, it is the least regulated of all businesses.

Sole proprietors may call themselves businessmen, businesswomen, business owners, shop keepers, entrepreneurs, self-employed, free-lancers, outside contractors, independent contractors, subcontractors, consultants, artists, craftspeople, tradesmen, manufacturers, employers, moonlighters, professionals, full-time, part-time, sideline, you name it. Legally, if you don't incorporate or form a partnership, you are a sole proprietor; your business is a sole proprietorship.

You, the owner of the business, the sole proprietor, are your own man (or woman). You make or break your business, which may sound singularly appealing to those of you instilled with the entrepreneurial, pioneering spirit. But you also have sole responsibility as well as sole control. You and your sole proprietorship are one and the same in the eyes of the law. Any debts or obligations of the business are the personal responsibility of the owner. Damages from any lawsuits brought against the business can be exacted from the personal assets of the owner. You should be fully aware of these legal aspects of the sole proprietorship. If you get your business into legal trouble or too far into debt, not only could you lose your business, you could lose your shirt.

The best definition of an entrepreneur is someone who spends 16 hours a day working for himself so that he doesn't have to work 8 hours a day for someone else.

—Mark Stevens, "Profit Secrets For Small Business"

There is only one way to avoid the unlimited personal liability of the sole proprietor, and that is to incorporate your business. Generally speaking, the debts, obligations, and legal liability of a corporation are limited to the assets of the business and are not the personal responsibility of the owner (or owners). Corporations are discussed later in the book.

The owner of a sole proprietorship cannot hire himself as an employee. This is a point of law often misunderstood by new business people. You may withdraw from the business (*i.e.*, pay yourself) as much or as little money as you want, but this "draw" is not a wage, you do not pay payroll taxes on it, and you cannot deduct the withdrawal as a business expense. The profit of your business, which is computed without regard to your personal draws, is your "wage" and must be included on your personal income tax return. If your business made a $10,000 profit last year, you personally owe taxes on $10,000. Even if you only withdrew $5,000 from the business, you still must pay taxes on $10,000. And if you withdrew $15,000, you still pay taxes only on $10,000. Owner's draw will be discussed in more detail in the bookkeeping and tax sections of the book.

The sole proprietorship itself does not file income tax returns or pay income taxes. You file a Schedule C, "Profit or Loss From Business," with your 1040 return, and pay personal income taxes on the profit. You also pay self-employment tax, which is social security-medicare tax, in addition to income taxes. These taxes are covered in detail in the tax section.

Licenses and Permits

The Lord's Prayer contains 56 words. Lincoln's Gettysburg Address has 268 words. The Declaration of Independence is 1,322 words long. Federal regulations governing the sale of cabbages are 26,911 words long.

When you open a new business, every government agency that can claim jurisdiction over you wants to get into the act. There are forms to file, permits and licenses to obtain, regulations and restrictions to understand and to heed. And, always, there are fees to pay.

Why all the government regulations? Why does water flow downhill? It's just the nature of government to regulate, license, permitize, officialize, "fees, fines and forms" you to death. Some of the laws were passed to protect the consumer public from unscrupulous or incompetent business people. Some were created solely to provide additional revenues to the government. Some...well, who knows.

Most business licenses and permits are required and administered by local governments: the city if you live within city limits; possibly the county. Some businesses must also have state and federal licenses. This chapter will describe the different types of licenses and permits typically required by states and municipalities and those currently required by the federal government. Regulations, however, vary from city to city and state to state; and they are changing and multiplying all the time. You should make it your responsibility to contact state and local government agencies (anonymously if you prefer) to learn the most recent requirements and restrictions.

If we don't have it, you're out of luck.
       —sign on a tiny general store in the middle of nowhere, Branscomb, California

---

If it's in stock, we have it.
       —sign in farm supply store, Ukiah, California

25

Fictitious Name Statement (DBA)

When a business goes by any name other than the owner's real name, the business is being operated under a "fictitious name" (also known as an "assumed name" or a "DBA"—doing business as). Country Comfort Carpentry, Johnson Plumbing, Ralph's Cleaners are all examples of fictitious names. People doing business under a fictitious name are required to file a Fictitious Name Statement (or Assumed Name Certificate or DBA or whatever it is called in your state) with the county where your business is located. The county will charge a filing fee. Filing a Fictitious Name Statement prevents any other business in the county from using the same business name (with a few important exceptions, covered in the chapter "Choosing A Business Name").

In addition to filing for the name, you will be required to publish the Fictitious Name Statement in a newspaper "of general circulation" in the area, the theory being that the public has a right to know with whom they are doing business. The county clerk can provide you with a list of acceptable newspapers. Publication costs can be relatively low if your county has one of those newspapers that specialize in running legal notices (and little else). If not, small-time newspapers almost always charge less than large-circulation dailies.

You will be required to renew your fictitious name periodically, usually once every five years. In many states, the county notifies you when your renewal is due. If you forget to renew, someone else can step in and file for your business name, and you will not be able to use it any more.

You don't have to register for a fictitious name statement if you use your full name as your business name, such as "Julia Smith." If, however, you are doing business as "Julia Smith Company" or "Julia Smith, Attorney at Law" or "Julia Smith's Bookstore," some states consider this to be a fictitious name, subject to regular fictitious name rules.

For the specific fictitious name requirements for your locality, contact the county clerk's office, usually located in the county administration building at the county seat.

Corporations, unless operating under a name other than the official name of the corporation, do not need to file a Fictitious Name Statement.

Local Business Licenses

Just about every business in the country must get a local business license, which is merely a permit to do business locally. "Local" may refer to either the municipal or the county level and sometimes to both. Local business licenses can cost anywhere from ten dollars to as much as several hundred dollars and must be renewed annually or bi-annually. Businesses operating under a fictitious name will usually not be able to get the local license until they have filed the Fictitious Name Statement. Contact city hall or the county clerk for specifics.

A few large cities impose an annual "Business Registration Fee" and issue "Business Registration Certificates" in addition to the regular business license. These clever cities have basically created a second business license, and local businesses must purchase both.

Bob Matthews, owner of Country Comfort Carpentry: "I never filed a fictitious name statement. I like the name, and right on the checks and letterheads it says 'Country Comfort Carpentry' with my name immediately under it. I felt that's good enough. I never got a business license. I'm in a rural area, twenty miles from town. I feel that business licenses are a tax on people who work in town, to make them conform."

Other Local Permits

Your business may be required to conform to local zoning laws, building codes, health requirements, fire and police regulations. Restaurants, night clubs, taverns, groceries, child care homes and businesses in shopping centers in particular are likely to be subject to these additional regulations. I suggest that you contact your local government *before* you open your doors. You may find the regulations so demanding that you cannot afford to meet them. If you do not get the proper permits or meet the building requirements, the police can shut you down.

Key Dickason is a partner in Major Dickason's Blend, a coffee store in Concord, California: "My partner is an honest, law-abiding person, and what he wanted to do is have everything A-OK. Then he found out that to put in what the health inspectors required would cost about twelve hundred dollars: a three-compartment sink, all of the walls smooth in the restrooms, a six-inch molding all around the bottom of the restrooms. The sink could not be in the location we wanted it, it had to be out in the storage room, the storage room had to be repainted. The main reason, well it's my opinion that the regulatory agencies are loaded with 'genus-clerks', and the only thing that they can see is the letter of the law. 'Genus' is Latin for family. It's a biological term. I say it's a sub-species of homo sapien, and you run across this type of person all the time. When they come in and you're serving coffee, they look up in their book and they say, 'Oh, serving beverages. It's a restaurant.' Then they say that you have to comply with this regulation and so forth and they cite book-and-verse.

"Now we've been in business a year and haven't done any of the things that they've recommended, but it was a big hassle. The reason we didn't do it is because we didn't have the money. When the health inspector comes, he looks around, he says, 'Oh, the place is clean, it's nice', this is it. There's no pressure at all to comply with the written directive which they gave us. If they plan to shut us down, then they'd say, 'You have thirty days in which to comply.' Well, then you do it.

"The laws are written—the health laws, the motor vehicle laws—for health reasons, for safety reasons. In the case of the health laws, it's to prevent people from getting sick from eating restaurant food. So they make these regulations and they apply to restaurants, but if you're just serving coffee in paper cups, well it doesn't apply. But you take a genus-clerk and they've got to enforce the law exactly. To the letter. You run into 'em everywhere. And the spirit of the law is to prevent illness. But, you see, they can't make that distinction."

State Occupational Licenses

Most sales businesses and many service businesses do not need state licenses.

States have traditionally licensed doctors, lawyers, CPA's, contractors and a few other professionals. Recently, however, demand for consumer protection has brought about state licensing of dozens of additional occupations. Auto mechanics, stereo and TV repair shops, marriage counselors, plumbers, even dry cleaners, to name a few, are often licensed. Occupational licenses are usually issued for one or two year periods and, as always,

for a fee. Some of the occupational licenses require the licensee to pass a test. Some have education and experience requirements. Contact the state agency administering consumer affairs to inquire about possible licensing of your business. State offices are always located at the state capital and usually in the larger cities around the state.

Sales Tax and Seller's Permits

Unless you live in a state that does not have a sales tax, you will be required to collect sales tax from your customers and remit the tax to the state. Every state's sales tax laws are a bit different. Many states exempt food, labor, and shipping charges from sales tax. Some states exempt manufacturing equipment. Some states tax leased property. Depending on the dollar volume of your business, you will have to prepare monthly, quarterly or annual sales tax returns on which you report your sales and pay the taxes collected. Some states let you keep a portion of the sales tax you collect as a payment for the cost of collecting it.

Every state that collects a sales tax issues "seller's permits" (also called "resale numbers" or "resale permits"), and every business that sells goods must have one. Some states will also require a security deposit from you before issuing you a seller's permit, which is the state's way of guaranteeing that you will collect and remit sales tax when you sell your goods to your customers. States will sometimes allow you to put your security deposit into a special interest-bearing bank account. If you don't want to tie up your own money or if the deposit is more than you can afford, you can often purchase a sales tax bond from an insurance company. The state will accept the bond in lieu of the deposit. When you apply for your seller's permit, the state will give you a full set of sales tax rules and procedures. Service businesses that do not sell parts or inventory are, in many states, not required to obtain a seller's permit.

Besides registering you as a seller, a seller's permit gives you the right to buy goods for resale— both finished products and raw materials—without paying sales tax to your supplier. Only goods that will be resold in the normal course of business can be purchased in this manner. You may not use your seller's permit to make tax-free purchases of office supplies, furniture, or goods to be used for personal, non-business purposes.

Businesses selling wholesale goods and raw materials must also obtain a seller's permit, which allows them to sell their resale goods to another business without charging sales tax. The wholesale business will usually be required to keep a record of all customers who make tax-free purchases (including their resale numbers). States usually provide wholesalers with a form for this purpose. A special note: don't confuse the word "wholesale" with "discount". Wholesale refers to a sale of goods by one business to another for resale or manufacture. The ads in the newspapers that say "Wholesale To The Public" or "Wholesale—Factory To You" or some other misuse of the word are actually referring to discount retail sales; that is, sales to the ultimate consumer.

In states where services are exempt from sales tax, some businesses have problems over the definition of what is a service (not taxable) as opposed to a product (taxable). For example, is an expensive custom-designed computer program a taxable product or a non-taxable service? The same question applies to the work of free-lance artists, graphic designers, typesetters, and the like. Be very careful to find out if this work is subject to sales tax. Sometimes the people in the sales tax office are unsure, so it is a good idea to see the rules in writing.

Out of state mail-order sales are exempt from sales tax. If, however, you have an office, warehouse or store in another state, you must abide by that state's sales tax laws in addition to your own state laws.

Mike Snead, owner of Ms. Perc Leather, San Francisco: "Our business grew incredibly fast, and word of mouth helped us a whole lot. So did the fact that we were one of a kind at a time, sociologically, when that kind of business was ripe to own. The hand-made crafts, the craftsman-entrepreneur concept was brand new and it generated a lot of curiosity, and the curiosity generated sales. I don't know if that can happen now. It's no longer unique. As a matter of fact, it's pretty much the status quo, and I suspect it's going to be one of the things people will rebel against on their way to the next new thing. And whoever it is who has some concept of what's coming next will be in the same position we were in."

It's an endless sequence of small details.
                                                    —*Kitson Logue*

Other State Regulations

In addition to occupational licenses and sales tax laws, some states have various other requirements for small businesses. Some of these state laws parallel or expand upon federal laws, particularly Federal Trade Commission regulations (discussed later). Here is a brief summary of *some* state laws. You are going to have to do some telephoning—try your state's Secretary of State office or Attorney General office for starters—to get answers.

Truckers and taxi cab operators must often register with the Public Utilities Commission. Businesses operating factories or other potential air and water polluting equipment must often meet state Air and Water Resources Commission requirements. Employers may be subject to state wage and hour laws and occupational safety and health laws administered by the state Department of Labor or Department of Industrial Relations. States often have laws regulating finance charges imposed on customers.

Well. Now that your family company is part of our family of companies, we've decided to let you go.

Federal Identification Numbers

Your business will be required to identify itself on tax forms and licenses by either of two numbers: your Social Security number or a Federal Employer Identification Number. A Social Security number is all the identification a sole proprietorship needs until you hire employees, or if you are required to file an excise tax return (excise taxes are covered in the Tax section of the book).

Then you will have to get the Federal Employer ID Number. To get an ID number, file Form SS-4 with the IRS. If you are in a rush, some IRS offices will issue you an ID number immediately, over the telephone. No fee is charged.

If you do file for and receive a Federal Employer Identification Number, the IRS will automatically send you quarterly and year-end payroll tax returns that you must fill out and return even if you

---

Form **SS-4**
(Rev. April 1991)
Department of the Treasury
Internal Revenue Service

Application for Employer Identification Number

(For use by employers and others. Please read the attached instructions before completing this form.)

EIN

OMB No. 1545-0003
Expires 4-30-94

Please type or print clearly.

1 Name of applicant (True legal name) (See instructions.)
Sam Leandro

2 Trade name of business, if different from name in line 1
Music Photo Service

3 Executor, trustee, "care of" name

4a Mailing address (street address) (room, apt., or suite no.)
P.O. Box 322

5a Address of business (See instructions.)
640 Bell Springs Road

4b City, state, and ZIP code
Laytonville CA 95454

5b City, state, and ZIP code
Laytonville CA 95454

6 County and state where principal business is located
Mendocino, California

7 Name of principal officer, grantor, or general partner (See instructions.) ►
Sam Leandro

8a Type of entity (Check only one box.) (See instructions.)
[X] Individual SSN 123-45-6789
[ ] REMIC
[ ] State/local government
[ ] Other nonprofit organization (specify) ____
[ ] Other (specify) ► ____

[ ] Estate
[ ] Plan administrator SSN ____
[ ] Personal service corp.
[ ] National guard

[ ] Other corporation (specify) ____
[ ] Federal government/military
If nonprofit organization enter GEN (if applicable) ____

[ ] Trust
[ ] Partnership
[ ] Farmers' cooperative
[ ] Church or church controlled organization

8b If a corporation, give name of foreign country (if applicable) or state in the U.S. where incorporated ►

Foreign country

State

9 Reason for applying (Check only one box.)
[ ] Started new business
[X] Hired employees
[ ] Created a pension plan (specify type) ►
[ ] Banking purpose (specify) ►

[ ] Changed type of organization (specify) ► ____
[ ] Purchased going business
[ ] Created a trust (specify) ► ____
[ ] Other (specify) ► ____

10 Date business started or acquired (Mo., day, year) (See instructions.)
June 14 1988

11 Enter closing month of accounting year. (See instructions.)
December

12 First date wages or annuities were paid or will be paid (Mo., day, year). **Note:** If applicant is a withholding agent, enter date income will first be paid to nonresident alien. (Mo., day, year) . . . . ► January 1, 1992

13 Enter highest number of employees expected in the next 12 months. **Note:** If the applicant does not expect to have any employees during the period, enter "0." . . . . ►

Nonagricultural	Agricultural	Household
1	0	0

14 Principal activity (See instructions.) ► photographer

15 Is the principal business activity manufacturing? . . . . [ ] Yes [X] No
If "Yes," principal product and raw material used ►

16 To whom are most of the products or services sold? Please check the appropriate box.
[ ] Public (retail)   [ ] Other (specify) ►   [X] Business (wholesale)   [ ] N/A

17a Has the applicant ever applied for an identification number for this or any other business? . . . . [ ] Yes [X] No
Note: If "Yes," please complete lines 17b and 17c.

17b If you checked the "Yes" box in line 17a, give applicant's true name and trade name, if different than name shown on prior application.

True name ►   Trade name ►

17c Enter approximate date, city, and state where the application was filed and the previous employer identification number if known.

Approximate date when filed (Mo., day, year) | City and state where filed | Previous EIN

Under penalties of perjury, I declare that I have examined this application, and to the best of my knowledge and belief, it is true, correct, and complete.

Telephone number (include area code)
(707) 984-6060

Name and title (Please type or print clearly.) ► Sam Leandro, owner

Signature ► Sam Leandro

Date ► December 14, 1991

Note: Do not write below this line.   For official use only.

Please leave blank ► | Geo. | Ind. | Class | Size | Reason for applying

For Paperwork Reduction Act Notice, see attached instructions.   Cat. No. 16055N   Form **SS-4** (Rev. 4-91)

All employers, partnerships, and corporations must have a federal identification number, obtained by filing Form SS-4 with the IRS.

have no employees. So don't apply for an Employer ID Number until you need one.

Partnerships and corporations must have federal and/or state identification numbers whether they hire employees or not. See the separate chapters in the Growing Up section.

Federal Permits and Regulations

Federal "watch dog" agencies and the rules and regulations generated by these agencies are growing at a tremendous rate. The U.S. Government section of the San Francisco telephone book lists over twenty-four major agencies and departments that in some way regulate or oversee business activity. Most of this government intervention is aimed at large corporations, but some small businesses are also subject to federal licensing and regulation.

Federal Licenses

Most small businesses do not need any federal licenses.

The federal government licenses all businesses engaged in common- carrier transportation, radio and television station construction, manufacture of drugs, preparation of meat products and investment counseling. You should contact the Federal Trade Commission, Washington, D.C. 20580 for specific licensing requirements.

Exporting and Importing

Businesses that export goods to foreign countries must fill out a Shipper's Export Declaration (SED) if any commodity in the shipment is valued at more than $2,500. If you export certain military or scarce goods, or if you ship to a handful of trade-restricted countries, you will have to obtain a Validated Export License. More information about exporting is available from the Department of Commerce, Washington D.C. 20233.

You do not need any special permit to import goods into the United States, but you should be aware of customs procedures—which are lengthy if the value of your shipment is over $250 including shipping costs—and customs duties, which can run from nominal amounts to as much as 110 percent of the value of the imported goods—more than doubling your cost!

Import and export businesses must abide by all the rules and regulations, tax laws, etc. covered in *Small-Time Operator*. Just about everything in this book applies to businesses in the import and export trade. But importing and exporting also involves an entire world of international laws, special tax incentives, international trade procedures, and various "middlemen" (agents, brokers, freight forwarders) that domestic businesses never encounter. *Small-Time Operator* does not cover these unique laws and dealings of international trade—that's an entire book in itself.

Employers

Some employers are subject to the minimum wage and equal-opportunity employment laws which come under the Department of Labor's Fair Labor Standards Act. These laws are discussed in the Hiring Help chapter.

Finance Charges

Businesses that impose finance charges on credit customers must explain those charges in carefully worded statements according to the Federal Trade Commission's Truth in Lending Act. Finance charges and Truth in Lending requirements are discussed more in the "Credit Selling" chapter.

More Federal Trade Commission Rules

Small businesses that guarantee merchandise, sell by mail, sell or manufacture clothes or fabrics, sell or manufacture packaged or labeled goods, or do certain types of advertising are subject to Federal Trade Commission regulations. Here is a brief run-down:

Product guarantees and warranties must be specifically worded according to the Consumer Products Warranty Law.

Mail order businesses must comply with a Federal Trade Commission rule designed to crack down on undue mail order shipping delays. Mail order sellers must ship ordered merchandise within their stated time (or thirty days if no time is stated) or notify the buyer of any shipping delay, and give the buyer an option to cancel the order "via an adequate cost-free means."

Textiles, fabric, wool, furs and clothing must be labeled according to a variety of Federal Trade Commission rules. Generally, a label must state

(1) the composition of the fabric—the fiber content, (2) the country of origin, (3) the names or registered identification numbers of the manufacturer and the business marketing the fabric, and (4) detailed instructions for care and cleaning.

All packages and labels on goods must conform to the Federal Fair Packaging and Labeling Act. Basically, a label must identify the product, name the manufacturer, packer, or distributor, and show the net quantity of the contents. The Act specifies how the label must be printed and where on the package it must appear.

Advertising of credit terms is regulated by the Federal Trade Commission. See the discussion under "Direct Credit."

Current information on all of the above Federal Trade Commission regulations is available free from the FTC, Washington, D.C. 20580. You should be aware that FTC regulations are constantly changing.

Although all businesses, big and small, are subject to the various Federal Trade Commission rules, enforcement of the laws is directed primarily at large companies that, due to their size, can and do take advantage of many, many people. As one Federal Trade Commission official explained to me, "We're too busy keeping track of large businesses to worry about a mom-and-pop grocery store in Kansas City which may be violating one of our laws. We've found that small businesses, though they may not adhere to the letter of the law—most of them don't even *know* about a lot of these laws—tend to be much more honest with their customers. We rarely get a complaint about a small business."

Insurance

Before you open your doors, you should thoroughly investigate the insurance needs of your business. Insurance replaces a large, uncertain loss with a small but certain cost—the insurance premium. The different kinds of insurance available to you include:

Basic Fire Insurance covers fire and lightning losses to your equipment and inventory and to your premises. Fire premiums vary widely and are based upon the location of your property and the degree of fire protection in your community, the type of construction of the building, the nature of your business and the nature of neighboring businesses. If you move into a building next to a wood-

working, upholstery or dry cleaning shop, your fire premiums will be high even if your business is a low fire risk. A sprinkler system in your building will sharply reduce your premium.

Extended Coverage protects against storms, most explosions, smoke damage, riot, and damage caused by aircraft or vehicles.

Liability Insurance pays for claims brought against your business because of bodily injury. A customer in your store slips and falls, breaks a leg and slaps you with a $100,000 lawsuit; it's not uncommon. Premiums for merchants usually are based upon the square footage in the store. The bigger the store, the higher the premium. If you are a manufacturer or a contractor, premiums increase as your payroll increases. Liability insurance does not cover you, the owner, nor any of your employees.

Property Damage Liability provides coverage for damage to property of others. There are two different types of property damage liability, and it is important that you understand the differences. The first type, which is usually covered under regular liability insurance, is damage to property that is not under your control or in your custody. A fire starts in your small office. The damage is minimal but smoke and water destroyed $30,000

worth of Persian rugs in the business next door. Property damage liability covers this situation.

The second type of property damage liability, which is not covered by regular liability insurance, is damage to others' property that is under your control or in your custody, such as property leased or rented to you, and—especially important for repair businesses—property that belongs to your customers. Insurance for this second type of property liability must be written as a special, separate policy.

Fire Legal Liability covers fire damage to your landlord's building—the portion you occupy only. The rest of the building would be covered by property damage liability.

Vandalism and Malicious Mischief Insurance.

Theft Coverage provides protection from burglary (theft from your closed and locked business) and robbery (theft using force or threat of violence). The cost of theft insurance depends largely on the type of merchandise you stock and on the type of theft protection on your premises—alarms, bars on the windows, door locks, etc. An investment in some security protection is certainly as important as an investment in theft insurance.

Products Liability refers to insurance coverage for any product manufactured or sold by the insured once the product leaves the business' hands. It covers the business in case the ultimate user of the product sues for bodily injury or property damage. The courts generally hold manufacturers strictly liable for any injury caused by their product, sometimes even when the product has not been used correctly. Even retail stores and restaurants can sometimes be liable for products they sell. If the insurance company does not consider your product to be hazardous, the premium could be low. Premiums increase as sales increase.

Business Interruption. If your business closes due to fire or some other insurable cause, business interruption insurance will pay you approximately what you normally would have earned. The premiums, especially when part of a complete insurance package, are low. There is similar insurance that provides coverage if you are hospitalized and have to shut down your business. You can also purchase "extra expense" insurance, which pays the extra cost of keeping a business operating (such as renting temporary quarters) after a fire or other building damage. "Overhead insurance" pays you for business overhead expenses you incur during long periods of disability. The IRS has special rules,

however, about the different "business interruption" policies. If the policy is paying business expenses (the "extra expense" and "overhead" policies), the premiums are deductible, but any insurance company payments to you are taxable as ordinary income.

If the policy is paying you for lost earnings, the IRS says the premium is not deductible as a business expense, and any insurance claims paid to you are not taxable income. But the IRS also says that such insurance claims, even though they are not subject to income tax, are subject to self-employment tax.

Bonds. Surety bonds guarantee the performance of a job. If you are unable for any reason to complete a job, your surety company must do so. Many contractors have such bonds to protect their customers and require them of subcontractors. Surety bonds are most often used in the construction industry and are always required on public construction projects. Surety bonds are difficult to obtain unless you have $30,000 or more of liquid assets, such as cash and inventory.

Fidelity bonds are placed on employees, insuring the employer against theft or embezzlement by the bonded employees.

Workers' Compensation Insurance provides disability and death benefits to employees injured or killed on the job. Most states require employers to carry workers' compensation insurance for all employees. You, the employer, must pay for this insurance. It does not come out of your employees' pockets.

You, as the owner of a sole proprietorship, cannot be covered under workers' compensation in most states. Partners in partnerships, in some states, may elect to be covered. If you can and do get coverage for yourself, however, neither partners nor sole proprietors are allowed a tax deduction for their own workers' comp. If you own a small corporation, you are an employee of the corporation and generally must be covered by workers' compensation—and it *is* a deductible expense for the corporation.

The minimum premium to obtain a workers' compensation policy, even for one part-time employee, will cost about $300 a year. Premiums increase as your payroll increases (how many employees you have and how much they earn) and vary dramatically with the occupation. Workers' compensation insurance for a roofer is roughly ten times higher than for a grocery clerk. You can keep your initial premium at or near the minimum, particularly for part-time and hourly employees, by giving the insurance company a low payroll estimate, since you really don't know how many hours your employees will be working. Once or twice a year, the insurance company will examine your payroll records, comparing your actual payroll to your original estimate. Your premium will be adjusted retroactively. Some insurance companies also pay dividends (refunds) after the end of the year if you have a satisfactory loss record.

Some states offer workers' compensation insurance through a state-operated insurance fund. If you have only one or two employees, you will probably find the state-operated insurance less expensive than insurance from a private carrier, because the state usually charges a lower minimum premium to write a policy. If you have several employees or if you are purchasing an entire insurance package, you'll often get a better rate from a regular insurance company. To locate the offices of the state fund, look in the Yellow Pages under "insurance" or contact the State Department of Employment or Department of Human Resources.

A special warning if your employees will be working at their own homes (not at the employer's home): Your workers' compensation premium will probably be triple the normal rate. The insurance companies view this as a high risk situation because the employee is at the workplace 24 hours a day and can too-easily claim that any injury at home is work related.

Special note to building contractors: If you hire subcontractors, in some states you are responsible for the subcontractor's workers' compensation coverage if the subcontractor does not have the insurance. Ask to see a Certificate of Insurance from each subcontractor.

Vehicle Insurance. Liability coverage is mandatory in most states. The same coverage available to you on your personal auto is available on a business vehicle. The premiums, however, are usually higher for business vehicles. If you use your personal vehicle for business, check with your insurance company to make sure you have coverage that includes business use.

"Non-owned" auto liability insurance protects you if one of your employees injures someone or damages someone's property while driving his own car on your company business. This coverage does not protect the employee, who should have his own insurance as well.

You should check with the state, your landlord and your bank (if you plan to get a loan) to determine what kinds of insurance you *must* carry. Many leases specify that the tenant must carry liability insurance naming the landlord as an additional insured. Landlords often require their tenants to carry plate glass insurance and sometimes even fire insurance on the landlord's building. When banks loan you money, they often require you to carry life insurance naming the bank as beneficiary. They will also require you to insure any property purchased with the loan money. Car and equipment leasing firms often require you to obtain liability and/or property insurance on leased equipment.

Over and above any mandatory insurance, liability coverage is unquestionably the most important to a business. One lawsuit by an injured customer can wipe you out—your business and you personally. Even if you win the lawsuit, without insurance it could still cost thousands of dollars in lawyer's fees.

Most insurance companies offer a "business owner's package," combining many of the above coverages in one policy. Some insurance companies offer "all risk" insurance, which includes fire, extended coverage, vandalism, theft and all other damage not specifically excluded in the policy. Insurance companies are competitive, offering different rates, packages and premium payment plans. It is a good idea to shop around. Talk to several insurance agents.

I am partial to independent agents because they are not tied to one company and can piece together the best insurance package to fit your needs and your pocketbook. I suggest you pick an agent who will devote time to your individual problems, who will at no extra cost survey your entire situation and recommend alternative methods of insurance, pointing out the advantages and disadvantages of each.

Self Insurance

In an attempt to reduce insurance costs, business owners sometimes attempt self insurance. Basically this means you are not insured at all but have set aside funds to cover possible losses such as fire or theft or a liability claim against the business. Some people call these funds a "reserve". While self insurance certainly saves on insurance premiums, the money set aside or in the reserve is not considered a business expense and is not tax deductible. At the time you actually sustain a loss or have to pay on a claim or lawsuit, you may or may not have a tax writeoff, depending on the nature of the claim or loss. For example, stolen or destroyed furniture and equipment can be written off only to the extent it hasn't already been written off or depreciated; inventory must be written off as part of cost-of-goods-sold; legal fees are probably fully deductible, but depend on the circumstances. The chapters on Inventory, Cost of Goods Sold, and specific items in the Tax section of the book explain how to deduct different kinds of losses.

Remember, too, that it is unlikely your self insurance reserve will be large enough to cover a large loss or lawsuit. That's why people purchase insurance in the first place. Also, insurance required by law, such as auto insurance and workers' compensation, and insurance required by contract with your bank or landlord, must be purchased from an insurance company. Self insurance will not suffice.

Choosing A Business Name

Thinking up a name for your new business can be a lot of fun, an opportunity to let your creativity and your imagination take charge. A business name, however, should be selected with care. I suggest three key guidelines:

1. Choose a name that is both pleasant and easy to pronounce. If your customer chokes on your name every time he mentions it to someone else, fewer people will hear about you.

2. Choose a name that will do a little advertising for you, that will tell people what you do. Wallpapers Plus, Strider Real Estate, Madrone Jewelry, say what they need to say, clearly and simply. "Acme Enterprises" tells people absolutely nothing.

3. Most important, choose a name that will not severely limit you, a name that will stand up to the passage of time. I know two jewelers who named their business "The Silver Workshop." They made high quality silver and turquoise necklaces and bracelets. Silver, however, is not as popular as it was three years ago, and The Silver Workshop is now making gold and beaded jewelry. These jewelers now find themselves with an albatross around their necks: the business name. On the one hand, the old customers recognize the name. But new customers, looking for gold jewelry, assume that

The Silver Workshop makes silver jewelry, and they stay away.

When you finally settle on a name you like, go to the county office that handles fictitious names and ask to see their alphabetical list of all fictitious names registered with the county. If you live in a large urban area, you may find that your first, second *and* third choices are all already taken. You can, if you want, try to contact the person who owns the business name and find out if the business is still in existence. If it isn't, and if the owner of the name consents, an Abandonment of Fictitious Name Statement can be filed, whereby the prior owner gives up all rights to the name. You may simultaneously file a Fictitious Name Statement for the name. The Abandonment of Fictitious Name Statement procedures are identical to the Fictitious Name Statement procedures, including the requirement to publish the statement in the newspaper. The former owner will probably want you to pay the cost of filing the statement of abandonment and may even want you to pay him a fee for his trouble.

You should be aware of possible trouble if you select a business name that is already being used by an out-of-county or even an out-of- state business. Corporations are usually granted exclusive state- wide use of a business name, assuming they were the first in the state to choose the name. Your state's Secretary of State maintains a list of business names claimed by in-state corporations and by out-of-state corporations licensed to do business in your state. Contact the Secretary of State and inquire if your proposed business name will conflict with one already in use.

A bigger possible problem involves federal trademarks of business names and products. Most large and even some very small businesses obtain trademarks from the U.S. Patent & Trademark Office. Trademark law is complex (and covered in more detail in the Appendix) but generally, a business with a federally registered trademark sometimes has exclusive use of that name throughout the United States. Large public libraries usually have a copy of the Federal Trademark Register. Locate a copy and look up your proposed business name. If it is the same as or very similar to a trademarked name, you may have future problems. This is particularly true if your goods or services are similar to those carrying the trademark and if you are both selling in the same part of the country.

What happens if you start your business and find out later that some other business has prior claim to your business name? What almost always happens is that you will get a letter from some lawyer telling you that you are in violation of the law and that you must cease using that business name, or else they'll take you to court, sue you, etc. and etc. At that point you can decide if you really are in the wrong, and right or wrong, do you want to fight it in court. There are few clear-cut answers in this area of law. Often, unfortunately, it comes down to who has the most money for lawyers.

Another suggestion: check local telephone directories, and check national trade directories for your type of business. Trademark or no trademark, avoid a business name already in use.

We went out and did something like a Nielson survey. We asked people which names they thought would be best for a bookstore. That narrowed it down to four or five. Then we took those four or five names and did another survey, asking people which of these bookstores they'd been in. Twenty per cent of the people surveyed said they'd been in a Crown Books store—and that was before we opened. So we said if 20 per cent of the people think they've already been there, that's the name.

—Robert Haft, Crown Books

The Burroughs Corp. picked a new name, after soliciting suggestions from its employees and getting 31,000 of same. Unisys. That is what they chose. Unisys. As if we needed another name of that sort. Unisys would be a great name for some kind of intestinal tract condition, but for a company, it is real snooze material. It is also highly uninformative. You are not considered to have a good corporate name these days if anyone can guess what you do. This is partly because most companies are not in the business of doing anything. They are in the business of adding another layer of nothing between you and something you want.

—Colin McEnroe, San Francisco Chronicle

Initial Cash Outlays

Getting your business started is going to require cash outlays right at Day One. The largest and most obvious expenses, of course, will be for your initial inventory and equipment purchases, for rent and possibly a rent deposit for your shop or store, and for insurance premiums. All those licenses and permits—$10 here, $25 there—can also run into a lot of money.

Here is a chart of typical start-up expenses, a rough estimate of what the costs may be, and a blank column so you can fill in the actual costs.

Type of Expense	Cost Estimate	Actual Cost
1. Inventory		$ _____
2. Equipment		_____
3. First month's rent		_____
4. Lease deposit		_____
5. Insurance premiums:		
liability	$150–500	_____
fire and extended coverage	150–300	_____
6. Telephone installation	25–100	_____
7. Telephone deposit	0–50	_____
8. Gas and electric deposit	0–50	_____
9. Seller's permit—fee	0–25	_____
10. Seller's permit—deposit	50–300	_____
11. Local license fee	10–100	_____
12. Fictitious name statement—fee	10–50	_____
13. Fictitious name statement—publication	15–50	_____
14. Business cards, stationery, sales books, check printing, etc.	50–200	_____
TOTAL START UP COSTS		$ _____

The Business Plan

If you've read this entire section of *Small-Time Operator*, followed through on all the suggestions, done your "market research," estimated your start-up expenses and your inventory needs, tried your hand at the cash-flow guessing game (covered in the Bookkeeping section), and wrote it all down, you would have yourself a respectable business plan. If this plan helps you organize your thoughts and observations, shows you problems that require more thought and analysis, helps you find all the jigsaw pieces and fit them together, it will be a valuable exercise.

It is extremely important to understand the limits of a business plan, particularly one this early in the game. The ideas are only that—untested ideas. The numbers are guesses—your own inexperienced, optimistic guesses. Don't rely on them too heavily. Proceed with all caution, keep your eyes open, and let experience, not some written plan, be your guide.

If you are trying to raise start-up capital from individuals or a bank, a written business plan will help you get your ideas across to prospective lenders and investors. Someone who is considering putting money into your venture will most likely want to see some sort of plan in writing. Basically they'll want to see a plan that includes:

1. Your business idea.
2. Why you think it is a good idea.
3. Your background, experience, contacts, etc.
4. Where you plan to locate.
5. How you will obtain or manufacture inventory.
6. How you'll find and keep customers.
7. The status of the competition.
8. How much money you will need to start, broken down into broad categories and also into finer detail.
9. How much time and how much of your own money you plan to commit to the business.

10. How much you will pay yourself.
11. How you plan to repay the loan or investment.

After you've been in business awhile, you may want to draw up a new business plan to help you make some major decision, such as reorganizing or expanding your business or trying out some new, bold idea; or a banker may want to see a business plan if you are applying for a loan. By then, you will know your business very well, and you will be able to create a much more reliable plan.

Business plans can be and often are much more elaborate and detailed than what I've described here. Entire books are dedicated to the many considerations, formulas, options and everything else you can conceivably fit onto graphs, charts, schedules, computer screens, and densely packed pages, to create some mighty impressive plans indeed—some of which are quite valuable and some of which are utterly useless. Sometimes, too much "information" will work against you, unable to see the forest for the trees.

In conclusion, I'd like to suggest that every new business person take the time, at the very beginning when you are still just considering your business idea, to put together a business plan—in your head if you like, on paper if you prefer, maybe just late night thoughts, maybe just scribbled notes, maybe something elaborate right out of the business plan books and computer programs. The form the plan takes is not important; it's the conclusions you reach that are important.

Never make forecasts, especially about the future.
—Sam Goldwyn, founder, MGM

Statistics are no substiturte for judgment.
—Henry Clay

Section Two
BOOKKEEPING

The best memory is not so firm
as faded ink.

Chinese proverb

"If you take one from three hundred
and sixty-five, what remains?" asked
Humpty Dumpty.
"Three hundred and sixty-four, of
course," said Alice.
Humpty Dumpty looked doubtful. "I'd
rather see that done on paper,"
he said.

Alice In Wonderland by
Lewis Carroll

Warming Up to an Unpopular Subject

Bookkeeping seems to be the one aspect of business that so many people dread. Columns upon columns of numbers, streams of adding machine tape, balancing the books (whatever that means), and "I'm a shopkeeper not an accountant." Whenever I try to explain or defend the paperwork end of business to a new business person, I always feel I have two strikes against me before I even open my mouth. But once a person understands why a business requires a set of ledgers and how these records can be kept with a minimum of time and effort, the fear vanishes, the work—somehow—gets done, and you are left with the satisfaction of seeing the total picture and of having done it yourself. And that is a nice feeling.

Bookkeeping is an integral part of business, of *your* business. To attempt a definition, bookkeeping is a system designed to record, summarize and analyze your financial activity—your sales, purchases, credit accounts, cash, payrolls, inventory, equipment. Your "books"—your ledgers and worksheets—are the bound papers on which the bookkeeping activity is recorded or "posted."

Why Keep a Set of Books?

Most new businesspeople think that they must keep books only because the government (meaning the Internal Revenue Service) requires them to. Well, it's true, the IRS does require every business to keep a set of books. (The IRS's basic bookkeeping requirement is, "You must keep records to correctly figure your taxes.") But there is a bit more to bookkeeping than taxes and tax law requirements.

The real reason you'd *want* to keep a set of books, as you will learn soon enough, is because you *need* the information to run your business. Can you ever expect to make a good decision based on incomplete information? Your books are your only source of complete information about your business. It is virtually impossible to keep all your business information in your head. You may think you know your business like the back of your hand, but you would be very surprised to see how much you don't know unless you can see the total financial picture, on paper in front of you. This is especially true of a business operated out of your home where personal and business expenses can get intermingled and confused.

Business failures have been blamed, time and again, on a lack of accurate financial records. Bob Willis, former owner of Booknews, a defunct bookstore: "Our biggest mistake was that we didn't keep a regular set of books. Half of our records were on scraps of paper and receipts. We didn't know whether some accounts were paid or not. We thought we were making a profit, but a good set of books would have shown us the truth: we were going broke. And you know, had I realized that, I could have taken steps to change things, to head us in a better direction."

Without a complete set of books, you find yourself trying to evaluate your business by looking at isolated areas, such as cash and inventory—these being the most observable (and also the most misleading). If, for example, you price your product based solely on its cost to you plus some arbitrary markup—a common mistake with beginners—you could be selling at a loss and not even know it. This happened at Booknews: "We knew what the books were costing us, but we didn't have any real idea of what our total overhead was—rent, insurance, supplies, utilities, payroll taxes, the rest. We sold a lot of books because we sold at a discount, and I thought we were doing well. Do you know it took me four months to realize that every single book we sold, we sold at a loss."

A good bookkeeping system will provide you with information essential to the survival of your business. Only with a complete set of books will you be able to evaluate your business and make any needed changes and plans for the future.

Joe Campbell, Resistance Repair: "Everybody who runs a business should sit down and figure out what it costs them to turn the key in that door every morning. Overhead. And do it on a daily basis. I never knew until I sat down and calculated exactly what my expenses were, what it costs me to have that place down there. And it's fifty dollars a day. When you walk in there in the morning you know exactly what you gotta do before you start putting bread on the table. You gotta make fifty bucks for the man. And then you start making money for yourself."

Setting Up Your Books

Where do you begin? How much bookkeeping do you need? If your business is a one man, one woman or husband and wife operation—no partners, no employees—your records can be kept quite simple. A bank account, a set of income and expenditure ledgers and a few worksheets are about all you will need. Do you sell on account? You will want to keep records of each credit customer. If you hire employees, you will need payroll records for each employee. Partnerships must keep records of each partner's contributions and withdrawals. Partnerships must file separate income tax returns and are sometimes required to prepare year-end balance sheets. Corporations, even small ones, often need entire forests to supply all the necessary paper to make everything run smoothly.

But let's take things one step at a time. *None* of the bookkeeping records need be too complicated for most people to keep themselves and to understand. This section of *Small-Time Operator* will show you, step by step, how to keep your own books and how to use the information once you have it. The Ledger Section in the back of the book includes sample income, expenditure, equipment, depreciation, and payroll ledgers, and year-end summaries that you can actually use. You will also learn how you can custom design your own ledgers, using low-cost accounting worksheets or blank ledger books, to meet your special requirements.

Computerized Bookkeeping

Keeping your books on a computer is very similar to keeping your books by hand. Computers are faster than you are and not likely to make mathe-matical errors, but the ledgers they produce for you will be virtually identical to those you would produce without a computer. Electronic spreadsheets in particular enable you to set up your ledgers on your computer exactly as described here. The same principles of bookkeeping apply whether your ledgers are kept by hand or on a computer. In either case, you should understand your bookkeeping completely. Everything in this bookkeeping section is applicable to computerized as well as hand-posted bookkeeping. When first using a computer, I strongly suggest that you keep duplicate hand-posted ledgers for at least a month, just to be sure your computer program is error-free and producing correct information.

There is a lengthy chapter in the Appendix on computers and spreadsheet applications.

Business Bank Account

As soon as you start your business, before you open your doors, go to the bank and open a separate business checking account. Keep your business finances and your personal finances separate. Nothing can be more confusing or cause you more trouble than mixing business with pleasure, financially. If you plan ahead and open your account a few weeks before starting business, you can have your checks all printed up with your business name and address, ready to use on opening day.

Many states require you to have your fictitious name statement before you can open a bank account in your business name. Talk to your banker ahead of time and find out all the legal requirements.

Ask your banker what the bank charges will be. Business accounts are handled differently from personal accounts. At my bank, a personal checking account with a $300 minimum deposit has no service charge. A business account, however, must have a $1,000 minimum deposit to have no service charge. Some banks charge substantially more than others; some offer free checks printed with your business name and address; some will provide you a free rubber stamp for endorsing checks. There are three Important Rules to follow:

Rule One: Pay all your business bills by check. Your expenses are more easily recorded and better documented when paid by check. Some payments, of course, will have to be in cash, but keep them to a minimum. A chapter at the end of this section explains how to set up a petty cash fund for your cash payments.

Rule Two: Deposit all your income, checks and cash, into the business bank account. You will have a complete record of your earnings.

Rule Three: When you take money out of the business account for non-business or personal use, it is known as "withdrawal" or "personal draw." When you want to spend some of your hard-earned money on yourself—to meet the car payment, buy groceries, see a movie—withdraw the money from the business account by writing a check payable to yourself or payable to "cash." Then cash the check or deposit the money in your personal account. Try not to use the business account to pay personal, non-business expenses. It is just too confusing (and doubles the time spent on bookkeeping) when business and personal expenses are paid from the same account.

A Few Bank Account Rules-of-Thumb:

1. Balance your bank account every month. It is too easy to make an adding error. You certainly don't want to bounce a check on your most important supplier because you thought you were down to the last ten dollars when you were really down to the last dime. Never balanced a bank account? There is a chapter in the Appendix explaining how to do it.

2. Keep your bank statements and canceled checks at least three years. They are the best documentation you have if you ever need to support your records. Three years is the normal statute of limitations set by the Internal Revenue Service for income tax audits.

3. Never write a check payable to "cash" unless it is a personal draw. Checks written to "cash" leave you with no record of how the money was spent.

4. Expenses that are partly personal and partly business, such as automobile expenses, or rent and utilities on your home when you use part of your home for business, or your credit card bill if it includes business and non-business purchases, are partly deductible—the business portion. These expenses can be handled in one of two ways: (1) Pay these bills from your personal checking account, then post the business portion to your business ledgers (explained in the Expenditure section); or (2) Pay the bills from your business checking account; post the business portion to its proper column in the expenditure ledger, and post the non-business portion to the "Non-Deductible" column (also explained in the Expenditure section).

Joe Campbell, Resistance Repair: "My problem was that I would look in our checking account, our one and only checking account, and I'd say, Jesus Christ, there's a thousand dollars in there. Let's go buy the new tires we need for the car. And then I'd say the kids can stand to have a new pair of shoes, and I go buy them a new pair of shoes. And I see we still have $700 in the bank; we're in good shape. Then all the parts bills come in, and I owe $800 worth of parts bills. And then I have to put creditors off. Having that parts money in a separate account tells you exactly where you are. And to me it's a tremendous feeling of security. It works like a charm. Plus it's emergency cash if you have to go in and get it."

Bookkeeping Simplified: An Introduction to the Single Entry System

The ledgers in *Small-Time Operator* are simple "single entry" ledgers. For any transaction, only one entry is made, either to income or to expenditure. Single entry bookkeeping keeps the paperwork and the arithmetic to a minimum while still providing you with the basic information you need to manage your business and prepare tax returns.

There are two disadvantages to this simple bookkeeping system. Single entry bookkeeping will provide a record of your income and expenditures but will not provide a complete record of inventory on hand, equipment, outstanding loans or other assets and liabilities. The other drawback to single entry bookkeeping is the lack of a built-in double check of arithmetical accuracy. These disadvantages, however, are partially offset by the additional asset records that the depreciation worksheets and the inventory ledgers provide, and also by the Total columns in the ledgers that provide a partial math double check.

The alternative to single entry bookkeeping, the well known and elaborate system called "double entry" bookkeeping, compares to our single entry system as a fancy stereo compares to a portable cassette player. Double entry is a complete bookkeeping system that provides cross checks and automatic balancing of the books, that minimizes errors, and that transforms business bookkeeping from a part-time nuisance into a full-time occupation. In double entry bookkeeping, every transaction requires two separate entries, a "debit" and a "credit." These terms originated in double entry bookkeeping, along with the expression "balancing the books:" total debits must equal total credits for the books to be "in balance."

Double entry bookkeeping is a science. It is *the* perfected bookkeeping system, and it requires a full semester in college to master. Simplicity is our goal. I find that most small businesses are better off without the refinements (and the headaches) of a double entry system.

Cash Accounting Vs. Accrual

Regardless of whether your books are single entry or double entry, you must choose between two accepted accounting methods: "cash" or "accrual." Under the cash method of accounting, income is recorded when the cash is received, and expenses are recorded when paid. (In accounting terminology, the word "cash" refers to checks and money orders as well as currency). Thus, credit sales for which you haven't yet been paid, and credit purchases you haven't yet paid for, do not show on cash-method ledgers. This can present an inaccurate and misleading picture of your income and expense. Accrual accounting, by comparison, records all income and expenses whether paid or not. Both credit and cash transactions are recorded when made.

Every sales and manufacturing business and any service business that stocks and sells parts is required by federal tax law to use the accrual method for its inventory. Small businesses with no inventory can use either method. Once a method is selected, it cannot be changed without written permission from the IRS.

For most small businesses, accrual accounting becomes a factor only at year-end. A sale made in December, for which you receive payment in January of the new year, must be recorded on December's ledgers and becomes taxable income for the old year. Of course, when the cash is received in January, it is not part of the new year's income and is not taxed a second time.

Accruing income at year-end can be tricky if you have a contract for a large job that is partially complete at December 31. For tax purposes, the completed part of the contract must be reported as December's income, the balance as next year's income. This will probably require some estimating and guess-work on your part.

Accrued expenses at year-end—those you've incurred but not paid for by December 31—become tax deductions for the year just ended, not the year paid. There is, however, a very important exception for inventory. Inventory cannot be written off until sold, regardless of when you bought it. This is covered in detail in the Tax section, under "Cost of Goods Sold," and is something you should understand thoroughly. You cannot run out at December 31, buy a truckload of merchandise, and expect to write it off immediately.

Another exception to the accrual rules are deductions for property taxes. Business property taxes cannot be deducted until paid under both cash and accrual accounting.

If you don't buy on credit or extend credit to your customers (other than credit card sales, which are handled as cash sales for bookkeeping purposes—explained later in this chapter), then all transactions are cash transactions, and the ledgers, whether you call them cash or accrual, are exactly the same. Life is simplified.

But part of the goal of *Small Time Operator* is to help simplify your life—your bookkeeping life anyway—whichever method you use. The income and expenditure ledgers in the Ledger section can be kept by either the cash or the accrual method. And to make things easy for inexperienced bookkeepers, the posting instructions in this Bookkeeping section are exactly the same for both methods—until year end. The year-end instructions explain how to adjust your ledgers so they are, at your choice, either cash or accrual.

This simplified system will work fine as long as you don't need precise figures at the end of each month. Since you only make your adjustments at year-end, at any time during the year the figures may be off slightly.

Corporations: Regular corporations with sales of $5 million or more per year must use accrual accounting. "Personal service corporations" operated by doctors, lawyers, engineers, architects, veterinarians and similar professionals, should use accrual accounting, and not cash accounting, to avoid special IRS restrictions.

Recording Income

Income is recorded in two steps. Step One: at the time you make a sale, record the sale on an invoice, cash receipt or cash register tape. Step

Two will be to summarize the sales in your income ledger. Let's first examine Step One in depth.

The manner in which you record each sale depends primarily on your volume of sales. A writer or cabinetmaker, for example, may have only a few sales each month. For this kind of low volume activity, a special invoice can easily be prepared for each sale. Way at the other end of the spectrum, a grocer may have several hundred sales each day and would go plumb crazy if he had to write out a receipt for every sale. The grocer needs a cash register tape to record his sales. The typical small business falls somewhere between the two examples. For most small businesses, use of preprinted cash receipts or invoices is the simplest and most efficient way to record sales.

Below are step-by-step procedures for recording sales for low, medium and high volume businesses.

Low Volume of Sales

If your business is of the type having only a few sales, you can easily prepare a special billing for each sale. The billing should be marked "Invoice" and prepared in duplicate. The invoice should include:

1. Your name or business name, address and telephone.
2. Date of sale.
3. Customer's name and address.
4. Description of sale.
5. Amount, showing any sales tax separately.
6. A space to indicate when paid.

If you offer return privileges or discounts for prompt payment, these should be spelled out on your invoice. If you offer credit terms, federal law requires you to disclose, clearly and in detail, your credit terms and finance charges (see "Credit Sales").

Give the original invoice to your customer and keep the duplicate copy for your records. Depending on your inclination and your finances, your invoices can be prepared on specially printed and custom-designed forms, or you can just type the information on plain paper.

Medium Volume of Sales

Most everyone is familiar with the small cash receipt books (invoice books) many businesses use to record individual sales. The books contain fifty or one hundred pre-numbered forms, in duplicate—one for the customer, one for you. Such books are ideal for small businesses with more than just a few occasional sales. These books are standardized and available in any stationery store. You can usually order the books with your business name custom-printed at the top; or you can purchase a rubber stamp and mark each receipt individually.

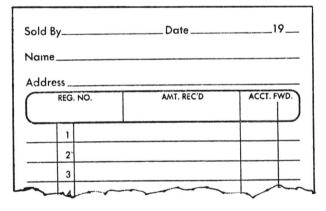

Typical cash receipt forms, sold in books of 50 or 100

Note: Don't confuse this book of cash receipts with other books labeled "Cash Receipts" that are in fact ledgers for recording income totals.

The procedure for using your cash receipts book is simple:

1. If the receipts are not already pre-numbered, number them as you use them.
2. Use a separate receipt for each sale.
3. Make a carbon copy of each receipt.
4. Write down the date and the amount of the sale. If there is any sales tax, it is very important

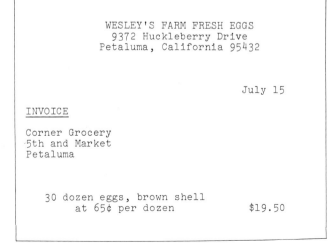

```
        WESLEY'S FARM FRESH EGGS
           9372 Huckleberry Drive
         Petaluma, California 95432


                              July 15

INVOICE

Corner Grocery
5th and Market
Petaluma


   30 dozen eggs, brown shell
         at 65¢ per dozen        $19.50
```

A simple typed invoice may be all you need if you have a low volume of sales.

to show the amount of the tax separately.

5. If this is a credit sale, write "CREDIT SALE" on the receipt.

6. A description of the sale is not necessary unless the customer desires it or you need it for your own information, such as for inventory control (discussed at the end of this section).

7. Give the original to your customer. *Leave the duplicate copy in your receipt book.* The duplicate copies will later be summarized and posted to your income ledger.

8. If you void any invoice, do not throw it out. Mark it "VOID" and retain it in your receipt book. Although you should not include the voided receipt in your summary total, you should keep a record of it here.

You can also purchase individual invoice forms from a local stationery store or printer. You can design your own, or buy standard forms with your name imprinted on them. These forms are used in the same way as the cash receipts.

Those of you with computers can quite easily design and print your own invoices on the computer. The simplest computer programs, however, cannot easily prepare invoices in automatic numerical sequence. You may have to key in the invoice numbers by hand, which may or may not be a nuisance. Computer-generated invoices should contain the same basic information described here.

Throughout the book, the terms "sales slips," "sales receipts," "cash receipts" and "invoices" are used interchangeably. They all refer to individual sales records.

Large Volume of Sales: Introducing the Cash Register

Few small businesses have a large enough volume of sales to justify the use and the expense of a cash register. But if you are opening a grocery, restaurant, auto parts store, or any similar retail business making many small sales a day, a cash register will be indispensable.

Cash registers can be as simple (and as useless, I should add) as the old-fashioned ones where the sale amount "pops up" in the little glass window, the bell jingles and the cash drawer flies out at you—but there's no tape, and no totals are recorded. And they can be as space-age-complicated as the new $5,000 mini-computers that do everything from updating inventory records to automatically weighing vegetables.

A cash register that is going to be useful to you must be a combination money box and adding machine. Each time you ring up a sale, the amount is recorded on a two-part cash register tape. Everyone is familiar with the part of the tape that pops out when the sale is rung and the cash drawer opens. That part of the tape is the customer's receipt. The other part of the tape, a duplicate of the customer receipt, stays inside the register and becomes the merchant's sales record. At the end of the day, the register is "totaled" and "cleared." Pushing one key on the register will total all the sales rung up during the day and print the total on the tape. Pushing the key also clears the total from the machine so it will start afresh the next day with a zero balance. As you can well imagine, such machines are not cheap. Even used ones will cost at least a few hundred dollars. If your business demands use of a cash register, shop for a machine with the following features:

1. A double tape as described above.

2. A separate total for sales tax if you are required to collect sales tax.

3. If some sales are subject to sales tax and others are not, as is the case with many groceries, an additional mechanism that separates these sales totals. Such a register will give you three totals: sales subject to sales tax, tax on those sales, and sales not subject to sales tax.

You should also realize that even the finest cash registers can and do break down once in a while. So be especially careful in selecting a register; be wary of cheap looking or very old machines. Does the register come with a guarantee or a repair contract? Before you buy it, work it fast and hard for a few minutes. Does it operate smoothly? Or does it feel like it's about to jam up any minute?

Recording Income, Step Two: The Income Ledger

The income ledger is a summary record of your sales invoices, cash receipts or cash register tapes. It is one of the most important business records you have. It tells you, monthly and at year-end, how much income you've earned and how much sales tax you've collected. It helps you manage your business by showing you the days and the months that are slow or busy so that you can better plan your expenditures, advertising, sales, even vacations. It is a guide to preparing cash flow

INCOME LEDGER Month of _June_

1 DATE	2 SALES PERIOD	3 TAXABLE SALES	4 SALES TAX	5 NON-TAXABLE SALES FREIGHT	6 WHOLESALE	7 TOTAL SALES
1		173 24	10 39			183 63
2		217 36	13 04	7 00		237 40
3						
4						
5	3rd – 5th	577 82	34 67	18 00		630 49
6		118 71	7 12			125 83
7	closed					
8		266 94	16 02	14 19	275 00	572 15
9						

information (cash flow and financial management are discussed at the end of this section). The income ledger also saves you time preparing your sales tax reports and your income taxes.

The ledger section in the back of this book includes sample income ledgers and a year-end summary. The ledgers were designed so they may be adapted to your individual needs and your state's sales tax requirements. Use a separate ledger page for each month. Each page has seven columns:

1. *Date.* You may post daily or periodically. How often you post the income ledger depends on you and the volume of sales you have. Discussed below.

2. *Sales period.* If you are posting daily, use the line corresponding with the date. If you are not posting daily, note the sales period here, such as "January 1-7." This is explained below. This column can also be used for any special notations you may want to make.

3. *Taxable sales,* excluding sales tax. If you live in a state that does not collect sales tax, or if you sell services or goods exempt from sales tax, use this column for total sales and ignore the rest of the columns.

4. *Sales tax collected.*

5 and 6. *Non-taxable sales.* Some states require your non-taxable sales to be broken down into categories, such as labor, freight, wholesale, etc.

7. *Total sales amount,* including sales tax. This column serves as a double check on your totals: the sum of the amounts in Columns Three, Four, Five and Six should equal the amount in Column Seven.

You will be summarizing your individual sales (from Step One of Recording Income) and posting the summary totals to the income ledger.

Daily Posting

If you have a moderate or heavy volume of sales, you probably should post the income ledger daily. Add up your sales slips for the day and post your totals to the proper columns in the ledger. Compute separate totals for taxable sales (post to Column Three), sales tax (Column Four), non-taxable sales (Columns Five and Six), and total (Column Seven). No need to make any entries under Sales Period (Column Two). After you have posted the ledger, add the daily totals in Columns Three, Four, Five and Six together. They should equal the total in Column Seven, which is the grand total for the day. If you get a different amount, you will have to locate your adding error. The procedure is a lot simpler in the doing than in the explaining. You really should have no trouble getting the hang of it.

———

ALWAYS POST YOUR LEDGERS IN PENCIL AND KEEP A CLEAN ERASER HANDY.

Posting Every Few Days or Once a Week

If you have only a few sales each day, you may wish to post the ledger once every few days or once a week. Whatever period you choose, total all your sales for the period, separating taxable sales, sales tax, and non-taxable sales. Enter the totals on the line corresponding with the last day of your sales period. For example, if the sales you are combining are for January 1 through January 5, post your totals on the January 5 line. Under Sales Period (Column Two), note the period: "January 1 through January 5."

Don't feel that you must stick to one method of posting once you have started. If daily posting becomes too tedious, try posting every three days or five days. And if you normally post your income ledger every few days, and a very busy time comes along, switch over to daily posting for the busy period. The posting only becomes a nightmare if the paperwork is allowed to accumulate. All of a sudden there's a three week backlog, all the receipts are mixed up, some billings are missing and, oh, how I hate bookkeeping. It doesn't have to happen that way if you keep your ledger up to date.

How to Post Sales Returns

Sales returns, both cash and credit, should be handled as if they were negative sales:

1. Prepare a separate sales slip for each return, and mark it clearly and in large letters, "RE-TURN" or "REFUND" or " CREDIT MEMO."
2. Write down all the information that was on the original sales slip, including the amount of sales tax.
3. Include the return slip (credit memo, or whatever you call it) with your *current* batch of sales receipts.
4. When you add up the current receipts to post to the income ledger, subtract the amounts on the return slips from the total.

End of Month Procedure

No matter how frequently or infrequently you do your posting, run a monthly total at month-end, even though it may not be a full five or seven days since your last regular posting. Never let a posting period cross months. As with your daily or period

totals, your monthly totals in Columns 3, 4, 5 and 6 should be cross-checked against the total in Column 7, and any error should be located and corrected.

Year-end Procedure

Record the twelve monthly totals on the year-end summary page. Cross-check your yearly totals in Columns 3, 4, 5 and 6 to Column 7 and correct any errors.

If you are keeping books on the accrual method (see the chapter Cash Accounting Vs. Accrual), that's all there is to it. No year-end adjustments are needed. You can skip the rest of this chapter.

If you are using the cash method, you must adjust your year-end total by backing off (subtracting) any credit sales that are still *unpaid* at year end. Since you haven't been paid yet for these sales, they shouldn't appear on cash ledgers. (If this doesn't make complete sense to you, please go back and re-read the chapter Cash Accounting Vs. Accrual). Keep these unpaid sales in a separate folder. When they are paid in the new year, record them along with current new year's income.

If these cash method adjustments turn into a headache for you, or you find them too confusing, you can simplify things by not posting *any* credit sales until you receive payment. In this way your income ledger is perpetually on the cash basis, and no year-end adjustment is needed.

Altering The Ledgers

Feel free to alter the income ledger to suit your needs. Many businesses post taxable sales and sales tax (Columns 3 and 4) as one combined figure in one column, and then back off the sales tax from the monthly totals. Some businesses want a separate column for each product or group of products they sell, or for different services they provide. You may not need the non-taxable sales information (Columns 5 and 6) or you may want to re-title them. And for some businesses, the total column may be all you want and need, period.

Filing Your Sales Receipts

Keep your sales receipts (and all other business records) at least three years. These are the source documents that support your tax returns, and you may need them if you are ever audited. If your

invoices are not already bound, batch and bind them monthly (staples, rubber bands, manilla envelopes—whatever will keep them together and in order) before filing them away.

Other Incoming Funds

The income ledger has one limitation. It is not a complete record of incoming funds. Any loans received and any of your own money put into the business are not recorded on the income ledger. Loans and "contributions" (your own funds) are not income to your business, and you pay no taxes on this money. Record business loans and personal contributions as memo entries in the income ledger, below the total for the month. Do not include these amounts as part of your sales totals.

Return Checks

If a customer's check bounces on you, find out first why the check was returned. Your bank will include an explanation with the returned check. "Insufficient funds" means that there is not enough money in the customer's account to pay the check. Often, this is not an intentionally written bad check. Get in touch with your customer and tell him you will redeposit the check after a certain number of days. If it comes back once more, however, the bank will not accept it a third time. Be aware that banks may impose a service charge on you if your customer's check bounces—two charges

if it bounces twice. "Account closed" means just that. Your customer either switched banks and had the wrong checks with him by mistake or switched banks and had the wrong checks with him intentionally. If the check came back from the bank marked "Stop Payment," the customer deliberately stopped payment. In either case, try to contact your customer and get payment. "Return to maker" is a general term; usually it means the same as "insufficient funds."

One possible way to collect on a bounced check is to "put it in for collection," a procedure that is very effective when you are dealing with well-meaning customers who are always down to their last penny. You give the bounced check back to your bank and request that it be held for collection. Your bank then sends the check back to your customer's bank, which will hold the check for up to a month. If any funds are deposited to the customer's account during this holding period, any checks held for collection will be paid first. Some banks charge for this service.

If all attempts at collection prove futile, file the bounced check in a folder marked "Bad Debts." Bad debts will be a year-end expenditure entry, explained in the expenditure ledger instructions. Make no entry in your income ledger.

Credit Sales

There is no doubt that offering credit to your customers will increase sales. "Buy Now Pay

Later" has virtually replaced "In God We Trust" as America's slogan. Many, many people have come to expect, even demand, that they be allowed to buy on credit. Shoppers may not go out of their way to find a store that offers quality merchandise at low prices, but they will always be on the lookout for a store that will sell to them on credit. And they are often willing to pay higher prices for the privilege: we all know people who will buy gasoline only at a station that takes their credit card, even though the gas is 5 cents per gallon cheaper at the station across the street.

There are two ways to extend credit: directly; or via a credit card such as Master Charge, VISA or American Express. This chapter is about *direct credit,* credit you extend directly to your customers. Credit cards are covered in the following chapter.

Almost all wholesale businesses extend direct credit to their business customers. Many retail stores also still extend direct credit to regular customers.

Direct credit involves more work and bookkeeping on your part and a much larger expenditure of energy. You must decide who you will and will not extend credit to and how flexible or inflexible your credit policy will be. It is a good idea to have a formal, written credit policy that applies to all customers, although you will find, time and again, that each customer is different and may require special handling. Any customer seeking credit should be made aware of your policy, which should clearly state (1) maximum credit allowed, (2) payment timetable, and (3) finance charges if any.

Federal Laws—Finance Charges

If you do impose finance charges, you must abide by the rules of the Federal Truth in Lending Act, the Fair Credit Billing Act and the Equal Credit Opportunity Act. If you will not be trying to collect finance charges from your customers, you can happily skip this section.

The purpose of the Truth in Lending Act, according to the Federal Trade Commission, "is to assure that every customer who has need for consumer credit is given meaningful information with respect to the cost of that credit." The Fair Credit Billing Act requires you to make prompt correction of a billing mistake. Equal Credit Opportunity prohibits discrimination against an applicant for credit on the basis of age, sex, marital status, race,

color, religion, national origin, etc.

These acts specify what information must be presented to the customer—right down to the exact wording and size of the print—and when the information must be made available. The acts also regulate advertising of credit terms and handling of cancellations.

The Truth in Lending Act, the most far-reaching of the three laws, states that before the first transaction is made on any open-end credit account (an account with no specified last payment date), the creditor (you, the merchant) must disclose in writing (1) the conditions under which a finance charge may be imposed, (2) the method of determining the balance upon which a finance charge may be imposed, (3) the method of determining the amount of the finance charge, (4) the minimum periodic payment required, and (5) your customer's legal rights regarding possible errors or questions he may have about the bill. Good lord...

In addition to the above laws, you may also have to abide by the Consumer Credit Protection Act, Fair Credit Reporting Act and Fair Debt Collection Practices Act. You can get information about all of these wonderful laws from the Federal Trade Commission, Washington, D.C. 20580.

Credit Ledger

If you do not have a large number of credit sales, you can easily set up a credit ledger to keep track of unpaid accounts. The credit ledger must be kept in addition to your income ledger. Credit sales will have to be posted to both. The ledger section in the back of the book includes a sample credit ledger page that you can use as a prototype. The ledger has six columns:

Column One: Date of sale.

Column Two: Customer's name.

Column Three: Invoice number.

Column Four: Total amount of sale (*including* sales tax).

Column Five: Date paid.

Column Six: Memo (for any notes you want to make).

Each credit sale should be recorded on a separate line on the credit ledger. Post Columns One through Four from the credit sales slip, either when you make the sale or when you post to your income ledger. (Be sure to write the words "CREDIT SALE" on the sales receipt when you

CREDIT LEDGER

1	2	3	4		5	6
SALE DATE	CUSTOMER	INV. NO.	TOTAL SALE AMOUNT		DATE PAID	MEMO
1-18	Brenneman	113	53	12	2-10	
1-23	S. Ross	128	17	92		notice sent 3-1
1-24	Rygh	134	8	82	2-28	
2-12	Miley	186	10	71		

make the sale.) Post Column Five when you get paid. At any time, you can glance down your credit ledger and, by looking at Column Five, tell who still owes you money. Now, collecting that money—that's another story.

An Alternative Credit Record

Remember: Credit sales must be posted to your Income Ledger as well as to any credit ledger. The Income Ledger is your only complete record of income from all sales.

An alternative to the credit ledger is to make extra copies of credit sales invoices and use them in lieu of a ledger. Order your invoices in three-part, rather than two-part forms, and use the third copy as your record of credit sales. File the third copy of all credit sale invoices in a folder marked "Unpaid." When you receive payment, pull the copy from the "Unpaid" folder and then either file it in a "Paid" folder or throw it away. Once paid, this "third copy" is an extra. There is no reason to keep it unless you want a record of paid-up customers. This method eliminates the need for a credit ledger, but it involves more pieces of paper (which can be easily lost) and more expensive forms.

If you only have a two-part sales invoice (one for the customer, one for you) you should *not* put your one remaining copy in a credit file. It should stay batched with the rest of the sales receipts. If you start shuffling receipts around, some here, some

there, and lose numerical control, you are just asking for trouble. The result of such haphazard bookkeeping is usually an incomplete set of records and unsupportable ledgers.

Businesses that regularly make a large number of credit sales may want a more elaborate credit system. Stores with regular credit customers often keep a separate card on each customer with a complete record of sales and payments. Such cards can be informal or can be part of a complicated system of billings and monthly statements. For you not-so-small-time operators who need to keep close track of credit sales, there are several commercially designed systems for recording credit sales. Most computer bookkeeping systems also include some type of credit ledger.

You and Your Credit Customers

The hardest part of direct credit is trying to collect past-due accounts from slow or non-paying customers. I can think of no single aspect of business that is more upsetting than trying to deal with people who can't or won't pay their bills. You begin to resent the customers and they begin to resent you. Bad and sometimes bitter feelings build up. You must decide for yourself where you draw the line, where you decide that the money is no longer worth the aggravation.

In fact, extending too much credit can actually destroy a business. I know a small grocery store, owned by a nice and eager-to-please couple, that offered credit to everyone in the neighborhood. Quite a few customers ran up large bills they couldn't pay, until the shopkeepers finally cut off their credit. The customers, unable or unwilling to face the store owners, not only didn't pay their bills, they stopped coming in the store completely. They bought their groceries elsewhere. The poor couple not only never collected on the old sales, they lost out on new sales as well. The couple went broke and the store folded. A few months later, a brand new but much wiser owner reopened the store—and, lo and behold, all the old deadbeat customers came back to shop! It wasn't the new owner's responsibility to collect the old owner's debts, this was a new business. The new owner extended limited credit to reliable customers and never let the accounts get too high or too far behind. She had the rare talent of being able to look a negligent customer right in the eye, and say, friendly yet firmly, "Pay up." And they did. And she prospered.

Posting Uncollectible Accounts

At year-end, you should review all unpaid credit sales and determine which are uncollectible. If you keep a credit ledger, write "Uncollectible" and the year in Column Six next to those accounts that are uncollectible. Add up the uncollectible accounts for the year, and record the amount in your Bad Debts folder (see the previous discussion of Return Checks). If you keep the third-part sales receipt copies instead of a credit ledger, pull out the uncollectible receipts from the unpaid file and mark each "Uncollectible." Add up the total sales amount from all the uncollectible receipts. Staple the uncollectible receipts together, write the total on the front (or attach the adding machine tape total), and file in your Bad Debts folder. Bad debts are an expense of your business and are computed at year-end. The additional procedures are explained in the expenditure ledger section.

A note regarding uncollectibility: only include in your list of uncollectible accounts those that you are certain are uncollectible. If you are unsure, let it ride until next year. You can write off a bad debt in any future year that it becomes definitely uncollectible.

Credit Cards

Accepting credit cards such as MasterCard and VISA will eliminate most of the headaches of direct credit selling. You will not need credit ledgers, and you will never have to hound people to pay up. The banks handle all the paperwork. The fee may vary depending on your dollar volume and number of transactions a month. It usually runs 3% to 6% of the sale amount. Sometimes there is also a one-time sign up fee and a fee for the imprinter—the machine that imprints the sales slips with the information on the customer's credit card. The bank provides all the forms and the "We Accept..." signs, usually free.

VISA and MasterCard sales are handled by most banks. They can be processed through your regular checking account if it's in a bank that handles the credit card; or you can set up a special "merchants account" in another bank just to process credit cards.

When you make a VISA or MasterCard sale, you deposit the credit tag in your bank account just as if you were depositing cash. The bank does the rest. They process the tags and credit your account for the amount deposited (the total amount on the credit card tags). Once a month, the bank sends a statement of activity for the month and charges your account a monthly fee—the bank's percentage of all transactions for the month. Instead of all this paperwork, you can purchase a credit card terminal from your bank that hooks up to your regular telephone line (no special wiring needed) and processes all credit card transactions electronically, including depositing the money in your bank account. The terminal will automatically reject any invalid card, which means you will no longer have to spend time looking up invalid numbers and making telephone calls for approvals. Many banks offer a lower service charge to businesses that use electronic terminals because they eliminate so much expensive paperwork.

You usually will not be responsible for unpaid credit card accounts or for stolen or invalid cards if you follow the procedures required by your bank, such as checking signatures, expiration dates, etc.

But be warned that following all the rules does not guarantee payment. Banks routinely dishonor invalid cards even if the cards are not on their invalid lists. The only sure way to avoid this is to get telephone approval for every charge or use the electronic terminal, which will automatically reject any invalid card. Also, if your customer refuses to pay your bill for any plausible reason—claiming that the merchandise was never received, or it was damaged, or it was returned, or never even ordered—the bank will side with the customer every time. If the dispute is not resolved to the customer's satisfaction, the bank will chargeback your account, and there is little or nothing you'll be able to do about it.

American Express credit cards are handled directly by American Express. You do not go through a bank. You send the credit card tags to American Express, and they mail you a check. The company is quite cooperative, even with very-small-time operators, and pays promptly.

Lara Stonebraker, Cunningham's Coffee, Oakland: "We thought about having accounts for people who were in the neighborhood and then decided that was just a can of worms. We just didn't want to mess with it. It would take a lot of bookwork, keeping track of these accounts and what they owe and all. But we do have both MasterCard and VISA. We have to have both because people just don't carry the cash around any more. We have a $10 minimum. With the 3 percent they take out, it doesn't pay us to do it for smaller amounts. I think people are much more willing to spend money if they can charge it because they kind of feel they won't be billed for a long time."

Nick Mein, owner of Wallpapers Plus in San Francisco: "I don't think the credit cards are worth it. We must have had $600 of credit sales at the very most. We had to open a separate merchant's account, and it wasn't at my bank. And they take three percent, which is a lot for a mini-merchant like me. Three percent does mount up. I think it's kind of a rip-off. Everybody has a checking account, right? I'd rather take checks than MasterCard. In my business it's easy for me to take checks because the kind of people who buy our stuff are usually fairly responsible. We've never had a bounced check."

"It's a jungle up here, Martha!"

The Expenditure Ledger

The expenditure ledger is your record of all business expenses, business loan repayments and personal draws (money you pay to yourself). The most important function of the expenditure ledger is to separate and classify different types of expenditures. The columns in the ledger represent categories of expenditure—such as inventory, supplies, rent, etc.—and each item must be posted to its appropriate column. For this reason, you will not be able to summarize a number of transactions on one line as you can with sales in the income ledger.

There are literally hundreds of different categories of expenditure on which small businesses spend their money. The tax section of this book lists over one hundred of the more typical items. But you certainly don't want to post a ledger with 100 columns, or even with 50 or 25 columns. Visions of green eyeshades, tall stool and columns and columns of numbers. Not necessary. The secret is to use only the categories you need and want. Some categories of expenditures must have their own column because they are required to be shown separately on your income tax return. Other categories should also be listed separately because they are used repeatedly or in large dollar amounts. You will want to know where your big dollars went and so will the tax people. Occasional or small expenses can often be combined under a single title. And, of course, there is good old "miscellaneous" for the fifty bucks you loaned your brother-in-law that you know you'll never see again. (That's not really a legitimate business expense, but you get the idea.)

EXPENDITURE LEDGER

DATE	CHECK NO.	PAYEE	TOTAL	1 INV.	2 SUPPLIES, POSTAGE, ETC.	3 LABOR NON-EMPL.	4 EMPLOYEE PAYROLL	5 ADVERTISING	6 RENT	7 UTILITIES	8 TAXES & LICENSES	9	10 MISC.	11 NON-DEDUCT.
1-2	101	Postmaster	12 18		12 18									
1-2	102	R. Jones	150 00						150 00					
1-6	103	Silver Supply	137 50	137 50										
1-7	104	Daily Journal	32 00					32 00						
1-7	105	Acme Supply	83 30	83 30										
1-8	CASH	UPS (delivery)	2 20		2 20									
1-9	106	City of S.F. (bus. license)	35 00								35 00			
1-10	107	Wilson Equip. Co. (drill)	83 69											83 69

The sample expenditure ledger in the back of this book has been specially designed for small businesses. It separates expenditures into eleven categories, specific enough to give you a good idea of how your money was spent and provide adequate information for preparing your income taxes, yet general enough to make the ledger useful to a large variety of small businesses with little or no alteration.

As with the income ledger, your own experience will soon guide you to the best schedule for posting the expenditure ledger. To start you off, here is a recommended system of posting that I think will work best for most small businesses:

Payments in currency: Record the expenditure in your ledger when you make the payment. Don't put it off even a few hours—it is too easy to forget.

Payments by check: When you write a check, record the information in your checkbook—check number, date, amount, paid to, and a brief description of what the payment is for. You must then re-copy the information from your checkbook into the expenditure ledger. How often you sit down and take the time to do the copy job depends again on you, your time schedule and the volume of checks you write. If you write a large number of checks, post daily. It is a good idea to post your expenditure ledger the same time you post your income ledger. The same warnings about posting apply here: whatever schedule you choose, stick to it. Don't get behind in the paperwork.

Checkbook and Ledger Combined?

Probably some of you are already asking why have both a checkbook and an expenditure ledger. The expenditure ledger provides you with important information that your checkbook does not show, such as expenditures paid by currency and money order and unpaid expenses at year-end. The ledger format also makes it easy to summarize and review your important categories of expenditure. Your checkbook cannot readily show you how much you spent on inventory or parts last month, or on office supplies; it doesn't even show the total combined expenditures.

Your checkbook, on the other hand, provides a very important record that the expenditure ledger is not designed to show—your running bank balance. The checkbook also has space for ticking off the canceled checks, for recording void checks and adding errors, and for posting deposits.

You can buy commercial bookkeeping systems that combine the expenditure ledger and checkbook. A lot of small businesses use and like them. I personally find them unwieldy and too complicated, particularly for people with no bookkeeping experience. The method I describe here takes more time and more pencil pushing, but it is easy for a beginner to understand. Once you have mastered bookkeeping and feel comfortable with your ledgers, which will take three to six months, then you are in a better position to experiment with different methods.

Posting the Expenditure Ledger

There are sample expenditure ledgers in the ledger section at the back of the book. Each page of the ledger provides space for 39 entries. The first column is for the date. The second column is for the check number. If you pay by currency, write "cash" in this column; if you pay by money order, write "M.O." The third column shows to whom the money was paid. This column can also be used to record any special notation. The fourth column shows the total amount of the payment. This column will provide a double check of your monthly and year-end totals. All payments should be posted to this "Total" column and to one or more of the following detail expenditure columns:

Column One—Inventory. If you make or sell a product, this column will be the one showing the most activity. Record in Column One all the goods you purchase for resale or for manufacturing, including any delivery charges. Also include all the related materials that go into or are consumed in the process of preparing your product for sale such as a dressmaker's thread and a jeweler's solder. Include packaging materials if they are an integral part of your product. If your packaging costs are only occasional or incidental, record them in Column Two. Do not include in Column One office supplies, tools, equipment or any material purchased for reasons other than resale.

Column Two—Supplies, Postage, Etc. These are expenses incidental to your work. Office supplies, paper, pencils, coffee, small tools that will not last more than a year. Do not include the supplies that become part of your product or are consumed in making your product; such expenses belong in Column One. Draws for Petty Cash should also be posted to Column Two. Petty cash is explained later in this chapter.

Column Three—Labor: Non-Employees There are two types of payment for labor: payments to employees, where you withhold income taxes, social security, etc.; and payments to non-employees such as outside contractors, where nothing is withheld. The Growing Up section of *Small-Time Operator* includes a chapter, "Hiring Help," that explains in detail the difference between these two types of labor.

To record payments to non-employees, simply write down the full amount of the payment here. Employee payroll is recorded in Column Four. Remember, any payments to yourself should not be shown in Column Three or Four. Your own "wage" is not an expense of your business (unless you incorporate). Record payments to yourself in Column Eleven-*Non-Deductible.*

Column Four—Employee Payroll. You must record employee payroll both here in Column Four and in a separate payroll ledger (discussed in the "Hiring Help" chapter). The separate payroll ledger must show the full detail of the payment: gross, amounts withheld and net pay. Column Four, however, should show only the *net* amount

of the payroll check (the employee's take-home pay).

Payroll taxes that you withhold from your employees are also recorded in Column Four, but only at the time you pay them to the government. Withheld taxes include federal income, social security, Medicare, state income and possibly state disability. You should not confuse these withheld payroll taxes with payroll taxes that you, the employer, are required to pay, such as employer's portion of social security, Medicare and federal and state unemployment taxes. Employer-paid payroll taxes are posted to Column Eight—*Taxes and Licenses.* This is a confusing area because employees' and employer's taxes are reported to the government on the same form and paid with the same check.

Column Five—Advertising. Includes advertising, promotion, business gifts and entertainment.

Column Six—Rent. Rent on any business property is fully deductible, except for some lease-purchase contracts, which may require special tax calculations. If you own the building your business occupies, you must depreciate the building (covered in the Tax section).

Home businesses: Before you take a rent deduction, you must first determine if you qualify under the Internal Revenue Service's home-business rules. They are explained in the Office-In-The-Home chapter in the Tax Section. If you do qualify, you then determine what percentage of your home is used for business. The percentage must be based on the amount of space devoted to business. For example, if you rent a five-room house and one room is used totally for business, one-fifth or twenty percent of your home can be considered used for business, and twenty percent of your rent expense can be charged to your business.

You can pay your home rent from your personal checking account or from your business checking account; but only the business portion is posted as a business expense in Column Six. The personal portion is not deductible (either post to Column Eleven or do not post at all).

Column Seven—Utilities. When your business is operated out of your home, the business portion of your utilities is the same percentage as the business portion of your home (see Column Six above). If you are not eligible for a home office deduction, you also cannot deduct home utilities.

Telephone can be included in this column or given its own column. For home businesses, the basic monthly rate on the first telephone line into your residence is not deductible. You may deduct business-related long distance charges, special equipment, extra services (such as call waiting), and the full cost of any additional business lines into the house. See the *Home-Based Business* chapter in the appendix.

Column Eight—Taxes and Licenses. Record any tax payment or license fee here except withheld payroll taxes (see instructions under Column Four). Be sure to note in the "Paid To" column what the payment is for; you will need this information for your income tax return.

Regarding sales tax: the only sales tax that should be posted to Column Eight is the amount you remit to the state, collected from your sales. Any sales tax you pay when purchasing supplies, equipment or anything else should be included as part of the price of the goods purchased. For example, if your business cards cost $12.00 plus 72 cents sales tax, you should enter $12.72 in Column Two. Nothing should be entered in Column Eight.

Column Nine is blank. I cannot possibly foresee all your needs, so here is one extra untitled column to use or not to use as you see fit.

Column Ten—Miscellaneous. The ol' catch-all. For unusual expenditures or expenditures that do not recur enough to justify their own column. Include in Column Ten payments for insurance, bookkeeping and other professional services, dues and organization fees, out-of-town travel, education expenses, minor repairs, loan interest (repayment of the loan principal should be posted to Column Eleven—*Non-Deductible*). A more detailed list of items to post to Column Ten can be found in the tax section. Any expense that you are posting to Column Ten that starts to recur regularly should be moved to its own column. Either use Column Nine or another column you are not using. Feel free to change the heading of any column in the ledger to suit your needs.

Column Eleven—Non-Deductible. Use this column for:

1. Personal draws—money you pay yourself.

2. Furniture, tools, equipment, machinery, buildings and other fixed (depreciable) assets. These expenses *are* deductible, but may have to be depreciated over a period of years. Some people post these asset to the Miscellaneous column; some set up a separate column just for fixed assets. But whatever column you use, these purchases should also be recorded on the Depreciation Worksheet/Equipment Ledger in the Ledger Section. Depreciation and the Depreciation Worksheet are explained in detail in the Tax Section.

3. Repayment of business loans—principal only. A loan is not income when received and is not an expense when paid. Any interest paid on a business loan *is* a valid expense and should be posted to Column Ten.

4. Legal fines or penalties, including traffic tickets. These may be "valid" expenses of your business, but they are not deductible for income taxes.

5. Accounts Payable. This relates to year-end adjustments to bring your ledgers up to full accrual. The full details are explained at the end of this chapter.

6. If you write a check on your business account for personal, non-business expenses; or if you write a check for something that is part-personal and part business—the non-business portion is not deductible and should be posted here. The business portion is fully deductible (unless it is one of the exceptions covered here or in the Tax section of the book) and should be posted to its appropriate column.

Recording Vehicle Expenses

There are two ways to record car and truck expenses. You may keep track of actual expenses, or you can take a standard mileage allowance. The "Car and Truck Expenses" chapter in the tax section explains both methods. If you decide to take the standard mileage allowance, you do not have to make any entries in your expenditure ledger until year-end. If you plan to keep track of actual expenses, you should record all vehicle expenses as they are incurred. Use Column Nine in your expenditure ledger to record these expenses. Note that the cost of the vehicle and any major repairs should not be included in Column Nine. These costs may have to be depreciated along with other fixed assets (see Column Eleven above and the Depreciation chapter in the Tax Section). If you use the Standard Mileage Allowance, however, you do not depreciate your vehicle.

Monthly Totals

As with the income ledger, total all the columns of your expenditure ledger each month. Cross-check the monthly totals to the Total column, and correct any errors. Do not, however, start a new expenditure ledger page for each new month. If a month ends and only half a page is used, double-underline your total, skip two lines and start the next month on the same page.

Year-End Procedures

You must make several year-end ledger entries. None are difficult. The Year-End Expenditure Summary in the ledger section has been designed to help you post the year-end entries.

Step One: Post the monthly totals in their proper columns to the summary sheet.

Step Two: This step is only for people using accrual accounting. People using the cash method of accounting can skip to Step Three. People who are unsure what I am talking about should re-read the chapter Cash Accountintg Vs. Accrual.

This step is the adjustment to bring your books up to full accrual. You will recall that under accrual accounting, all expenses are recorded whether paid or not. Throughout the year, for ease in posting, only the paid expenses have been recorded. So now you must post any unpaid bills to your ledger. List the bills individually, one to a line, and post to the appropriate columns. As you record each unpaid bill, clearly mark it "ACCOUNTS PAYABLE." Any other unpaid expense for the year just ended, such as payroll taxes, should also be recorded on this year-end summary, one to a line, even if you have not received a bill.

Step Three: Add up the Total column and Columns One through Eleven. Cross-check your totals: the sum of the totals in Columns One through Eleven should equal the total in the Total column.

Step Four: For accrual accounting, total the return checks and the uncollectible accounts in your Bad Debts folder (discussed earlier in this section) and post in the Total column. If, however, you are using the cash method, include the bounced checks but do not include any unpaid credit sales.

Step Five: If you use the standard mileage allowance for vehicle expenses (discussed in the tax section), calculate the vehicle expense on the summary sheet and post to the Total column.

Step Six: If you take depreciation, record the depreciation expense from the depreciation worksheets (discussed in the tax section) in the Total column. If your accountant figures you depreciation for you, just skip this step.

Your work is done.

Accounts Payable

This Accounts Payable chapter is for accrual method businesses only. Cash method businesses can skip to the next chapter.

The unpaid bills and unbilled expenses that you posted to the Year-End Expenditure Summary require special handling when paid next year. These expenses are deductible the year they were incurred, which is the year just ended. They may not be deducted again next year, even though they will be paid next year. When the bills are paid—you will recognize them because you marked them "ACCOUNTS PAYABLE" when you posted them to the summary—they must be posted to Column Eleven-*Non-Deductible.*

Altering the Ledgers and Designing Your Own

After a year's experience with these ledgers, learning which categories of expense you need and don't need, you can easily design your own ledgers. Do you need the non-employee labor column, or the payroll column, or the advertising column? Instead, maybe you want a separate column for equipment purchases, or freight charges, or travel, or some other category important to your business. Many small businesses set up their expenditure ledger columns to exactly match the categories on their income tax forms. For my own business, I try to use as few columns as possible to minimize my book work; and yet I've met business owners who felt they had to have 18 different columns to keep their expenditures straight.

You can make inexpensive ledgers using accounting ledger paper. Ledger paper—also called "accountants' work sheets"—usually comes in fifty-sheet pads, with numbered lines (about 40 to a page), blank spaces for column headings and punched holes for loose-leaf binding. The ledger paper is available with anywhere from two to twenty-five columns. Every stationery store carries a selection of these pads.

Ledgers get a lot of use and abuse. The loose leaf ledgers do not hold up well, the pages tear out easily and the ledgers are often awkward to work with. If you can afford a higher quality ledger, purchase a heavy duty cam-lock post binder and heavy duty ledger sheets. By the way, thrift stores are great places to find old (and excellent quality) ledger binders. I found two in a Salvation Army store, complete with unused sheets, for $1.50 each. And, of course, all varieties of commercial ledgers and prepackaged bookkeeping systems are available in most stationary stores.

Petty Cash

A petty cash fund provides a systematic method for paying and recording out-of-pocket cash payments and payments too small to be made by check. ("Cash" in petty cash refers to currency, *not* to checks; which is just the opposite of my earlier definition. Nobody's perfect.)

I suggest, for starters, that you do not have a petty cash fund. It's more bookkeeping, more paperwork, more procedures to remember. Pay the nickel-and-dime expenditures out of what cash is on hand, and record them directly and *immediately* in your expenditure ledger. Any respectable accountant would roll over in his subsidiary ledgers, so to speak, if he heard me say this, because the absence of a petty cash fund can result in poor cash control, increasing the possibility of incomplete records and "misappropriation" (that means theft) of funds. But if yours is a one person business or if you alone have access to the money, the importance of cash control is outweighed, I feel, by the need for a simple set of books.

If a petty cash fund is what you want or need, I have devised a relatively simple system for handling petty cash. It is a compromise between no system at all and a bookkeeper's dream, and it requires you to follow three rules. One, keep no more than twenty dollars in the fund. Two, make payments out of the fund only for miscellaneous supplies and postage—expenses that normally would be posted to Column Two in the expenditure ledger. Three, use the fund as little as possible and only when there is no practical way to write a check instead.

If you promise to follow those ground rules here is the procedure:

1. Write a check payable to "Petty Cash" for $20. Cash the check at your bank and put the money, a piece of accounting worksheet paper and a pencil in a separate cash box or cigar box—whatever is handy and relatively safe.

2. Record the $20 check as an expenditure in your ledger, posting it to Column Eleven-*Non-Deductible*.

3. Every time you make a payment from the petty cash fund, record the date, payee and amount on your accounting worksheet, which has just become your petty cash ledger. Get receipts for the payments if possible and put them in the box with the cash.

4. When the fund starts to get low, total the payments recorded on the worksheet, and add up the remaining cash in the box. The worksheet total and the remaining cash should equal $20. If you are out of balance, you either made an adding error, recorded a payment wrong, failed to record

PETTY CASH LEDGER

Period __3/26 – 4/30__   Page __1__ of ____

DATE	DESCRIPTION	AMT.	BAL.
	Beginning Balance	20.00	20.00
3/26	Stamps	1.30	18.70
3/29	COD Charge	1.87	16.83
3/29	office supplies	.53	16.30
4/2	donation to Boy Scouts	1.00	15.30
4/8	coffee for the office	3.57	11.73

a payment, or else you've been robbed. If you can't find an error, adjust the worksheet total so that your petty cash fund is back in balance. Staple all the petty cash receipts to the worksheet and file it away.

5. Write a check payable to "Petty Cash" equal in amount to the total (or the corrected total if there was an error) from the worksheet. Cash the check and put the money in your petty cash box with a new worksheet. Sharpen the pencil.

6. Record the check in your expenditure ledger in Column Two—*Supplies, Postage, Etc.*

Thereafter, whenever your petty cash fund gets low, and also at year-end, repeat steps Four through Six.

Calculators and Adding Machines

A pocket calculator is an excellent business tool. It can be carried around with you and it will give you instant answers. If you are often computing package deals or bulk prices, figuring discounts, sales tax, etc., a good pocket calculator will be indispensable to you.

But when it comes to posting ledgers, adding columns of figures, balancing bank accounts or any typical business activity involving the addition or subtraction of more than just a few numbers, the pocket calculator leaves much to be desired. Most of the calculators are very small, and their keyboards are tiny. It is easy—*too* easy—to make an adding mistake. Many of the calculators have keyboard buttons smaller than the tip of your finger and no spaces between the buttons. Punch a 6, and your finger strays onto the 5. Try this: get out your calculator and add a column of twenty-five numbers. Note your answer, and then add the numbers a second time. Got two different answers, didn't you? Happens to me all the time. Now, which amount is correct? Here lies another problem inherent in the little calculators. There is no way to check your figures, no tape to look at. An adding machine tape is indispensable for checking your totals, locating errors and keeping a record of your calculations.

Here are some guidelines to follow when shopping for a ten-key adding machine:

1. Buy a machine with a large, easy to operate keyboard, one well-spaced to accommodate your hand, allowing maximum speed and minimum error. If the machine includes a digital display, try

to find one with an LED display (real lights, usually green) instead of an LCD or liquid crystal display (the silvery and often dim-looking numbers that are difficult to read in bright light).

2. Test out the machine. Add some numbers and see how the machine feels. The keys should not "stick"—that is, the response should be smooth and rapid. A major difference between quality and cheap adding machines is how well they respond to the touch.

3. Adding machines vary in the number of digits they can handle. Select one with at least an eight-digit capacity.

4. It is very important that your machine be able to handle negative amounts. If you subtract 100 from 90, the machine total should either be a 10 in red or a 10 with a large minus mark next to it, or both. Printing the negative balance in red is preferable because it stands out better. Some older adding machines and some of the very cheap new ones may either give a total of 10 with no indication that it is a minus or else give no total at all. Avoid such a machine.

Basic ten-key adding machines can be purchased new at reasonable prices though a good used machine is better than a cheap new one.

Financial Management: Using Your Ledgers

Your books are more than just a record of your business activity and an aid to preparing income tax forms. They are valuable tools to help you manage your business successfully.

Profit-and-Loss Analysis

Without a schedule of profit and loss, it is difficult for the owner of even the smallest business to determine whether or not the business is making a profit. Your cash balances and the day-to-day cash income and outgo, as important as they are, are not a good indication of profit or loss. Cash flow can, in fact, give you a totally misleading picture of how your business is doing.

Simple profit and loss statements, prepared monthly from your ledgers, can tell you a great deal about your business. A profit and loss statement is, basically, a schedule showing your income and your expenses and the difference between the two. Here is a procedure for preparing a very simple profit and loss statement:

Income. The income on the statement is the

```
                    Profit & Loss Statement

                    Bear Soft Pretzel Company

                    January thru September


              Month of September              Year-to-Date


Income from ledger              $2,095                    $13,724

Beginning inventory    $  900              $   310

Purchases               1,230               6,710

                       $2,130              $7,020

Estimated inventory
   September 30        (1,000)             (1,000)

      Cost-of-goods-sold          1,130                     6,020

         GROSS PROFIT           $  965                    $ 7,704

Other expenses:

   Rent                $50                 $450

   Supplies             13                   74

   Other                 0                   27

   Total Other Expenses           63                       551

      NET PROFIT               $  902                    $ 7,153
```

monthly income total from your ledger (Columns Three, Five and Six in the income ledger). You should exclude sales tax, loan income and any money you put into the business from your own personal funds.

Expenses. Expenses should be separated into two groups: inventory (Column One in the expenditure ledger) and all other expenses (Columns Two through Ten). Column Eleven should not be included.

If you have inventory, you must estimate the cost of the inventory on hand at the end of the month. If it is only an insignificant amount, you can ignore it. The inventory on hand at the beginning of the month, *plus* the current month's purchases from Column One, *less* your estimate of inventory on hand at the end of the month gives you your actual current inventory expense. This expense is called "cost-of-goods- sold" and is covered in much greater depth in the tax section.

"All other expenses" includes everything in Columns Two through Ten except sales tax paid (recorded in Column Eight—*Taxes and Licenses*). Be sure not to include any expenditures from Column Eleven—*Non-Deductible*.

Your income *less* the cost-of-goods-sold (inventory expense) gives you what is known as "gross profit." Gross profit *less* all the other expenses gives you your net profit or loss. By showing both a gross and a net profit or loss, you can tell more easily how your expenses relate to income. If you are losing money, you can readily determine if it is the cost of the inventory (cost-of-goods-sold) or the other expenses that are responsible for the loss. A service business that has no inventory does not have to compute cost-of-goods-sold or gross profit. For such a business, income less "all other expenses" equals net profit or loss.

A statement prepared in the above manner will give you profit and loss information for the month just ended. Some business owners like to see a second column in their profit and loss statements that shows the year-to-date cumulative activity. The year-to-date column is prepared in almost the same way as the monthly column. Year-to-date income is the sum of all the monthly income totals in income ledger Columns Three, Five and Six from January to date, including the month just ended. Cost-of-goods-sold is slightly different. It is the inventory on hand *at January 1, plus* the sum of all the monthly totals in expenditure ledger Column One, *less* the same ending inventory that you estimated for the monthly column. "All other expenses" is the sum of all the monthly totals in Columns Two through Ten (again excluding sales tax payments in Column Eight).

Your profit and loss statement should look something like the Bear Soft Pretzel Co. illustration. This type of profit and loss statement is only approximate. It does not include unpaid expenses or expenses computed at year-end such as depreciation, and it should not be used for preparing income tax forms.

Cash Flow

One of the most damaging things that can happen to a business is a cash shortage. If you don't have the cash to pay your bills or replenish depleted inventory, your business will suffer. I know of profitable businesses actually forced to shut down for a lack of immediate cash.

```
            Estimated Cash Flow Projection

                  Month of June
```

	Cash In	Cash Out	Balance
Cash on hand June 1........			$800
June 1 rent payment.......		$250	
June 1 utilities..........		20	$530
Receipts first week........	$500		
Inventory purchase 1st week		$500	
Supplies first week........		30	$500
Receipts second week.......	$500		
Payroll second week........		$200	$800
Receipts third week........	$500		
Supplies third week........		$50	$1,250
Receipts fourth week.......	$500		
Payroll fourth week........		$200	
Inventory purch. 4th week..		500	
Personal draw.............		400	$650
Cash on hand June 30.......			$650

INVENTORY RECORD

Item _#3 Silver Buckle_   Supplier _L. J. Silver Co._

DATE ORDERED	QUANTITY ORDERED	DATE REC'D.	QUANTITY REC'D.	QUANTITY SOLD	BALANCE ON-HAND
1-31	50				0
1-31	15	2-13	35		35
				13	22
				4	18
		3-1	15		33
				10	23
3-12	50				23

To help avoid a sudden cash squeeze, many businesses prepare monthly "cash flow projections." Cash flow projections are estimates of cash that will be coming in and cash that must be spent during the upcoming month. These projections show approximately how much cash will be on hand during the month and alert you to possible cash shortages.

During the first few months your business is in operation, cash projections will be difficult for you to make. You cannot yet estimate how much income will be coming in nor will you be familiar enough with your regular expense requirements. But the first few months are a critical time for any business. You should make some attempt to estimate and be prepared for cash needs. Here is a good way to project your first month's cash flow:

First determine how much cash you will need to get your business off to a good start. The chart of start-up costs in the Getting Started section should help you calculate these initial cash outlays.

If yours is a sales or manufacturing business or a service business that stocks parts, estimate how much additional inventory you will need during the first month of business. Unless you initially purchased a large inventory, figure on doubling the original amount.

Next, add the expenses that must be paid during the first month, such as supplies and payroll, and those that must be paid by the first of the next month, such as rent and utilities. Then add another $200 for unanticipated expenses.

The sum of the above items should give you an estimate of your first month's expenses. Now, how much income do you anticipate during the first month of operation? Obviously, this can only be a guess, but be conservative. And once you've arrived at a good guess, knock it down by twenty-five percent—almost all new business owners are overoptimistic.

Comparing the "guess-timated" income to the projected expenses will give you some idea of your cash needs. It is a very rough idea, admittedly; but it is better than no idea at all. Once you have a few months' actual experience behind you, cash flow projections will become easier and more accurate. A good ongoing procedure is to estimate your income and expenditures week by week, showing the balance of cash on hand at the end of each week.

The main purpose of a cash flow statement is to warn you *in advance* when cash might get dangerously low. If you know of a big cash outlay coming up next month—such as a loan payment or a tax payment—or a predictable seasonal drop in sales, the cash flow statement will show you whether your regular income will provide enough cash to meet expenses.

If the statement predicts a cash shortage, you can plan in advance to avoid the problem. Postpone a payment that is not immediately necessary, or plan a sale to generate more income, or seek a short-term loan. Short-term bank loans are relatively easy to get. Banks are usually willing to loan short-term funds (usually thirty days or sixty days) to profitable businesses. What's more, the fact that you have actually prepared a cash flow statement indicates to a banker that you are knowledgeable about your business and, therefore, a better risk than someone who has no financial knowledge at all.

Inventory Control

Any business that sells or manufactures goods and any service business that stocks parts must have some sort of inventory control, some way of knowing what has been ordered, what is on hand, and when it's time to reorder. For a very small business or one selling only a small variety of items, the inventory purchase records in your expenditure ledger (Column One) and your day-to-day observations of the stock on hand will probably provide you all the information you need to maintain adequate inventory control. A periodic count, or "inventory," is the easiest and quickest way to determine what is still on hand and what must be reordered.

Larger businesses and those selling a large selection of merchandise, however, will need more formal procedures for controlling inventory. Such businesses should maintain a written record of all stock ordered, received and sold. "Perpetual inventory" records, as they are called, can be kept on index cards—one card for each type of item in stock—or in inventory ledgers, with a ledger page for each different item. Both the cards and the ledgers have the same format. An up-to-date and accurate inventory record can tell you at a glance your balance on hand, what is still on order, and how long it takes to receive an order.

How to Keep an Inventory Record

When you place your order, record the quantity and the date of the order in the Ordered column. When you receive the order, line out the entry in the Ordered column and enter the information in the Received column. Posting the date received will give you an idea how long it takes your suppliers to send you an ordered item. If you receive only part of your order, record the undelivered back-ordered quantity and the original order date in the Ordered column.

On the sample inventory record, 50 silver buckles were ordered on January 31. A partial shipment of 35 arrived February 13. The 35 received were recorded in the Received column, the order for 50 was lined out, and the balance of 15 still on order was recorded in the Ordered column. The 15 finally arrived on March 1, at which time the 15 still showing in the Ordered column was lined out. Got it? The number of items sold should be recorded either when the sale is made or at the end of the day, summarized from the day's sales slips.

At least once a year, and preferably every six months, the perpetual records should be proven by taking a physical count. If there is a discrepancy, the records should be adjusted to agree with the count. If the difference is substantial, you know something is wrong. Either you have not been updating the records correctly, or your inventory is being stolen.

Inventory control, like cash flow, is a management tool only. It is meant to help you run your business. The methods I have described for inventory control are only suggestions. Feel free to alter or ignore them. Any system or non-system that works for you is probably a good one.

Computerized Inventory Control

Businesses with large or varied inventories have found computer inventory programs extremely useful; some say essential. Computer inventory records should look very similar to the hand-posted ledgers shown here, and they should provide you with *exactly* the information you need. Shop around for a program that meets your needs. If you compromise, I can almost guarantee that you will soon be looking for a different program. Computer inventory records should be proven by taking physical counts on a regular basis, just like hand-posted records; a computer record is just as likely to be incorrect.

Joe Campbell, Resistance Repair: "Here's one example of not running a service business like a regular business. For years I've had parts around, and I'd use one of them and I'd say, 'I think these things cost about fifty cents, so I'll charge 65 cents for them.' But it wasn't at all consistent. I had absolutely no idea how much I was spending for parts. If you get back only what you paid for it, you've lost money. Because it's taken time to order it, write the check for it, put it into stock, keep track of it and pay taxes on it. Now, I've got a little plastic box for every part that I stock. Inside that plastic box is the part and a card telling me where I got it, what the number is, what I paid for it. We use a uniform markup: 100 percent. We're selling things that cost us 30 cents. If we sell them for 40 percent more, for 42 cents, that hasn't even paid for hassling the damn things. Every week when we tally up the income, we break it down into parts and labor. And we get separate totals. We have a separate checking account and we take 60 percent of the parts income total and deposit it into the parts account. This way, we'll be able to replace the part and have 10 percent left over. It gives a little bit of wiggle room. It'll pay our resale taxes. That's about how it works out. Plus we know exactly how much money we've got to buy parts with. You look at it and say the balance is $400 and we need $300 worth of parts. Can we afford it? Yes, we can afford it. It's very simple, it's very efficient, and it works."

———

Larry Campbell, of Ingram Book Company, a large book wholesaler who sells to, and works with, owners of very small bookstores: "One of the quiet, simple programs at Ingram seems to be a step back in time: the Card in Book system. Under it, booksellers pay three cents for a card sent with each shipment, to go in each book. When a retail customer buys a book, the clerk takes the card. At the end of the day, the store can easily reorder sold titles. It's low-tech. If you're a small store, you don't need computers but still need an inventory management program."

Section Three
GROWING UP

Most people would succeed in small things
if they were not troubled with great
ambitions.

—Longfellow

Growing Up

"LEARN the many different methods and little known techniques used today by experienced businessmen in building small companies into Powerful Places in Industry."

-from the cover jacket of another book on starting a business

---

Well, maybe John D. Rockefeller did start with a two-pump filling station and some spectacular ambitions. After all, *bigger and better* has been a trademark of this big country of ours for as long as most of us can remember. For years we have associated big business, big industry, big government with prosperity, happiness and the good life.

But today it seems that America's "powerful places in industry" are just too powerful and are choking—not helping—our economy. In the last few years we have witnessed huge corporations laying off thousands of employees without warning; other corporations doubling and tripling their prices—and their profits—with us apparently powerless to stop them; big city governments unable to pay their bills, on the verge of financial collapse. Bigger is no longer synonymous with better, and big business no longer seems to be able or willing to provide us a good way of life.

Small-Time Operator is not going to be much help to those Rockefellers among you with dreams of building your business into "powerful places in industry." I feel that small business can offer you personal satisfaction and a good livelihood. But "small" does not have to mean that you are forever the one person business, unable to grow. Nothing in this world is intrinsically good or bad. Business growth can be a positive and pleasant experience for everyone concerned. Business growth, however, can also be mistimed and miscalculated, turning against you and doing you in.

A few years ago, I was associated briefly with a small music magazine. It was doing well—good circulation, good advertising—and it was making a healthy profit. The owners of the magazine, feeling the power of success, simultaneously launched two other ventures: one was experimental films, the other a fashion magazine. Both new ventures were major undertakings, and both catered to a small audience. And both started losing money immediately and consistently until the entire company, music magazine and all, was at the brink of collapse. Major surgery saved the business. The unsuccessful sidelines were discontinued; friends loaned money to pay the creditors; the number of employees was cut back; and many of the extra luxuries added during the early success were eliminated. Only the original magazine remained, and still being very popular, it saved the company, which eventually emerged again, healthy, happy and much wiser.

Success is heady, and the owners of the successful magazine believed—as many overly ambitious small-time operators do—that success necessarily breeds success. They soon learn that things don't always work out that way.

Very often a business expands because a situation presents itself that the owner "just can't pass up": the adjacent store-front becomes vacant, and the landlord offers to knock out the separating partition and rent both stores to you; a competitor is failing and offers to sell his business to you, cheap. Or it may be that your customers have been encouraging expansion, suggesting that you offer some related product or service. And as frequent a reason for expansion as any, you're out to catch a bigger fish; success in your present business is tempting you on to bigger and better success (bigger and better?).

He is well paid that is well satisfied.
—Shakespeare from Merchant of Venice

**Too Big, Too Fast:
Excerpts from the Financial Pages**

Publishers Weekly:

The former president of now-defunct Pinnacle Publishing reported, "Pinnacle was caught in the situation that we were in a tremendous growth cycle. As we were building the receivables, a constant cash infusion was required to continue that growth. The bigger we got, the more we owed. The growth continued, but so did the liability to creditors."

San Francisco Chronicle:

"My Child's Destiny Fails": My Child's Destiny, on the fancy end of Grant Avenue, was a store of plush mauve carpets, books, toys, computer learning software, expensive velvet dresses, hand-knit sweaters, and Italian children's shoes. It seemed like a good idea at the time: quality children's products, good service, a national mail-order catalog and relatively high prices. They hoped to attract thousands of well-to-do, two career parents, many having their first child late in life. They plunged into mail-order and conventional retailing at the same time, opening what was really a small department store for children in an expensive downtown location. But the dream came crashing down this month when they filed for bankruptcy…"It's over. I'm looking for a job," said [the owner]. "If we had to do it all over again, we'd start a bit slower or a bit smaller. Launching eight categories all at one fell swoop was a bit much, in hindsight…I never had the thought that it could possibly fail."

San Francisco Chronicle:

"A Fine Food Failure"—The interior of Hoffman & Husband specialty food store is dark and sumptuous, the shiny brass setting off the wood and wallpaper like the handles on a fancy casket. And that is just what Hoffman & Husband has become, a coffin for an idea that seemed almost foolproof: supplying high-style, high-priced comestibles for the cash-heavy professional horde spending its way down from Pacific Heights. What went wrong? Almost everything. The store was designed to have the feel of a series of small shops, and the result was a labor-intensive operation. Frequently, the staff outnumbered the customers, payroll ran $250,000 a year, "and we never took a salary." Start-up expenses were high. The Hoffmans relied on a series of consultants, each highly recommended, each delighted to find clients who understood you have to spend money to make money. You walk in and you see the quality, but you have to sell a lot of pate to pay for the fixtures. "We had no experience in the food business, and we didn't understand the cost-control side." It took a mere 15 months for the store to descend into bankruptcy. "We lost our shirts."

San Francisco Examiner:

Banana Republic Inc., the offbeat, homegrown retailer that bolted into a national success, is under siege. The 101-store chain, propelled into prominence selling "safari style" attire, is refusing to talk about its unraveling sales, layoffs, the remodeling of stores, and alterations in merchandise. It's a classic example, industry analysts say, of an entrepreneurial start-up that explodes in phenomenal growth and is forced to make a jarring leap from free-wheeling alliance into big business. The owners spent millions underwriting expansion. Then last year, sales per store declined and expenses jumped out of whack. Retail analysts say Banana Republic's merchandise was overpriced when the safari-look, after ten years of successful sales, fizzled. "After all, how many khaki shirts do you need?", commented one observer. "Retailing is an evolution. It has to keep moving with the rest of the world. I don't think Banana Republic is different from anybody else."

Image Magazine:

"They Lost Their Britches": Aca Joe's warehouse, a huge space, is virtually empty. Stand by its deserted loading bays and you can hear the quiet inside. Three years ago, Aca Joe was the fastest rising star in retail. Today it's on the edge of ruin. The warehouse on Eichler Street is a monument to oversized ambition and dubious judgment. The most glaring trouble spot was manufacturing and supply. The company, with some 75 stores, was having trouble paying for enough merchandise to stock them. And with the $145,000 a year rent on the warehouse, the $1 million computer system, another $1 million a year in legal and accounting fees, total overhead was running about $5 million a year—when annual sales were only $13 million. Aca Joe needed to have 150 stores open just to cover its overhead, but how could it when the company couldn't get merchandise into the 75 or so stores that were already open. "We were building up in anticipation of our growth," said [the former owner]. "Our financial condition just deteriorated much faster than we realized. We got swallowed up by everyone's greed."

You should put in some real thinking time before making a decision about expanding:

1. Just as your present business was slow going at first, maybe even losing money, the expanded business will take time to get on its own feet. You will probably be making less money for a while, possibly even losing money for a year or two. Are you prepared for a repeat of the early, lean days?

2. Any expansion is going to require more capital. It means investing your savings or borrowing.

3. If you plan to acquire a second business location, be prepared for a *major* increase in the amount and type of work you will have to do. Someone will have to be hired to run one of the stores for you, and suddenly you will find yourself not only buyer, seller, bookkeeper, market analyst and the rest, but manager also. Some real skills are required to manage a multi-store operation, not the least of which is being able to deal with employees—hiring, training, delegating authority and responsibility, and sometimes firing.

4. The paperwork—bookkeeping, payrolls, forms—will just about double. How well do you handle it now? You may need to hire a bookkeeper.

5. Your own leisure time away from business will be reduced, possibly eliminated.

A re-warning about financial commitments: in the eyes of the law, you and your unincorporated business are one and the same. Any liabilities of your business, financial or otherwise, are also personal ones.

Hugo said, "Caution is the eldest child of wisdom." Think this decision through. Don't let any outside factors lure you into a move that you aren't ready for. Whether you choose to stay small or take a chance on expansion, be totally satisfied that you have made the right decision.

Small-Time Operator is primarily written as a guide for the very small and the new business.

"Growing Up" encompasses a world of new challenges and difficulties, the subject of an entire book itself. This Growing Up section covers three areas many small—and growing—businesses need to know about: hiring help, starting partnerships, and incorporating.

Hiring Help—How to Save Time and Money By Not Becoming an Employer

Hiring employees will just about double the amount of your paperwork. As an employer, you must keep separate payroll records for each employee, withhold federal income and social security-Medicare taxes, withhold state income and possibly state disability taxes, prepare quarterly and year-end payroll tax returns, pay employer's portion of social security and Medicare taxes and unemployment taxes, purchase workers' compensation insurance and prepare year-end earnings statements for each employee. It's been estimated that the employer's taxes, worker's comp insurance and paperwork will cost you an additional thirty percent of your payroll. In other words, if you pay a wage of $7.00 per hour, it's really costing you about $9.00.

Businesses hiring employees are also more closely controlled and regulated than one-person businesses. Federal and state governments demand prompt payroll tax returns and require strict adherence to employment laws. If you are late filing your income tax return, it might easily be six months or more before you even hear from the government, and then it will just be a letter of inquiry or a bill. If, however, you are late filing your quarterly payroll tax return, in just a few weeks you could find your business under lock and key and your bank account impounded.

Who are employees? From the Internal Revenue Service: "Anyone who performs services that can be controlled by an employer (what will be done and how it will be done) is an employee. This is so

---

We have assumed that, because the country is big and the economy is big, everything should be big. It has been the conventional wisdom that bigness is goodness. Some bigness is dictated by the nature of things; in manufacturing it can bring wider distribution of goods and potentially lower prices. But a good deal of bigness is bad for the economy and bad for the free enterprise system. The large miscellaneous conglomerates that absorb independent businesses and engage in predatory competitive practices do not serve the best interests of the economy or the country.

—former Senator Gaylord Nelson

even when the employer gives the employee freedom of action, if the employer has the legal right to control the method and result of the services. Employers usually provide the tools and place to work and have the right to fire an employee."

Some businesses such as restaurants and larger retail stores must have employees; there is no getting around it. You can't possibly do all the work yourself, and the people you hire—dishwashers, waitresses, clerks—definitely fall within the legal definition of "employee."

Some small businesses can sometimes get outside help without hiring employees. These businesses often hire "outside contractors" (also called independent contractors), people in business for themselves, people who sell their services to you. When you hire an outside contractor, you pay the contractor his or her fee in full. You do not withhold taxes, pay employment taxes or file payroll tax returns.

Who is an outside contractor? The IRS says, "Generally, people in business for themselves are not employees. For example, doctors, lawyers, contractors and others who follow an independent trade are usually not employees."

Here are two hypothetical examples to illustrate employees vs. non-employees:

Example I: The Clever Leather Company (that's you) needs help making belts. You want someone to cut the leather into two inch wide strips so you can devote your talent to the design work. You hire your buddy for $5.00 an hour, sit him down in your shop, and tell him to cut out 250 two inch wide belts, each three feet long.

The Clever Leather Company has just become a bona-fide employer. When you pay your friend, you must withhold income, social security and Medicare taxes, send the withheld taxes to the government, pay employer social security, Medicare and unemployment taxes, maintain payroll ledgers, prepare earnings statements at year-end. Ugh.

Example II: The More-Clever-Than-Ever Leather Company (that's me) needs help making belts. I want someone to cut the leather into two inch wide strips so I can devote my talent to the design work. I call up the Leather Cutting Company (that's *my* buddy) and order up 250 of his standard two inch wide, three foot long belts. The Leather Cutting Company produces the belts on its own work schedule and delivers the completed order to me.

The More-Clever-Than-Ever Leather Company just conducted business with an outside contractor. More-Clever-Than-Ever Leather wrote a check for the full amount billed and recorded it in the expenditure ledger.

Seriously, it is important that you carefully determine the legal status of your hired help. A person who falls within the definition of an employee *is* an employee no matter what you call him. Says the IRS: "If an employer-employee relationship exists, it does not matter what it is called. The employee may be called a partner, agent or independent contractor. It also does not matter how payments are measured or paid, what they are called, or whether the employee works full or part-time."

A key determining point, as far as the IRS is concerned, in deciding whether a person is an outside contractor or an employee: Does the person perform service for more than one business? A person working solely for you is usually your employee. A person providing services to several businesses is probably an outside contractor. Another determining factor is whether the contractor has invested heavily in his own tools and equipment as opposed to using yours. Little things also often help, such as contractors having their own business licenses and even having business cards.

When hiring someone you plan to pay as an outside contractor, it is also important that the person fully understands what you are doing—that he or she is not your employee, that he considers himself in business for himself, that he knows he is responsible for his own taxes and insurance and social security, and that he will not be eligible for unemployment insurance when the job is finished.

Many small businesses have gotten into expensive trouble with the federal and state government because their former "outside contractors" (who really should have been paid as employees) complained to the IRS when they were turned down for unemployment insurance or when they were fined for not paying their own social security.

There is another and much more serious problem if you hire people and treat them as outside contractors when the law says they should be employees. If one of these people gets injured on the job and is not covered by workers' compensation insurance, you could find yourself with medical bills and a large lawsuit.

RENTAL AGREEMENT

MONKEYWRENCH MOTORS (hereinafter "Owners"), doing business in Berkeley, California, and _____ (hereinafter "Lessee") in consideration of the premises, agree as follows:

FIRST: Lessee agrees to rent from owner a mechanic's stall and the immediate surrounding area necessary to perform the normal functions of an automobile mechanic for the daily rental of _____ per cent of the lessee's daily gross receipts.

SECOND: Lessee shall provide owner with evidence of sufficient liability insurance coverage.

THIRD: Lessee shall hold harmless owner for any and all losses owing to fire, theft, water hazard, earthquake, or any disaster.

FOURTH: Owner shall provide all supplies and materials necessary for the normal operation of an automobile garage, excepting tools and personal equipment, which shall be supplied by lessee.

FIFTH: Lessee is an independent contractor leasing or renting space in the Monkeywrench Motors' garage for the purpose of conducting the business of an automobile mechanic, and lessee shall be responsible for filing all necessary tax returns.

SIXTH: This rental agreement may be terminated by either party by giving one day's oral notice of the intention to terminate this rental agreement to the other party.

DATED:_____

MONKEYWRENCH MOTORS

_____
                                        Owners

_____
                                        Lessee

This rental agreement was drafted by a lawyer for the specific purpose of clarifying the relationship between the owner of a garage and the people working in that garage. The lawyer claims that this agreement defining the "lessees" as independent contractors and not as employees will hold up in tax court. The Internal Revenue Service says that the agreement may or may not hold up depending on the actual situation.

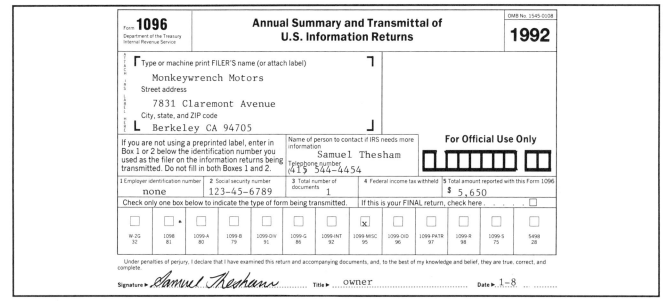

9595 ☐ VOID ☐ CORRECTED

Type or machine print PAYER'S name, street address, city, state, and ZIP code		

Type or machine print PAYER'S name, street address, city, state, and ZIP code

MONKEYWRENCH MOTORS
7831 Claremont Avenue
Berkeley CA 94705

1 Rents
$

2 Royalties
$

3 Prizes, awards, etc.
$

OMB No. 1545-0115

19 92

Statement for
Recipients of

Miscellaneous Income

PAYER'S Federal identification number	RECIPIENT'S identification number
123-45-6789	987-65-4321

4 Federal income tax withheld
$

5 Fishing boat proceeds
$

Copy A For Internal Revenue Service Center

Type or machine print RECIPIENT'S name

Crystal Rose

6 Medical and health care payments
$

7 Nonemployee compensation
$ 5,650

Street address

485 Buena Vista

8 Substitute payments in lieu of dividends or interest
$

9 Payer made direct sales of $5,000 or more of consumer products to a buyer (recipient) for resale ▶ ☐

For Paperwork Reduction Act Notice and instructions for completing this form, see Instructions for Forms 1099, 1098, 5498, and W-2G.

City, state, and ZIP code

San Francisco CA 94117

10 Crop insurance proceeds
$

11 State income tax withheld
$

Account number (optional)

12 State/Payer's state number
Calif.

Form **1099-MISC**

Do NOT Cut or Separate Forms on This Page

Department of the Treasury - Internal Revenue Service

Form 1099-MISC must be filed for every outside contractor (non-employee) who received $600 or more during the year and for outside sales people who purchased $5,000 or more in goods from you.

Form **1096**
Department of the Treasury
Internal Revenue Service

Annual Summary and Transmittal of U.S. Information Returns

OMB No. 1545-0108

1992

ATTACH IRS LABEL HERE

┌ Type or machine print FILER'S name (or attach label) ┐

Monkeywrench Motors

Street address

7831 Claremont Avenue

City, state, and ZIP code

└ Berkeley CA 94705 ┘

If you are not using a preprinted label, enter in Box 1 or 2 below the identification number you used as the filer on the information returns being transmitted. Do not fill in both Boxes 1 and 2.

Name of person to contact if IRS needs more information
Samuel Thesham
Telephone number
(415) 544-4454

For Official Use Only

1 Employer identification number	2 Social security number	3 Total number of documents	4 Federal income tax withheld	5 Total amount reported with this Form 1096
none	123-45-6789	1		$ 5,650

Check only one box below to indicate the type of form being transmitted. | If this is your FINAL return, check here . . . . . ☐

W-2G 32	1098 81	1099-A 80	1099-B 79	1099-DIV 91	1099-G 86	1099-INT 92	1099-MISC 95	1099-OID 96	1099-PATR 97	1099-R 98	1099-S 75	5498 28
☐	☐	☐	☐	☐	☐	☐	☒	☐	☐	☐	☐	☐

Under penalties of perjury, I declare that I have examined this return and accompanying documents, and, to the best of my knowledge and belief, they are true, correct, and complete.

Signature ▶ *Samuel Thesham*   Title ▶ owner   Date ▶ 1-8

A 1096 summary and Transmittal Form must accompany the 1099 forms sent to the IRS.

The IRS puts out a free publication, *Circular E-Employer's Tax Guide*, which includes all of their legal definitions and guidelines. When in doubt about the status of your "employee," you may request a ruling from the IRS on form #SS-8.

If you hire outside contractors, there is one extra bit of paperwork that you must do at year-end. For each person to whom you paid $600 or more during the year, you must file a federal form #1099-MISC. The form shows the contractor's name, address, social security number and amount paid. One copy goes to the IRS and another copy to the contractor. In addition, if your outside contractors are independent sales agents, you must report to the IRS each contractor who purchased $5,000 or more in goods from you. Use form 1099-MISC.

The 1099-MISC forms must be given to your contractors no later than January 31 of the new year. The IRS copies of the 1099 forms must be accompanied by a summary Form 1096, and must be sent to the IRS by the last day in February (although you can get a 30-day extension to file your 1096 with the IRS by filing Form 8809). Don't you love all these numbers?

The IRS provides a Form W-9 for your outside

contractor to fill out, showing his name and address and social security number (or Employer Identification Number if he uses one). By signing the form, the outside contractor certifies to you that he is giving you correct information. You keep the form in your files; it does not get sent to the IRS. This form is optional. The outside contractor is not required to fill out this form, but he is required to give you his social security or Employer ID number. If he refuses, you will most likely be required to withhold taxes from his pay.

A final word, about paying a worker "under the table". The term means that the worker is not on the payroll as an employee, that the payment is usually in currency, and that no record is made of the payment. This is usually illegal and can get you in more trouble than it's worth. If the worker is supposed to be an employee, not only can you get in the same trouble as the independent contractor problems mentioned above, you have no defense whatsoever when you get caught by the IRS. At least when you are mislabeling employees as outside contractors, you can argue the issue and possibly minimize the penalties. If your "under the table" worker doesn't file taxes, that's fraud, and you could well be implicated. And again, an injury on the job could be disastrous. On top of all this misery, since you don't record the payment, you lose the expense deduction and pay more income taxes. Have I said enough?

Special Situations

Subcontractors. Are subcontractors employees or outside contractors? This is a touchy area, and some states have special employment regulations just for subcontractors. For IRS purposes, the general rules regarding employees versus outside contractors apply to subcontractors. A subcontractor who is actually in business for himself, offering services to several building contractors, is most likely an outside contractor. Some states, however, require contractors to purchase workers' compensation insurance for subcontractors if the subcontractors do not have the insurance themselves, even if the subcontractor is legally considered an outside contractor. Some states require subcontractors to be licensed.

Statutory Employees. One strange exception to the above rules applies to certain people the IRS calls "statutory employees": commission truck drivers who deliver laundry, food, or beverages other than milk; full-time life insurance sales people; home workers such as maids and cooks; traveling sales people working full-time for one employer and selling to other businesses (not to consumers). Statutory employees are subject to regular employee social security and Medicare taxes, but otherwise are treated as outside contractors. They file tax Schedule C, like a sole proprietor, and are entitled to regular business deductions.

If you are a statutory employee, or someone employing a statutory employee, you should get more information from the IRS or a good accountant, to find out how to treat wages and expenses.

Statutory Non-Employees. The IRS has another special rule, applying only to travelling salespeople selling consumer goods (not selling to businesses) and real estate salespeople. The IRS will allow these salespeople to be outside contractors, in business for themselves, but only if there is a written agreement stating that they are outside contractors and responsible for their own taxes. The regular employee-versus-contractor tests do not apply.

Out-of-State Residents. If you hire an outside contractor who resides in another state, who comes into your state and performs contract work for you, you may be required by your state to withhold state taxes on the contractor. This is not an IRS law. It is a state law, only for some states, and only for state taxes. Check with your state's income tax or employment offices.

Steps to Becoming an Employer

To meet the legal requirements of becoming an employer, you will have to deal with the federal government and the state government, and you will probably have to obtain workers' compensation insurance. These are one-time-only procedures, but they require quite a bit of paperwork. If possible, start these procedures a month before you plan to hire your first employee.

One thing I hate is staff meetings. And, you know, you read all these things about motivating people. I hate doing that. What do I want to spend my time motivating people for? I want to make some deals, make some money, and have a good time.

—small business owner quoted in a local paper

Form W-4 — Employee's Withholding Allowance Certificate

Form W-4
Department of the Treasury
Internal Revenue Service

Employee's Withholding Allowance Certificate
▶ For Privacy Act and Paperwork Reduction Act Notice, see reverse.

1992

1 Type or print your first name and middle initial
Julia P.

Last name
Rose

2 Your social security number
222-22-2222

Home address (number and street or rural route)
640 Bell Springs Road

City or town, state, and ZIP code
Laytonville CA 95454

3 Marital status
[X] Single   [ ] Married
[ ] Married, but withhold at higher Single rate.
Note: *If married, but legally separated, or spouse is a nonresident alien, check the Single box.*

4 Total number of allowances you are claiming (from line G above or from the Worksheets on back if they apply) . . . **4** | 1

5 Additional amount, if any, you want deducted from each pay . . . . **5** | $

6 I claim exemption from withholding and I certify that I meet **ALL** of the following conditions for exemption:
- Last year I had a right to a refund of **ALL** Federal income tax withheld because I had **NO** tax liability; **AND**
- This year I expect a refund of **ALL** Federal income tax withheld because I expect to have **NO** tax liability; **AND**
- This year if my income exceeds $500 and includes nonwage income, another person cannot claim me as a dependent.

If you meet all of the above conditions, enter the year effective and "EXEMPT" here . . . . . ▶ **6** | 19

7 Are you a full-time student? (**Note:** *Full-time students are not automatically exempt.*) . . . . **7** [ ] Yes [X] No

Under penalties of perjury, I certify that I am entitled to the number of withholding allowances claimed on this certificate or entitled to claim exempt status.

Employee's signature ▶ *Julia P. Rose*   Date ▶ *April 8* , 19 *92*

8 Employer's name and address (**Employer:** Complete 8 and 10 **only if sending to IRS**)

9 Office code (optional)

10 Employer identification number

Each of your employees must fill out a W-4 form.

Federal Requirements

1. Contact the Internal Revenue Service and tell them you are about to become an employer. Request Form SS-4, "Application for Employer Identification Number." Ask for a free copy of publication #15, *Circular E-Employer's Tax Guide.* Circular E will give you detailed instructions for complying with federal requirements. Circular E also includes federal withholding tables.

2. Ask the IRS for several copies of Form W-4, "Employees Withholding Allowance Certificate." Each new employee must fill out a W-4 indicating marital status and the number of exemptions claimed. You keep the W-4's in your files (except for employees claiming eleven or more exemptions; or employees claiming to be exempt from withholding whose wages are expected to exceed $200 a week. These W-4 forms must be sent to the IRS).

3. All employers must comply with Occupational Safety & Health Administration (OSHA) regulations. If you have more than ten employees, OSHA will also require you to keep routine job safety records, although some retail businesses with low injury rates are exempt from this requirement. Write OSHA, U.S. Department of Labor, Washington D.C. 20210 for complete information.

4. Most employers are subject to the Fair Labor Standards Act. This act sets a minimum wage for covered employees and sets overtime pay at not less than 1.5 times the regular rate of pay. Generally, the following businesses are covered by the act: businesses that handle, ship or receive goods that have moved or will move in interstate commerce; businesses that regularly use the mail or the telephone for interstate communication; laundries, construction firms, hospitals, nursing homes, schools and preschools; other businesses with annual gross income of $362,500 or more. Specifically exempt from the act are most executives, administrators, professionals and outside sales people and some amusement park employees, switchboard operators, seamen and farm workers. For more details, write the Department of Labor, Washington D.C. 20210.

5. The Americans With Disabilities Act prohibits job discrimination against certain disabled people and requires employers to provide reasonable accommodations for disabled employees.

State Requirements

1. Contact your state department of employment and ask for their forms and instructions. Most states assign employers a state Employer's ID Number (this is in addition to your Federal ID Number).

2. Every state that has an income tax on wages requires employers to withhold state income tax. The states usually publish their own employer's tax guides including state withholding tables. Request a copy of these tables.

3. Some states have other required withholding

from employee wages. You should inquire about any such state laws.

4. Most states have employer-paid state unemployment insurance; this is in addition to federal unemployment insurance (discussed below). The state will require you to submit an application and receive an insurance rating. The rates vary from state to state and within states from occupation to occupation. The unemployment insurance rate for your business will initially be based on the prevailing rate in your particular occupation. For future years, your own business experience—that is, how many of your former employees receive unemployment insurance—will determine your rate. A "favorable" record will mean lower rates.

5. Most states require employers to have Worker's Compensation Insurance. Some states provide the insurance themselves, and some require that you obtain Workers' Comp from an insurance company. A detailed explanation of Worker's Compensation Insurance is included in the "Insurance" chapter.

6. Some states have laws similar to the Federal Fair Labor Standards Act. Again, contact your state department of employment.

7. Some states set their own minimum wage, higher than the federal minimum.

Federal Procedures and Taxes for Employers

Outlined here are the basic federal procedures most employers must follow. These laws have changed very little in recent years, but that does not preclude the possibility of changes in the future. It is your responsibility as an employer to read Circular E, *Employers Tax Guide* carefully and comply with all the instructions. Unlike income taxes, there is no "grey" or questionable area where payroll taxes are involved. There is only one way to do it—their way.

1. The Internal Revenue Service requires that you withhold income tax from each employee's paycheck. The amount you withhold is calculated from the tables in Circular E.

2. The Federal Insurance Contributions Act (FICA) requires employers to withhold social security tax (also known as OASDI—old age, survivors, and disability insurance) and Medicare tax (also known as Hospitalization). Social security tax is 6.2% on every employee's earnings, up to an earnings maximum of $55,000. The Medicare tax, levied in addition to the social security tax, is 1.45% on every employee's earnings, up to an earn-

ings maximum of $130,200. These are 1992 rates and maximums; they go up every year.

3. You are liable for an employer's portion of social security and Medicare taxes in addition to the taxes withheld from your employees. This is money you, the employer, pay out of your own pocket on behalf of your employees. The employer's tax is exactly the same as the employee's tax: 6.2% social security on each employee's earnings up to $55,500; and 1.45% Medicare tax on each employee's earnings up to $130,200. Do not confuse this employer's tax with the self-employment tax discussed in the Tax section of the book. They are different taxes.

4. Federal Payroll Tax Returns (Form #941) are due quarterly on April 30 for January, February and March; July 31 for April, May and June; October 31 for July, August and September; and January 31 for October, November and December. Taxes reported on Form 941 are the taxes withheld from your employees—federal income, social security and Medicare—and also the employer's portion of the employees' social security and Medicare (do not include self-employment tax). As long as the total taxes due in any one quarter are less than $500, the entire amount can be remitted with the return. If, however, at the end of any month in the quarter, total taxes due (combined employee and employer portions) are $500 or more, you must deposit the full amount by the fifteenth day of the next month. Deposits are reported on yet another form, #501, "Federal Tax Deposit, Withheld Income and FICA Taxes," and paid to an authorized commercial bank or to a Federal Reserve bank. You can obtain the names of authorized commercial banks at any local bank.

The deposit information is confusing enough to warrant an illustration. (Maybe it's confusing enough to go back and read the chapter, "How Not To Become An Employer.") In January, let's say you withheld from your employees $140 in income tax and $80 in social security and Medicare taxes. Your tax liability at the end of January is the $220 withheld plus $80—your employer's portion—for a total of $300. Since this amount is under $500 there is no need to file anything at that time. Okay so far? Now in February, let's say the same taxes recur: $220 withholding and $80 employer's portion, or $300. Your total tax liability is now $600 for the two months. Since you are now over the $500 limit, you must deposit the full $600 with an authorized bank by March 15. Taxes for March, the last month of the quarter, are due when you file the quarterly return on April 30—assuming that March's taxes are less than $500. If your payroll jumped in March, and March's taxes alone are $500 or more, a deposit of the full amount must be made by April 15.

Another and more complicated set of deposit rules apply if your undeposited payroll taxes exceed $3,000. Businesses with payrolls in this bracket should contact the Internal Revenue Service for instructions.

5. As an employer, you are also subject to Federal Unemployment tax (F.U.T.A.) if during the year you, (a) paid wages of $1,500 or more in any calendar quarter, or (b) had one or more employees for some portion of at least one day during each of twenty different calendar weeks (better re-read that slowly). Unemployment tax is imposed on you, the employer. It is not deducted from your employee's wages. An annual return must be filed

1 Control number		OMB No. 1545-0008								
2 Employer's name, address, and ZIP code			6 Statutory employee ☐	Deceased ☐	Pension plan ☐	Legal rep. ☐	942 emp. ☐	Subtotal ☐	Deferred compensation ☐	Void ☐
Music Photo Service PO Box 322 Laytonville CA 95454			7 Allocated tips				8 Advance EIC payment			
			9 Federal income tax withheld $327.50				10 Wages, tips, other compensation $4,300.00			
3 Employer's identification number 99-605342	4 Employer's state I.D. number CA 67-988		11 Social security tax withheld $266.60				12 Social security wages $4,300.00			
5 Employee's social security number 222-22-2222			13 Social security tips				14 Medicare wages and tips $4,300.00			
19 Employee's name, address, and ZIP code			15 Medicare tax withheld $62.35				16 Nonqualified plans			
Julia P. Rose 640 Bell Springs Road Laytonville CA 95454			17				18 Other			
20	21		22 Dependent care benefits				23 Benefits included in Box 10			
24 State income tax $67.70	25 State wages, tips, etc. $4,300.00	26 Name of state Calif.	27 Local income tax			28 Local wages, tips, etc.	29 Name of locality			

Copy 1   Department of the Treasury—Internal Revenue Service

Form **W-2 Wage and Tax Statement 1992**

A W-2 form must be sent to each employee, listing earnings and deductions for the year.

1 Control number 33333	For Official Use Only ▶ OMB No. 1545-0008				
☐ Kind of Payer	2 941/941E ☒ Military ☐ 943 ☐ CT-1 ☐ 942 ☐ Medicare govt. emp. ☐	3 Employer's state I.D. number CA 67-988		5 Total number of statements 1	
		4			
6 Establishment number	7 Allocated tips	8 Advance EIC payments			
9 Federal income tax withheld $327.50	10 Wages, tips, and other compensation $4,300.00	11 Social security tax withheld $266.60			
12 Social security wages $4,300.00	13 Social security tips	14 Medicare wages and tips $4,300.00			
15 Medicare tax withheld $62.35	16 Nonqualified plans N/A	17 Deferred compensation			
18 Employer's identification number 68 — 1234567		19 Other EIN used this year			
20 Employer's name Music Photo Service		21 Dependent care benefits			
PO Box 322 Laytonville CA 95454		23 Adjusted total social security wages and tips			
		24 Adjusted total Medicare wages and tips			
		25 Income tax withheld by third-party payer			
22 Employer's address and ZIP code (If available, place label over Boxes 18 and 20.)					

Under penalties of perjury, I declare that I have examined this return and accompanying documents, and, to the best of my knowledge and belief, they are true, correct, and complete.

Signature ▶ *Sam Leandro*   Title ▶ owner   Date ▶ 1-29-92

Telephone number (optional) _____

Form **W-3 Transmittal of Income and Tax Statements 1992**   Department of the Treasury Internal Revenue Service

A W-3 must accompany the W-2 forms sent to the Social Security Administration.

on Form #940, (or for many small businesses, the simpler Form #940 EZ), Employer's Annual Federal Unemployment Tax Return, on or before January 31 of next year. The rate is 6.2 percent of the first $7,000 of wages paid to each employee during the year. You may receive credit of up to 5.4 percent for state unemployment taxes you pay, so your net federal liability could be as low as 0.8 percent.

6. Ask the IRS to send you several copies of form W-2, "Wage and Tax Statement." The W-2 is a five-part form that you must prepare for each employee, annually at year-end. You must mail or give out the W-2 Forms by January 31. Three copies of the W-2 are given to the employee, one copy you retain, and one copy is sent to the Social Security Administration (the SSA). The SSA copies should be batched and sent with form W-3, "Transmittal of Income and Tax Statements," no later than February 28. W-3's are available from the IRS. You can get a 30-day extension to file your W-3 by filing Form 8809.

7. The Immigration & Naturalization Service (INS) Reform & Control Act makes it a crime to "knowingly hire any alien not authorized to work in the United States." When hiring any new employee, the employer must be shown "proof of employment eligibility" such as a social security card, military registration card, or immigrant "green card." Employers must record this information for each new employee on an Employment Eligibility Verification Form #I-9, available from INS offices, and retain the forms in your files. For more detailed information, see the INS publication #M274, "Handbook For Employers."

8. Special rule, for restaurant and nightclub owners only: Employees must report their tips to you, and you must withhold taxes on the tips just as you do on wages. If you have more than ten employees, you must also report gross income and other information related to tips, using Form #8027. Call a local IRS office for more information.

9. Agricultural employers come under a different set of federal laws, particularly regarding social security and Medicare taxes, minimum wage, and overtime pay. For full details, see IRS Publication #51, "Circular A—Agricultural Employer's Tax Guide."

Payroll Ledgers

Every employer must keep a separate payroll ledger in addition to the regular expenditure ledger. The payroll ledger must show all the details of every paycheck for every employee. Payroll ledgers can be purchased pre-lined and all headed up for you, or you can easily design your own. Included in the Ledger section of this book is a sample payroll ledger page that you can use as a prototype.

These payroll ledgers should become a permanent record of your business. Keep them as long as you own the business, even longer if possible. Long-gone employees can come back to haunt you years later, usually when there's some problem with social security retirement.

Use a separate ledger page for each employee. Head the page with the employee's name, address and social security number. Year-end W-2 Earnings Statements will be easier to prepare if all this required information is in one place. Also write down the employee's hourly or monthly rate of pay at the top of the page. If the rate changes during the year, show the new rate as well as the old and the date of change.

The payroll ledger should have a column for each of the following:

1. Date of paycheck.
2. Check number.

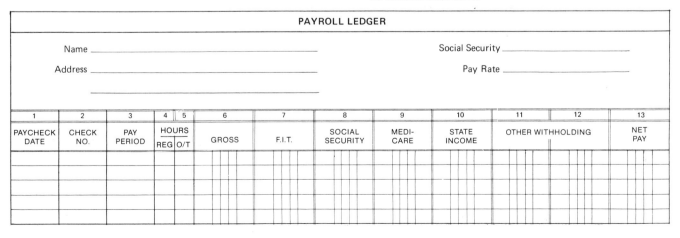

3. Payroll period.
4. Number of regular hours worked.
5. Number of overtime hours worked.
6. Gross pay.
7. Federal income tax withheld.
8. Social security taxes withheld.
9. Medicare taxes withheld.
10. State income taxes withheld.
11–12. Two extra columns for any other withholding.
13. Net "take-home" pay.

Remember that the *net* pay amount must also be posted to your expenditure ledger in Column Four.

Mike Madsen, Mike Madsen Leather: "When you're first getting started you don't always hire the best people. You don't know what you are looking for. You might hire somebody who is sympathetic to you or flatters you or somebody who is good looking. But they might not fit the job that you have. You've got to think in terms of what the job is, and hire the people for the job, and not hire friends. I'd say it's better always to make friends of those people that work for you, but never to hire friends."

Nick Mein, Wallpapers Plus, San Francisco: "A person's gotta be happy if he or she is going to work for you. The women working for me were terribly unhappy. This one woman who worked for me, who I really liked, was a great saleswoman. She'd been going to a Freudian shrink for about six years, and she switched to a Jungian psychologist. He said, 'Work's bad for you.' So she called up one day and said, 'I won't be in.' A lot of jobs depended on her charm; she brought a lot of people in the store. And she just sort of gave up on it. That's irritating. No 'stick-to-it-ivity' my father calls it; no perseverance.

"It's very difficult to be nice to your employees because they're going to take advantage of you. They're going to start coming in late. All the people who worked for me are perfect examples. I'd say, 'Get in at 9:30, do whatever ordering needs to be done, and open the doors at ten. I want you to be ready to sell at ten.' And they do that for a while, but then they say, 'I want to get in a little later because there's no ordering to do, there's no backlog.' I say okay. And then eventually, they'll be coming in at eleven. Because they felt nobody was coming into the shop until 11:00 or 11:30. And if you're not on it

everyday, you get screwed. You have to be on it all the time. And then, they leave early…

If you have somebody working for you you've got to make it absolutely plain that they're being paid for the specified hours. I find that really hard to do, keep people to that, because I'm a little bit like that myself. On a really slow day, I'd say, 'Go ahead, go home early.' Then it always happens: next day some woman would call and say, 'I came by your shop at 5:20 and you weren't there.' That's bad service."

Partnerships

Partnerships offer opportunities often not available to the one-person business: more capital, more skills and ideas, the extra energy generated when two or more people are working together. Partnerships are the traditional meeting ground of the "idea" person and the "money" person. Having a partner can relieve the sole proprietor pressures of having to do everything yourself. And, at last, you can take a little vacation without having to shut down the business.

Partnerships have their drawbacks as well. The independence and sole decision making that only the sole proprietor has must now be shared. There is more paperwork. Inter-personal relations with your partner or partners may require both time and tact. Most important, the legal consequences of having one or more partners can be serious.

General Vs. Limited Partnerships

There are two kinds of partnerships. The kind of partnership covered in this chapter, the typical business partnership, is called a "general" partnership. There is also something called a "limited" partnership, which is not a partnership in the usual sense. A limited partnership is really an investment financing arrangement, with one general partner who owns and operates the business, with full legal and financial responsibility, much like a sole proprietor; and one or more limited partners, who are investors only. The limited partners have no involvement in the management or operations of the business, and usually have no personal liability beyond their investment.

Limited partnerships are covered in the Equity Financing chapter in the first section of the book. The information in this Partnership chapter—the legal aspects, partnership agreements and partnership bookkeeping—are for general partnerships only.

Legal Aspects of General Partnerships

A partnership, like a sole proprietorship, is legally inseparable from the owners, the partners. Individual partners can be held responsible for financial debts and legal obligations of the partnership. The most important legal aspect of a general partnership is that all partners can be held personally, individually liable for the acts of any one partner acting on partnership business. If your partner, representing the business, goes to the bank and borrows $5,000, you can be personally responsible to repay the debt, even if you didn't sign the papers yourself, even if you didn't know about the loan. In a more serious situation, if your partner gets into legal trouble while on partnership business, you may also be in legal trouble.

Like sole proprietors, partners cannot be employees of their partnerships. Partners can draw a "wage" (called a "guaranteed payment"), or they can merely share in the profits of the partnership or some combination of the two. Profits and guaranteed payments are taxable to the individual partners. Partners are subject to self-emplyment tax (social security and Medicare tax), which is covered in the Tax section.

A partnership must have its own federal identification number, obtained by filing Form SS-4,

"Employer's Federal Identification Number." If the partnership will have no employees, note on the form that it is "FOR IDENTIFICATION ONLY." This will alert the IRS not to send you payroll forms.

Partnerships file a partnership income tax return, on form 1065, although the partnership itself pays no taxes. Partnerships will need business licenses, seller's permits, and if operating under fictitious names, fictitious name statements. Partnerships pay sales, employment, and local taxes.

Death or withdrawal of one partner or the addition of a new partner legally terminates a partnership. The business need not be liquidated, however. A new partnership agreement can be made. The original partnership agreement can include provisions for continuation of a partnership (discussed below).

Partnership Agreements

A partnership agreement is an "understanding" between partners as to how the business will be conducted. Many partnership agreements are nothing more than a handshake and a "Let's do it;" and often such agreements turn out to be more of a *mis*understanding than anything else. A written partnership agreement is not required by law, but it is something no partnership should be without. It reduces the possibilities of misunderstanding and future problems.

A written partnership agreement should be signed by all the partners and should specify:

1. What the business is and what are its goals. Be succinct: you should be able to pin this down in one paragraph. A simple, *written* statement of business goals is the first and most important step in any partnership agreement. Long range goals should be included as well. For example, one partner may want a business that will provide a good livelihood for many years; while the other partner may be dreaming of building up the business and when it becomes successful and established, selling it for a big profit. These two partners obviously have a serious conflict of interest. If partners do not agree on the basics, the partnership is doomed from the start.

2. How much each partner will contribute—in cash, in property and in labor. There are no federal laws requiring partners to make equal or simultaneous contributions.

3. How each partner will share in the profits and losses. The easiest and most common arrangement is an equal division of profits between partners. You may wish, however, to provide for an unequal division of profits to compensate for differences in time or money contributed or for differences in ability and experience. A partner can also draw a wage to reflect actual time spent running the business. The wage is known as a "guaranteed payment to partner." It is not a regular employee wage for tax purposes. There is no withholding, employee social security or unemployment insurance. It is part of the partner's total partnership income. Paying a wage is common when one partner works day-to-day at the business and the other doesn't or when partners do not put in equal time. After the wage is paid, any remaining profit (or loss) for the year is then divided between the partners according to your agreement. Specify in the agreement who gets a wage and the amount.

4. Procedures for withdrawal of funds and payments of profits—how much and when. Such an understanding will prevent situations in which one partner can arbitrarily withdraw substantial amounts of money from the partnership. There is no federal law requiring partners to make equal or simultaneous withdrawals.

5. Provisions for continuing the business if one partner dies or wants out. A prearranged agreement to buy out a departing partner can prevent the shutdown of the business. Your biggest problem is determining how much money the depart-ing partner (or his estate) should receive and over what period of time. For example, the business may be worth a lot of money because it is established and successful or because it owns a lot of inventory and equipment, but there may be little cash on hand to pay the departing partner.

Your agreement should state how a partner's share of the business is to be valued. Is it based on the value of the business assets; that is, what you actually have invested in the business? Or is it based on what the going business is worth on the open market, what an eager new owner might pay for it? And who will be the lucky person to determine this "worth?" Also, there are tax consequences to a partner buy-out and they vary depending on how the agreement is worded. The tax interests of the remaining and outgoing partners are often diametrically opposed. This tax aspect can be substantial if the business is worth a lot of money; it will require professional help. I suggest you talk to a competent accountant.

6. You may also want a clause specifying the financial and legal powers of each partner. Such a clause will not relieve any partner of partnership obligations entered into by other partners. The clause is not binding on outside parties, such as a lender. It only reduces the possibility of misunderstanding among the partners.

Most of the professional advice I have heard suggests that you hire a lawyer to draw up any partnership agreement. Certainly a *knowledgeable* lawyer—not all lawyers are familiar with partnership problems—will draft up an "iron-clad" agreement that leaves nothing to doubt. But you will pay a high fee for this service. I feel it is not really necessary to see a lawyer if the partnership agreement is a simple one (such as 50-50, equal sharing, equal contributions) and if you know your partner well enough to be confident you aren't being used.

You and Your Partners

My friend Rory said, "Having a partner is just like having a wife, only more so." Well, Rory is a long-time loner, but his words are basically true. Partnerships are more than business. They are often complex inter-personal relationships. And like marriages, partnerships can bring out the best and the worst in people. By acquiring a partner you are adding a whole new dimension to your business venture, one you should be fully prepared to deal with.

PARTNERS CAPITAL LEDGER

1	2	3	4	5	6	7
		HUCK — A		*PIPPI — B*		
DATE	DESCRIPTION	ACTIVITY	BALANCE	ACTIVITY	BALANCE	TOTAL BALANCE
1/1	Contrib.	$2,000	$2,000	$2,000	$2,000	$4,000
3/31	Contrib.	800	2,800	400	2,400	5,200
12/31	Income for yr.	4,000	6,800	3,000	5,400	12,200
2/5	w/Draw	(400)	6,400	—	5,400	11,800
5/1	w/Draw	—	6,400	(350)	5,050	11,450

Anyone who has lost a friend after an argument can quickly realize the possible problems and complications of having a business partner. It is not uncommon for partners to have a disagreement, a difference of opinion, or worse. You may feel that your partner is not working as hard as he should (and he may be feeling the same about you!). When trouble arises between partners, the most logical step is to try to work it out: sit down with your partner, get the problems "out front", and hopefully get them solved. Much more easily said than done. Like divorces, partnership dissolutions are more common than ever and often just as problematical. The alternatives—dividing up the assets and going out of business, or one partner buying out the other—can be difficult even with a good written agreement, can require lawyers, and almost always cause the business to suffer.

Marriage counselors can sometimes save a marriage. But it's a little out of my field, and there is little advice I can give you retrospectively. Knowing that such things happen should warn you to take every precaution prior to going into a partnership to reduce the possibility of problems later on. The best advice I can offer is to pick your partners *very* carefully. This advice may seem basic, just common sense; but a poor choice of partners is the root cause of many partnership failures. How well do you know your prospective partner? Are you old friends? Have you worked together before? What business experience does your partner have? What is his or her "track record?"

Partnership Bookkeeping

The basic bookkeeping for a partnership is the same as for a sole proprietorship. You will be able to use the ledgers and worksheets in the ledger section with no alteration. In addition to the income and expenditure ledgers, partnerships must keep a separate "partners' capital ledger" which provides a complete record, by partner, of all contributions and withdrawals and of each partner's share of profit or loss.

The partners' capital ledger has two columns for each partner. One column shows *activity* in the partner's account—contributions, withdrawals and the partner's share of profit or loss. The second column is the *balance* of the partner's capital remaining with the partnership. Contributions and withdrawals should be recorded when they occur. Contributions are shown as positive amounts and increase the partner's balance. Withdrawals are shown as negative, bracketed amounts and decrease the partner's balance. A partner's "guaranteed payment" (wage) is shown as a withdrawal. Each partner's share of the partnership profit or loss is posted to the partners' capital ledger once a year at year-end. A profit is posted to the Activity column as a positive amount; a loss is shown as a negative, bracketed amount. Profits and losses increase and decrease a partner's balance accordingly. The Total Balance column is the sum of all the individual partners' Balance columns.

The sample partners' capital ledger shows activity for 1992 and part of 1993 for Wesley's Farm Fresh Eggs, a new partnership owned by two partners.

Entry 1: The partnership began on January 1, 1992. Each partner contributed $2,000 to the business. Each partner's balance is $2,000, and the total balance is $4,000.

Entry 2: On March 31, Huck (Partner A) contributed another $800, and Pippi (Partner B) contributed another $400.

Entry 3: The partnership made a $7,000 profit in 1992. At December 31, 1992, the partners' shares of the profit were posted to their individual accounts.

Entry 4: On February 5, 1993, Huck withdrew $400 from the business. This is the first money either partner has taken out of the business.

Entry 5: On May 1, 1993, Pippi withdrew $350 from the business.

With each entry, the partners' individual balances and the total balance were adjusted.

A partnership income tax return must sometimes include a balance sheet (explained in the Appendix) and schedule of partners' capital. The Appendix also includes a chapter on husband and wife partnerships. For more tax information about partnerships, ask the IRS for a free copy of Pub. 541, "Tax Information on Partnerships."

Partnership Post-Mortem

Lara Stonebraker, former partner in Aromatica, Walnut Creek, California: "It's been my experience that partnerships rarely work, especially if there is an odd number of partners. Because it's always going to be two against one in all decision making, and there's always going to be an odd man out. Unless you have such well matched personalities that everybody is always good friends, it just creates incredible hassles. That was the most anxiety-ridden period of my life. There were three of us and I happened to be the odd one, because I was living in Berkeley and the other two were right there on the premises.

"And then one of the partners turned out to be a Jesus freak and was really just impossible to deal with. She'd bring her Bible to the store and talk to the customers about it, and there was just no way of stopping it. Finally she decided that she had to go to this retreat in the mountains to prepare for the holocaust, so she sold her partnership. I blotted out a lot of that whole experience."

Key Dickason, former partner in Xanadu, Concord, California: "I was in a partnership once before, and my partner and I disagreed, not on the running of the business, but on the way we handled employees. We bought out a data processing service bureau which had two employees, a key puncher and an operator/supervisor. One of the conditions of the sale was that we continue the old employees on and honor their vacations. But when the operator/supervisor got married and gave us notice she was quitting, my partner said, 'No one quits on me,' and he refused to pay her vacation. So I wrote a check for her vacation money.

"The keypuncher working for us got a four-year, fully-paid scholarship from the university; in May, she told us she would be leaving in August. And my partner fired her on the spot. That was fifteen years ago and I've never had another keypuncher who even approached her. He just arbitrarily fired her. Because I disagreed on that, it eventually led to the dissolution of the partnership.

"I also discovered that he was putting his personal debts into the business. I finally went to a CPA. He looked at the books and said, 'I'd advise you to see an attorney.' So I went to see my attorney, and he told me that if I got out of the business, closed the business up, I would be liable for all the debts, and the business would be defunct. So I just signed all the assets and everything over to my partner. The only way I could try and get my money out of it, which was gone, was to sue for dissolution of the partnership. Then once you go into litigation, according to my attorney, everything's tied up.

"The partnership agreement doesn't mean a thing unless both parties want to honor it. Jack and I disagreed on a philosophical—a better word is ethical—aspect of employee-employer relationships. To Jack, an employee was somebody you used and discarded. To me an employee was somebody you used but you also had an obligation and a commitment to. If you have this basic disagreement, no partnership agreement will handle it. Do you put in there, 'You agree to treat employees fairly?' Well, that doesn't mean anything. 'Cause to Jack, Jack was treating them fairly.

"The biggest mistake in the world is to start a partnership if there is disagreement in the beginning when you're laying the groundwork for the formation of the business. If you enter into basic disagreement on ethics, business management, or whatever the objective of the business is, if you disagree on that then you shouldn't go into business together. Putting your doubts about the situation into a partnership agreement doesn't accomplish anything unless you're prepared to fight, which isn't what it's all about."

Jan Lowe, former partner in Midnight Sewing Machine, Mendocino, California: "I went into business with my sister who is a dear person, and who taught me everything I know. I didn't sew a stitch in my life before we bought this dress shop, and she handed me a pattern and scissors and said, 'I'm going to lunch now. If you have any problems, let me know.' So I started off real cold there, which is no way to do it. I'd run into problems when people would want something intricate done or they'd want something altered, and I wouldn't know how to handle it. I wasn't really prepared to do what I did for a living.

"One of our basic problems was non-communication. My partner would borrow money from someone and I didn't know about it, which I thought was a cheap shot. You've got to be in constant communication. If somebody's going to lunch, they've got to tell you. We didn't have anything in writing between us. How things were going to be run was not made clear and that I think was another downfall. That should be made clear right from the start—exactly what do you want to see happen, how is it going to happen, who's going to make what work, who is best at handling what; and stick to it. I think you should be willing to bend when that system does not work. Face it immediately and try something else. To hang onto a system that doesn't work can get you into lots of trouble."

...And a Partnership That Works

"Kipple is a made-up word that means, um, kipple, the dumb stuff that you gather around you that you can't live without." Pat Ellington is a partner in Kipple, a small antique store in Berkeley, California: "We function pretty well as a four-way partnership. Miriam and I are old friends—friends for fifteen years or more. Her downstairs neighbor is the third partner, and a friend of hers is the fourth. Everybody's really working part time. But this way we can operate a full time business.

"When we first came into this, I was the only one with any kind of skill, any kind of business skill. Miriam never really worked at a job. Pam worked at a recycling center. She never held an office job or a business job of any type. Ann has been a housewife all her life.

"We've had personality troubles, but not serious ones, because we squashed them right away. The inter-personal stuff can be worked out if everybody agrees it's going to happen, that there's no blame attached to differences of opinion or feelings. We all agreed when we set out that everybody was going to make mistakes—some of them are going to cost us money—but no blame should be attached to anybody, and we would not throw it up to each other. When Ann joined us, Miriam made a lot of noises, 'She did this wrong, she bought that thing, she never should have bought it...' Pam and I would say, 'Miriam, you made your mistakes too, back off.' And she slowly but surely got over that. She felt, being the one partner with the most money in at that point, like the business was hers. None of this was conscious. People don't consciously set out to be that way about things, it's sort of inbred. The system's run that way, and no matter what your philosophy is, we all have moments of 'mine' mentalities: 'That's mine. She's threatening it.'

"Miriam is a crackerjack saleswoman. She can sell anybody anything. But she couldn't keep a set of books to save her soul. She can't balance a checkbook. But she can sell. That's a real asset. She doesn't have to keep books if she can do that. Pam's got a good eye when it comes to buying. She's good at that. And Ann, who's much better organized than the other two when it comes to shows and things like that, she's the one who says, 'Uh huh, we're going to do it,' and she sits down and makes out a list: we're gonna need lights, we're gonna need display material, we need this, we need that. Pam says, 'Well, we need so much inventory; where's the rest of it?' These are skills. And I'm the bookkeeper. And between the four of us we can really operate."

You, Incorporated: A Corporation Primer

The corporation is truly a misunderstood animal. People, even business people, have more misconceptions about corporations than about any other form of business. Some small-time operations will benefit by incorporating but many will not. In order for you to make an intelligent choice between "You" and "You, Incorporated," you will need a basic understanding of what a corporation is and what can and cannot be accomplished by incorporating.

"In Twenty-Five Words or Less"

A corporation is...just another business. The basic day-to-day operations, the management, the bookkeeping, are virtually no different from the operations of an unincorporated business. A corporation can be as tiny as the tiniest unincorporated business. It can be loose and easy and very personal. Just as there are grey-suits-and-elevators corporations, there are blue-jeans-and-pure-funk corporations.

A corporation is just another business... but the rules of the game are different. Owners of corporations are the stockholders (also called shareholders). They own shares of stock, pieces of paper. Your corporation may have one or more stockholders (one or more owners) with one or more shares of stock, depending on your needs and your state's laws (discussed later).

If you don't make mistakes, you aren't really trying.
—Coleman Hawkins

Corporate Myth Number One: You're going to lower you taxes by incorporating. Not so. The fact is, most small businesses will not save tax money by incorporating. Corporate profits are taxed *twice*: once as corporate income and again when distributed to the shareholders (owners) as dividends. In contrast, the profits from your unincorporated sole proprietorship or partnership are taxable only to you, the owner; the business itself pays no tax. So even though corporate tax rates are in some cases lower than individual tax rates, the effective corporate tax rate because of the double taxation is always higher. Small corporations do have a few ways to reduce the combined corporation and shareholder taxes (discussed later in this chapter), but none will result in taxes lower than those paid by an unincorporated business.

Limited Liability

Rules regarding liability are also different for corporations. These liability rules, which offer protection to the owners of corporations from lawsuits and creditors, are the most convincing reason for you to consider incorporating your business.

A corporation is recognized by law as a "legal entity," which means that the business is legally separate from its owners (the stockholders). If your corporation does not pay its debts, the creditors usually cannot get their money from your personal, non-business assets. In most cases you will not be personally liable for lawsuits brought against your corporation. Sole proprietorships and partnerships, on the other hand, are legally inseparable from their owners; the owners are personally liable for all business debts and obligations.

High-risk businesses, even very small ones, often incorporate solely to protect the owners from personal loss. Businesses borrowing a lot of "risk" capital and businesses that will owe a lot of money to suppliers and other creditors fall in this category. Businesses with a more than average likelihood of being sued—such as security businesses and manufacturers of potentially dangerous products—also incorporate for the liability protection. Partnerships often incorporate to protect individual partners against possible lawsuits and losses resulting from the actions of other partners.

Limited corporate liability, however, is not "blanket" or all encompassing. Officers of a corporation (in a small corporation, the officers are the owners) can be personally liable for claims against their corporations in some situations. A corporation will not shield you from personal liability that you normally should be responsible for, such as not having car insurance or acting with gross negligence. Professionals such as doctors cannot hide behind corporations to protect themselves from malpractice suits. And as to financial commitments, any bank lending money to a small corporation will require the stockholders or officers to co-sign as personal guarantors of the loan.

If you plan to incorporate soley or primarily with the intention of limiting your legal liability, I suggest you find out first, before you invest the time and money in incorporation, exactly how limited the liability really is for your particular venture. Hire a knowledgeable lawyer to give you a written opinion.

There are three other significant differences between corporations and other forms of business. None are as important as the limited liability rules, but all three are worth considering.

Change of Ownership

Incorporating a business eliminates much of the legal and tax complications of a change in ownership. New shareholders can be added easily (within certain legal limits, discussed later). Selling a business, or passing a family-owned business from generation to generation, or giving your employees an ownership interest (i.e. stock) in the company is much less difficult with a corporation than with an unincorporated business. Sale of stock or death of a shareholder will not end the business. The same corporation can continue in business with new shareholders. By comparison, a sole proprietorship ceases to exist when the owner sells or gives away the business, takes on a partner, or dies. A partnership ceases to exist when one partner quits or dies. Of course, a sole proprietorship or a partnership can be sold or otherwise acquired by new owners. But the result, legally, is a new business requiring new records, new valuation of assets and liabilities, new business licenses, etc.

Owner-Employees

A corporation is the only form of business that can hire its owners as employees. Corporations can pay their owner-employees a wage and even offer company-paid fringe benefits such as health insurance. Owners of sole proprietorships and partnerships, you'll remember, can never be employees of their businesses, and they are allowed only a partial deduction for health insurance. The income tax consequences of hiring owner-employees are numerous and difficult to explain. Briefly—I don't want to bog you down in corporate tax law before you have even decided to incorporate—hiring owner-employees is one method of reducing corporate income taxes. Every employee's wage, including that of an owner-employee, is a deductible expense of the business. The wage, of course, is taxable to the owner-employee as personal income. But unlike regular corporate profits, which are taxable to the corporation and again to the owners, wages paid to owner-employees are not subject to the double taxation. Any fringe benefits paid to owner-employees are also tax deductible expenses of the corporation. There is even a greater tax savings with company-paid fringe benefits because many fringe benefits are not taxable to the employees at all.

Retired people collecting social security know that they can lose part of their social security income if any other outside income--such as earnings from a small business—gets above a certain level. By setting up a corporation, you may be able to pay yourself a low enough salary so it stays under the social security limits. This arrangement cannot be accomplished with a sole proprietorship or a partnership, because all of the profits of an unincorporated business are considered personal income whether you take a salary or not. This is an area of tax law that you schould discuss with an accountant.

If you do become an owner-employee of your own corporation, you should be aware of IRS limitations on employee business expenses. Your corporation can take tax deductions for any allowable business expenses, as long as the corporation itself spends the money. If you, as an employee, spend the money, your tax deductions are greatly reduced, even though you may be the sole owner of the business and even though the expenses may be totally legitimate. It is important that you learn the IRS rules, because it's easy to avoid this trap. This is not a problem for sole proprietors or partnerships; you and your unincorporated business are one and the same, and any business expenses you pay out of your own pocket are fully deductible.

Retained Earnings:

The remaining significant difference between incorporated and unincorporated business is the corporation's legal ability to retain undistributed profits within the company, and not pay the profits out to the owners. Though the corporation must pay income tax on these "retained earnings," as they are called, the owners do not have to pay the "double" or second tax because the profits have not been paid out to them. Retained earnings can be reinvested in the business, distributed to the shareholders at a later date or retained indefinitely by the company. An unincorporated business can also retain the profits in the business, but the owners must pay income tax on the profits whether distributed to them or not. The laws regarding retained earnings are quite complex. Among other rules, there are strict limitations on the amounts that can be retained. This aspect of corporate law, however, is not a major consideration for or against incorporating a small business. It is yet one more potentially complicated area to deal with if you do decide to incorporate.

S Corporations

The type of corporation described above is commonly called a "regular" or "C" corporation. (Don't confuse a C corporation with a Schedule C tax return. The two C's are not related. Schedule C is for sole proprietors, not corporations.)

There is another form of corporation different from the type just described. It is sort of a hybrid between a regular corporation and a partnership, with some of the advantages of both.

The S corporation (so called because it is covered in Subchapter S of the Internal Revenue Code) has the same basic structure as a regular C corporation and offers the same limited liability protection to the stockholders. The S corporation, however, pays no corporate income tax. Like a partnership, all the profits of the S corporation pass through to the owners who are taxed at their regular individual rates.

Unlike a partnership, owner-employees of S corporations are treated similarly to owner-employees of regular corporations. If you work for your S corporation, you must be on the payroll as a regular employee with regular payroll deductions. Any S corporation profits in excess of your salary are also taxable directly to you, as dividends, but are not subject to employment taxes. Since you decide how much of a salary you earn, you obviously also get to decide how much of the corporation's annual profit is subject to payroll taxes, and how much escapes payroll taxes as "dividends". But look out: if the IRS thinks that your salary is too low and your dividends too high, they may declare that the dividends were a salary in disguise, and hit you for back taxes and penalties. This may require an accountant's help.

As an employee of your own S corporation, you may be eligible for some tax-deductible fringe benefits, but not medical insurance. Owners of S corporations come under the same health insurance rules as partnerships; they are only allowed a limited 25% deduction (explained in the Tax section). Employee-owners of regular C corporations, you will recall, are eligible for 100% tax-deductible health insurance.

There are three significant tax advantages to an S corporation. The first and most obvious is the elimination of the double taxation. Second, where regular corporate tax rates are higher than individual rates, as is the case in some tax brackets, S corporations allow you to have the corporate structure without the higher tax rates. The third advantage is due to some complex tax laws that allow current business losses to be carried back to prior years to offset prior years' taxes, bringing immediate tax refunds. Any business, corporation or otherwise, can avail itself of operating loss carryback laws (which are explained in more detail in the tax section). But if a corporation is brand new and sustains a loss, there are no prior years to carry the loss back to. In the case of an S corporation, the loss passes through to the stockholders, and they in turn can carry the loss back to their personal prior years' returns even though the business did not exist then. Losses of a regular corporation (or any other business) that cannot be carried back can be carried forward to offset future years' earnings, but the business must wait a full year or more to get the refund.

Only "closely held" corporations—those having 35 or fewer stockholders—can elect to become S corporations. There are special and very stringent requirements as to who may be a stockholder, how profits are to be distributed, how and when the election to become an S corporation must be made, what kind of stock can be issued.

For state income tax purposes, most states recognize the S corporation, but a few states do not and tax these businesses as regular corporations.

For more information on the federal requirements, ask the IRS for a free copy of publication #589, "Tax Information on S Corporations."

Steps to Incorporating a Business

The states, not the federal government, license corporations. The requirements vary greatly from state to state, as do the fees, which can run from minimal amounts in some states to as high as $2,500 in others. And unless you are willing and able to study all the incorporation laws, which can get complicated, and file all the necessary forms yourself, add another $200 to $600 for a lawyer's assistance.

Generally, the first and most important step in the required incorporation procedures is the preparation of a "certificate" or "articles" of incorporation. This document usually must show the following information:

1. The proposed name of the corporation. The state can reject your proposed name if it is too similar to another corporation's name or if it is deceptive so as to mislead the public—like if you called your corporation "Germinal Motors" or "U.S. Government Licensing Co." or something.

2. The purposes for which the corporation is formed. In some states, the wording of this section can be critical and, if improperly worded, can severely limit the type of business you can conduct.

3. Names and addresses of incorporators.

4. Location of the principal office of the corporation. Most small corporations obtain their charter from the state in which they are located. Much has been written about the benefits of incorporating in a state other than your own, particularly Delaware, where the corporate statutes are lenient and the filing fees minimal. Most states, however, require in-state corporations—particularly small corporations where the majority of stockholders are state residents—to abide by state laws, pay regular in-state incorporation fees, and pay resident corporate income taxes, regardless of where the business is officially incorporated. So, in most cases, small corporations should incorporate in their home states.

5. The names of subscribers (future shareholders) and the number of share to which each subscribes. This is known as a "limited offering" of stock. Corporate stock is issued either as a "limited offering" or as a "public offering". Most small corporations make limited offering of stock, with each shareholder individually named in the articles of incorporation. After the initial issuance of stock, you will need special permission from the state to sell new shares or to sell old shares to new stockholders.

A corporation that is "going public"—making a public offering—can sell stock to anyone. States charge much higher fees to charter public corporations. Public corporations must register with the Federal Securities and Exchange Commission (the SEC) and hire CPA's to prepare annual audited financial statements.

When a certified public accounting firm audits your financial statements, they make a thorough examination of your ledgers, checking accuracy, examining supporting documents, following the "paper trail," doing their best to prove that your figures are correct. Then they issue an opinion, that your financial statements are accurate and prepared in accordance with "generally accepted accounting principles." This, as you can imagine, is a rather expensive undertaking.

All public corporations are required by law to hire CPA's and publish audited financial statements. Most private corporations (those with the "limited offerings" described above) are not required to have their statements audited; and, of course, most don't.

6. The type and maximum amount of capital stock to be issued. Stock is typically classed as "common" or "preferred." Holders of preferred stock generally have prior or "preferred" claim on corporate assets over common stockholders. Preferred stockholders are often just investors with no interest in the corporation other than making money on their money. Stock can also have a "par value"—an arbitrary value per share—or "no-par value."

7. Capital required at time of incorporation. This is another important decision and requires a knowledge of corporate "equity", which is comprised of "stated capital" and "paid-in surplus." "Stated capital" is, basically, an amount of money that belongs to the corporation and cannot be paid out to stockholders until the corporation is liquidated. All corporations must have some stated capital. Some states specify the dollar minimum. Some states require the corporation to bank the stated capital in cash. Since stated capital is money with only limited use, most corporations try to keep stated capital as small as possible. "Paid-in sur-

plus" is money in excess of stated capital and generally is not restricted.

In addition to filing the articles or certificate of incorporation, many states require one or more of the following procedures:

1. Reserving a name with the state. This step, if required, precedes the filing of the articles of incorporation.

2. Filing a statement naming the elected officers. This usually must be filed after the first board of directors meeting.

3. Requesting formal permission to issue stock. This may require a description of how the stock will be distributed and how the proceeds from the sale will be used.

If a lot of this sounds like a duplication of information already included in the articles of incorporation, you're right—it is. But the states still require separate forms (and additional fees).

In most states, one person can incorporate a business. Some states require two or three people. But be it a one person corporation or a huge conglomerate, if you are going to incorporate you must play the corporate game entirely. You must hold meetings and keep written minutes of the meetings. Your corporation must have stockholders who elect directors (you must have directors), who are a policy making and overseeing group. The directors appoint officers (that's right, you must have officers), who run the business. Officers, in turn hire employees, who do the work. In a small corporation, one person often wears all four hats: stockholder, director, officer and employee.

It may all sound ludicrous to you, but that's the corporate game, and that's the way it must be played.

Incorporating an Existing Business

A business can incorporate when it first opens its doors or any time afterward. You can start you business as a sole proprietorship or a partnership, both of which cost much less to start and involve a lot less paperwork than a corporation; and incorporate the business later—after you know the business is going to be successful, and you can afford the additional cost, and you can see a real reason to incorporate.

Charles Dorton is an amazing man. He is a full time school teacher, enrolled in a doctoral program at the University of San Francisco, and raising a teenage daughter. And "on the side," Mr. Dorton operates Dorton Security, Inc., which grossed about $35,000 in its first year of operation:

"Starting a corporation was no big deal. I think most people misinterpret the law, or they feel that they've got to have an attorney do everything. I looked into the possibility of going to a lawyer. He wanted $400. I decided to see what I could do myself instead. I thought, well, I've got to find out something about state requirements. So I called one state agency and they said I had to call another agency, the Secretary of State's office. I called San Francisco, and they said if I want some information I have to write to Sacramento. They gave me the address, and I wrote. They sent back a little brochure indicating what the state required in terms of their articles of incorporation. It's very simple. I think there are about five articles that the state will accept. If you write in anything else, they'll have you take it out.

"I got my articles written up and took them up to Sacramento. The thing that bothered me, it costs $65 to file, but if you go to Sacramento and have them process your papers while you're waiting, it's $70—a $5 handling fee, which to me was sort of a rip-off. You must pay $800 prepaid franchise tax. Every corporation has to pay that, even if you are floundering financially. Every year you have to pay that $800. Because my typewriter ribbon wasn't dark enough, I had to have my articles typed over.

Joe's Janitorial, Inc.

Section Four
TAXES

"If the adjustments required by section 481(a) and Regulation 1.481-1 are attributable to a change in method of accounting initiated by the taxpayer, the amount of such adjustments, to the extent such amount does not exceed the net amount which would have been required if the change had been made in the first taxable year beginning after December 31, 1953, and ending after August 16, 1954, shall be taken into account by the taxpayer in computing taxable income in the manner provided in section 481 (b) (4) (B) and paragraph (b) of this section."

—Internal Revenue Code

Well as through this world I've rambled
I've seen lots of funny men
Some will rob you with a six-gun
And some with a fountain pen.

—Woody Guthrie

Deep In the Heart of Taxes

Throughout *Small-Time Operator* I've made enough comments—maybe more than enough—about the intrusion of government into all our affairs. And an introduction to Taxes is an ideal setting to get into it again. But I think enough's been said. The revolution doesn't seem to be coming, and the "system" is not quite ready to collapse yet. So it seems that taxes are here to stay awhile. Rather than criticize or defend them, I'd just like to give you some information to help you deal with them.

This tax section of *Small-Time Operator* will discuss the federal income, self-employment and excise taxes; state income taxes; gross receipts taxes; and other local taxes. Sales taxes and the various licenses and permits required of small businesses have already been covered in the "Technicalities and Legalities" chapter. Employment taxes were discussed in the Growing Up section.

Because of the nature of the beast—the non-stop modifications and the complexity of the tax laws—this tax section is handled differently from the rest of the book. The tax section is like a third grade reader, simple and basic. Rather than presenting a step-by-step "all you need to know" guide to taxes (which would require at least five times the space), the tax section will provide you with a general education about taxes, including specifics of some of the basic and more important federal laws.

Even if you take your tax problems to an accountant, I think you should familiarize yourself with the information in this tax section. There is more to taxes than just filling out the tax forms every April 15. Many of the tax laws outlined in this section relate directly to every day management of your business.   The federal income tax laws affect your bookkeeping and, through a knowledge of which expenditures are and are not tax deductible, your business profit. What's more, you will be of greater help to your tax account-ant—which means your tax accountant can be of greater help to you—if you have at least some familiarity with the federal income tax laws. In fact, the information here may help you think of some tax savings that your accountant may have overlooked.

The Tax Laws As They Apply to You

Many of the federal tax laws are designed solely to keep you from cheating the government out of what they think is rightfully theirs—your money. But a lot of these laws were enacted to save you money, to give you some sort of tax break. The Internal Revenue Service does make an effort—albeit a lame one—to educate people about beneficial tax laws; but basically it's up to you to dig in and find out how to save yourself tax dollars. The problem is that income tax laws tend to overwhelm most people because of their complexity and because of their sheer volume—so many different possibilities, so many "if's, and's and but's."

A lot of special effort has been put into this section of the book to help you understand the tax laws without getting trapped in the octopus tentacles of exceptions. This is accomplished by a four-step procedure:

Step 1: The basic tax rules—those that apply to most small businesses—are explained as simply as possible in plain English; no accounting double-talk and no "if's, and's and but's."

Step 2: Following the basic rules, any special situations, exceptions or tricky catches in the law are separately headed up—labeled "The Fine Print"—and explained. This is designed so you can skim over them rapidly and spot an area that may apply to you.

Step 3: Unusual and complex rules, most of which apply only to a minority of people, are mentioned in order to alert you to their existence but are not explained in detail.

Step 4: Free sources of complete tax information are listed so that you can pursue the subjects you need and want to know more thoroughly.

A Warning

This tax section does *not* provide complete information on all federal tax laws nor was it ever intended to. It is meant to be a general guideline to help you wade through the maze of rules and regulations that our government in its wisdom has seen fit to enact into law. Read the tax section with this warning in mind, and I think you will find it helpful and informative. And remember, the tax laws are in a constant state of change. It is your responsibility—and it could be to your benefit financially—to keep abreast of current tax law.

As additional help in using and understanding this tax section, you should get a copy of the Internal Revenue Service's *Tax Guide For Small Business* (Publication #334), available free from any IRS office. This is a surprisingly well-written tax guide, revised every year, and contains about 200 pages on income, excise, and employment taxes for sole proprietors, partnerships and corporations. If you use the IRS's *Tax Guide* in conjunction with this tax section of *Small-Time Operator* you shouldn't go wrong.

A warning about IRS help: Although IRS publications are usually accurate and reliable, the same cannot always be said of tax information the IRS gives out over the phone or in person. The IRS people do, on occasion, give out totally incorrect information. Tax laws are vastly complicated and even the experts make mistakes. Do not rely on verbal information unless you can verify it. Ask the IRS person for a reference in their *Tax Guide* or in one of their other publications, and look it up.

Please also keep in mind that these are federal laws, applicable to federal tax returns. For state returns, most state income tax laws are very similar or identical to these federal laws; but some states have different laws, different ways to compute depreciation, different deductions allowed or not allowed. Many of the differences are covered in this section. You should, however, study the instructions that come with your state tax forms. You might find additional state deductions that the IRS does not allow, and save some money on your state taxes. State taxes are covered more thoroughly at the end of this section.

A tax is a compulsory payment for which no specific benefit is received in return.

—U.S. Treasury

Accounting Period: Calendar Year vs. Fiscal Year

Every business must keep books and file tax returns based on what the IRS calls a "taxable year", which is either a "calendar year" or a "fiscal year." A calendar year begins on January 1 and ends on December 31. A fiscal year is a twelve month period ending on the last day of any month other than December.

Most small businesses use a calendar year simply because it's easier. All of the federal and state tax procedures are geared to the calendar year: issuance of W-2's, 1099's and dividend and interest statements, and publication of the new tax forms and instructions.

The calendar year is also preferred by the Internal Revenue Service. They have strict and rather complex rules about who can adopt a fiscal year and when the decision must be made. The rules vary depending on how your business is legally structured. Generally, sole proprietorships must use the same taxable year as the owner, which means the calendar year in most cases. The same rule applies to partnerships, S corporations, and "personal service" corporations (corporations that primarily sell services performed by the owner-employees), though the IRS will allow these businesses to adopt a fiscal year if there is a valid business reason for using a fiscal year. You must file IRS form #8716, "Election to Have a Tax Year Other Than a Required Tax Year." Regular corporations can choose either a calendar or a fiscal year.

Why choose a fiscal year at all? Some businesses have definite yearly cycles and find that coordinating their taxable year with the business cycle better reflects actual income and expenses. Large department stores have traditionally chosen a January 31 fiscal year so they can have their January "white sales", to reduce their stock of merchandise on hand, thereby making the year-end inventory count much easier and less expensive. Corporations sometimes choose a fiscal year coinciding with the month the business first began operation, in order to avoid a short-period tax return and extra taxes the first year.

The tax laws discussed in this tax section apply to both calendar year and fiscal year taxpayers, except where otherwise noted.

Who Must File A Tax Return

You must file a federal income tax return if your *net* earnings from self-employment (your business *net* profit) is $400 or more. Business income minus expenses equals *net* profit. If you operate more than one business, combine the profits and losses of the different businesses to arrive at the total net profit.

Filing Dates for Tax Returns

For calendar-year businesses other than corporations, the federal income tax return is due April 15. For corporations, the due date is March 15.

Automatic extensions to file returns (but not to pay the taxes) are available to all businesses and individuals:

Sole proprietors and partners in partnerships (not the partnership itself) can obtain an automatic four-month extension, to August 15, by filing IRS Form #4868, and paying the estimated tax due, on or before April 15. Beyond the automatic four-month extension, the IRS will sometimes allow an additional two-month extension, to October 15, but only for "very good reasons" (those are the IRS's words, and they make the decision). File Form #2688, but only after you first file Form #4868.

Corporations can obtain an automatic six-month extension, to September 15, by filing Form #7004 and paying the estimated tax due, by the March 15 due date.

Partnerships can obtain an automatic three-month extension, to July 15, by filing Form #8736 by April 15. Since partnerships pay no income taxes, no taxes are due with the extension. Partners should also file their own personal extensions on Form #4868.

All the above extensions (except Form #2688) must be filed by the original due date of the return and must include payment for all taxes due. If you underpay your taxes by more than 10%, the IRS will hit you with a penalty.

Fiscal year taxpayers: For businesses other than corporations, the federal income tax return is due on the fifteenth day of the fourth month following the end of the fiscal year. Corporate returns are due on the fifteenth day of the third month. The same extensions described above are available to fiscal-year businesses.

State tax returns: Many states offer extensions of time to file state returns. Some duplicate the federal rules, but some are different. Check your state income tax instruction book.

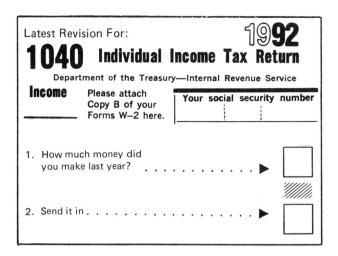

Tax Calendar for Businesses

The tax calendar lists due dates for federal and state tax reports. Each date shown is the last day on which to perform the required action without penalty. If the due date for filing a return, making a tax payment, etc. falls on a Saturday, Sunday or legal holiday, the date is moved to the next regular work day.

Tax deposits that are due weekly and monthly throughout the year are listed at the end of the calendar.

In order to help you spot the dates applicable to your business and skip over those not applicable, the first word in each description will tell who the information applies to, such as 'Employers,' 'Corporations,' etc. 'Individuals' refers to sole proprietors, partners (not partnerships), and corporate stockholders (not the corporations).

These dates apply to calendar year taxpayers. Businesses using a fiscal year must change some of the dates. See the end of the calendar.

These due dates don't usually change from year to year, but they can. Be sure to verify them before relying on them.

JANUARY 1-MARCH 16
Corporations that meet certain requirements may elect, during this period, to be treated as S corporations during current and future years. Use Form 2553.

JANUARY 15
Individuals must either pay the balance due on prior

year's estimated income tax or file an income tax return (Form 1040) on or before January 31 and pay the full amount of the tax due. See January 31.

Farmers and fishermen may elect to file declaration of estimated income tax (Form 1040-ES) for prior year and pay estimated tax in full, and file income tax return (Form 1040) by April 15. If declaration of estimated tax is not filed, see February 28.

JANUARY 31

Individuals should file an income tax return for prior year and pay the tax due, if the balance on their prior year's estimated tax was not paid by January 15. Use Form 1040. Farmers and fishermen, see February 28.

Employers' last day for giving every employee Form W-2 showing income and social security information. Also see February 28.

Employers deposit federal unemployment tax (FUTA) at an authorized bank if the tax is more than $100. If the amount is $100 or less, you are not required to deposit it, but you must add it to the taxes for the next quarter. Then, in the next quarter, if the total undeposited tax is more than $100, deposit it by the last day of the month following the quarter. Use Form 508.

Employers file Form 941 for income tax withheld and social security and Medicare taxes for the 4st quarter of the prior year and pay any taxes due. If timely deposits were made, see February 10.

Businesses liable for excise taxes must file quarterly excise tax return. Use Form 720.

Employers subject to federal unemployment tax file annual return for the prior year. Use Form 940. If timely deposits were made in full payment of the tax, see February 10.

All businesses: most state sales tax returns for the 4th quarter of last year are due.

Corporations that paid $10 or more in dividends or interest must prepare Form 1099 & give one copy to each recipient. See also February 28.

All businesses that paid $600 or more to an individual in commissions, fees or other compensation including payments to subcontractors must prepare Form 1099 & give one copy to each recipient. See also February 28.

All businesses that sold $5,000 or more of goods to independent sales agents must prepare Form 1099 and give one copy to each agent. See also February 28.

All businesses that paid $10 or more in interest must prepare form 1099-INT & give one copy to each recipient. See also February 28.

All businesses that paid $10 or more in royalties must prepare Form 1099-MISC & give one copy to each recipient. See also February 28.

Operators of fishing boats give each self-employed crew member a statement showing member's share for the year, using Form 1099-MISC. See also February 28.

FEBRUARY 10

Employers who made timely deposits in full payment of all income taxes withheld and social security and Medicare taxes due for the 4th quarter of the prior year file 4th quarter return. Use Form 941.

Employers subject to federal unemployment tax who made timely deposits in full payment of the tax file annual return for the prior year. Use Form 940.

FEBRUARY 28

All businesses that prepared Form 1099 (See Jan. 31) must file the 1099's along with transmittal Form 1096 with the IRS.

Employers must file Form W-3, Transmittal of Income and Tax Statements, with the Social Security Administration if you have issued Form W-2 (See Jan. 31). Copy A of each W-2 must accompany Form W-3.

Employers whose employees receive tips must report those tips on Form 8027.

Farmers and fishermen who did not file declaration of estimated tax on January 15 should file final income tax return (Form 1040) for prior year.

MARCH 15

Corporations must file federal income tax return, Form 1120, or application for extension, Form 7004, and pay to a depositary the balance of tax still due.

S Corporations must file federal income tax Form 1120S.

Corporations must file state income tax returns for the following states: Ala., Alaska, Calif., D.C., Ill., Maine, Mass., Md., Minn., Miss., Nebr., N.H., N. Mex., N.Y., N.C., Okla., R.I., S.C., Vt., W. Va., Wis.

MARCH 31

Corporations must file state income tax returns for the following states: Conn., Del., Fla., Ohio, Tenn.

APRIL 15

Individuals must file a federal income tax return for the prior calendar year. The tax due must be paid in full with this return. Schedule C must be filed (Schedule F for farmers), and in addition, Schedule SE must be completed. If you desire an automatic 4-month extension, file Form 4868 accompanied by payment of your estimated unpaid income tax liability.

Individuals must file a declaration of estimated income tax (including self-employment tax) for the current year and pay at least 25 percent of such tax. Use Form 1040-ES.

Partnerships must file a return for the prior calendar year. Use Form 1065 (no tax due).

Corporations deposit first installment of this year's estimated income tax.

Individuals must file a state income tax return for all states collecting income tax except Ark., Del., Hawaii, Va., La., and Iowa.

Corporations must file state income tax returns for the following states: Ariz., Colo., Ga., Idaho, Ind., Kans., Ky., Mo., N.J., N.D., Ore., Pa., Utah, Va., La.

APRIL 20

Individuals in Hawaii must file a state income tax return.

Corporations in Hawaii must file state income tax returns.

APRIL 30

Individuals living in Del., Va. or Iowa must file a state income tax return.

Corporations in Mich. and Iowa must file state income tax returns.

All businesses: most states sales tax returns for the first quarter are due.

Employers file Form 941 for income tax withheld and social security and Medicare taxes for the 1st quarter and pay any taxes due. If timely deposits were made, see May 10.

Employers deposit federal unemployment tax (FUTA) at an authorized bank if the tax is more than $100. If the amount is $100 or less, you are not required to deposit it, but you must add it to the taxes for the next quarter. Then, in the next quarter, if the total undeposited tax is more than $100, deposit it by the last day of the month following the quarter. Use Form 508.

Businesses liable for excise taxes must file quarterly excise tax return. Use Form 720.

MAY 10

Employers who made timely deposits in full payment of income tax withheld and social security and Medicare taxes due for the 1st quarter, file 1st quarter return. Use Form 941.

MAY 15

Individuals living in Ark. or La. must file state income tax returns.

Corporations in Ark. and Mont. must file state income tax returns.

JUNE 15

Individuals must pay 2nd installment of estimated income tax.

Corporations deposit second installment of estimated income tax.

JULY 31

Employers file Form 941 for income tax withheld and social security and Medicare taxes for the 2nd quarter and pay any taxes due. If timely deposits were made, see August 10.

Businesses liable for excise taxes must file quarterly excise tax return. Use Form 720.

Employers deposit federal unemployment tax (FUTA) at an authorized bank if the tax is more than $100. If the amount is $100 or less, you are not required to deposit it, but you must add it to the taxes for the next quarter. Then, in the next quarter, if the total undeposited tax is more than $100, deposit it by the last day of the month following the quarter. Use Form 508.

All businesses: most state sales tax returns for the 2nd quarter are due.

Employers with an employee benefit, pension, profit sharing, or stock bonus plan, file Form 5500 for the previous calendar year.

AUGUST 10

Employers who made timely deposits in full payment of all income tax withheld and social security and Medicare taxes due for the 2nd quarter, file 2nd quarter return. Use Form 941.

AUGUST 15

Individuals who received an automatic 4-month extension for filing last year's federal income tax return must now file the return. Form 1040.

AUGUST 31

Heavy-duty truck owners and operators must pay the federal use tax on highway motor vehicles used on the public highways. Use Form 2290.

SEPTEMBER 15

Individuals must pay 3rd installment of estimated income tax. Use Form 1040-ES.

Corporations deposit 3rd installment of estimated income tax.

Corporations that received an automatic 6-month extension for filing last year's federal income tax return must now file the return, on Form 1120, 1120-A or 1120-S.

OCTOBER 31

Employers file Form 941 for income tax withheld and social security and Medicare taxes for the 3rd quarter and pay any taxes due. If timely deposits were made, see November 10.

All businesses: most state sales tax returns for the 3rd quarter are due.

Businesses liable for excise taxes must file quarterly excise tax return. Use Form 720.

Employers deposit federal unemployment tax (FUTA) at an authorized bank if the tax is more than $100. If the amount is $100 or less, you are not required to deposit it, but you must add it to the taxes for the next quarter. Then, in the next quarter, if the total undeposited tax is more than $100, deposit it by the last day of the month following the quarter. Use Form 508.

NOVEMBER

Employers should request a new Form W-4 from each employee whose withholding exemptions will be different next year.

NOVEMBER 10

Employers who made timely deposits in full payment of income tax withheld and social security and Medicare taxes due for the 3rd quarter, file 3rd quarter return. Use Form 941.

DECEMBER 15

Corporations deposit the 4th installment of estimated income tax.

WEEKLY AND MONTHLY ALL YEAR

Corporations that meet certain requirements may elect, any time during the year, to be treated as S corporations in future years. Use Form 2553. To be treated as an S corporation this year, see Jan. 1.

Employers: tax deposits of social security and Medicare (NOT self-employment) and withheld income taxes required monthly (by the 15th of the following month) whenever amounts due are $500 or more; required 8 times a month whenever amounts due are $3000 or more.

Businesses liable for excise taxes are required to make monthly deposits on the last day of the month when more than $100 in excise taxes is collected. For more information, see IRS publication #510.

FISCAL YEAR TAXPAYERS

Individuals: federal income tax return 1040 is due the 15th day of the 4th month after the end of your tax year.

Partnerships: federal tax return 1065 is due the 15th day of the 4th month after the end of your tax year

Corporations: federal income tax return 1120 or 1120-S is due the 15th day of the 3rd month after the end of your tax year.

All fiscal year businesses: many states follow the same schedule as the federal government for filing state income tax returns, but some states have different dates. Consult your own state.

Individuals: federal estimated tax payments are due on the 15th day of the 4th, 6th, & 9th months of your tax year, & on the 15th day of the first month after your tax year.

Corporations: federal estimated tax payments are due on the 15th day of the 4th, 6th, 9th & 12th months of your tax year.

Corporations electing to be S-Corporations must file Form 2553 by the 15th day of the 3rd month of the tax year.

Employers maintaining an employee benefit, pension, profit sharing, or stock bonus plan, must file Form 5500 by the last day of the 7th month following the end of the taxable year.

Business Expenses

All legitimate business expenses, except those specifically disallowed by law (covered in this Tax Section), are deductible in computing your taxable income as long as they meet the Internal Revenue Service's three basic rules:

One: The expenses must be incurred in connection with your business. Personal non-business expenses are not deductible.

Two: The expenses must be, in the words of the IRS, "ordinary and necessary." "Ordinary" does not mean that the expenses must be recurring or habitual; only that similar expenses are common or accepted in your particular type of business. A "necessary" expense, according to the IRS, is one "that is appropriate and helpful in developing and maintaining your trade or business."

Three: The amounts must be "reasonable."

Expenditures that are partly personal (non-business) and partly business can be prorated and the business portion expensed or depreciated. Sometimes your home or your automobile fall in this category. Proration of rent was explained in the bookkeeping section. Proration of automobile expenses is explained in this tax section. Business expenses that you pay on your personal credit card are also fully deductible.

Any asset that you originally purchased and used for non-business purposes that you are now using for business or using partly for business can be written off or depreciated as of the date you began using the asset in your business. It does not matter when you purchased the item. The depreciation chapter has complete information.

Start-Up Expenses

Business expenses incurred before you start your business (called start-up expenses, though they are really pre-start-up expenses) come under two different tax rules.

General preliminary costs incurred before you actually pick a specific business, such as investigating different business possibilities and checking out locations, are usually not deductible at all. The IRS considers these "personal expenses," no tax write-off ever.

Once you've decided on a particular business, the start-up expenses (not including the general preliminary costs mentioned above) are deductible, but not 100% the year you incur them. You have the option to capitalize them, which means no deduction at all until you quit or sell your business, or to write them off (amortize them) over a 60-month period (or longer if you prefer) starting with the month the business actually begins operation.

To figure your deduction, divide your total start-up costs by the number of months in the write-off period (at least 60, but more if you want to spread the tax deduction over a longer period). The result is the amount you can deduct each month. Use Form 4562, the part labeled Amortization, to show your calculations. To get this amortization option, you must start taking the deduction the first year you are in business. Otherwise, you lose the option and will be required to capitalize the start-up expenses.

Start-up expenses are a real sore spot for new businesses, because the expenses include any and all business expenditures incurred before you are open for business. They include organizational expenses, such as hiring an accountant or a lawyer to draft up legal documents; and even conventional pre-opening expenses such as rent, telephone, advertising, stationery, etc.

The IRS has often wrangled with taxpayers over which costs are and aren't "start-up," and at what point a new venture is actually "in business." The IRS has stated that a business hasn't actually started until it produces income. Tax Courts have disagreed and have ruled that once a business is set up and "open for business," it is officially started even if it has not made a sale yet. This is an area to discuss with an accountant. I suggest you put off as many expenses as possible until after the business is operating.

One way around some of the start-up expense hassles is to start your business at home if that's feasible, just as small an operation as possible to meet IRS requirements. Once you have generated a little income, *then* spend your money on finding a new location, on stationery and forms, on furniture and equipment, and on accounting and legal advice. Since you are now officially in business, the expenses are deductible as regular business expenses and no longer subject to the start-up rules.

If you do incur start-up expenses but never actually start a business, the expenses may, in some situations, be deductible as a capital loss under the IRS's capital gains and loss rules. Here also, you will probably need an accountant's help.

100 Typical Business Expenses

Below is an alphabetical listing of over 100 typical business expenses that can be deducted on your income tax return. Those items marked with an asterisk (*) are explained in more detail on the following pages. The number following each expense corresponds to the column number in the sample expenditure ledger, so you can tell at a glance in which column to post the expense. "Y/E" after an item means that the expense is recorded on the year-end summary only. Year-end procedures were explained in the bookkeeping section.

A list of typical business expenses can never be complete. *Any* expense that meets the IRS's three rules (incurred in connection with your business, complies with "ordinary and necessary" test, is "reasonable"), if not specifically disallowed, should be taken whether it is on this list or not. Those expenses specifically disallowed are listed later in this section.

Account books (2)
Accounting fees (10)
Advertising (5)
Auditing fees (10)
*Automobile expenses (9 or Y/E)
*Bad debts (Y/E)
Bank service charges (2)
Bonding fees (10)
Bookkeeping services (10)

Books (useful life one year or less) (2)
Burglar alarm service (10)
*Burglary (see Casualty losses)
Business associations (10)
Business cards (5)
*Business gifts (5)
*Business interruption insurance (10)
Business license (8)
*Casualty losses (see discussion)
Charitable contributions (10)
Cleaning (2)
Clothing, special (2)
Coffee service (2)
Collection expense (10)
Commissions (3)
Consultant fees (3)
Contractor's fees (3)
*Conventions (see Travel away from home) (10)
*Cost of goods sold (1)
Credit bureau fees (10)
Credit card fees for merchants (10)
*Depreciation (Y/E)
Dues, business associations (10)
Dues, professional societies (10)
Dues, union (10)
*Education expenses (10)
Electricity (see Utilities) (7)
Employer's taxes (8)
Employment agency fees (10)
*Entertainment (5)
*Equipment (see Depreciation) (Y/E)
*Extended coverage insurance (10)
Fees for services (3)
Fees to organizations (10)
*Fire insurance (10)
*Fire losses (see Casualty losses)
*Floor tax (inventory tax) (8)
*Freight (1 or 2—see discussion)
Garbage (see Utilities) (7)
Gas (see Utilities) (7)
*Gross receipts tax (8)
Heating (see Utilities) (7)
*Insurance (10)
*Interest on business debt (10)
*Inventory (see Cost of Goods Sold) (1)
*Inventory (floor) tax (8)
Janitorial service (10)
Ledgers (2)
Legal expenses (10)
*Liability insurance (10)
License fees (8)
Loss on sale of business assets (Y/E)
*Loss of useful value (see Depreciation) (Y/E)
*Machinery (see Depreciation) (y/E)
Magazines (2)
Merchant's associations (10)

SCHEDULE C (Form 1040)

Department of the Treasury
Internal Revenue Service (T)

Profit or Loss From Business
(Sole Proprietorship)

► Partnerships, joint ventures, etc., must file Form 1065.
► Attach to Form 1040 or Form 1041.   ► See Instructions for Schedule C (Form 1040).

OMB No. 1545-0074

1992

Attachment Sequence No. 09

Name of proprietor	Social security number (SSN)
Samuel Thesham	123 : 45 : 6789

A Principal business or profession, including product or service (see instructions)
auto repair

B Enter principal business code (from page 2) ► 8 9 5 3

C Business name
Monkeywrench Motors

D Employer ID number (Not SSN)

E Business address (including suite or room no.) ► 7831 Claremont
City, town or post office, state, and ZIP code   Berkeley CA 94705

F Accounting method: (1) ☐ Cash (2) ☒ Accrual (3) ☐ Other (specify) ► ....

G Method(s) used to value closing inventory: (1) ☒ Cost (2) ☐ Lower of cost or market (3) ☐ Other (attach explanation) (4) ☐ Does not apply (if checked, skip line H)

	Yes	No
H Was there any change in determining quantities, costs, or valuations between opening and closing inventory? (If "Yes," attach explanation.)		X
I Did you "materially participate" in the operation of this business during 1991? (If "No," see instructions for limitations on losses.)	X	
J If this is the first Schedule C filed for this business, check here		► ☐

Part I   Income

1 Gross receipts or sales. **Caution:** If this income was reported to you on Form W-2 and the "Statutory employee" box on that form was checked, see the instructions and check here ► ☐	1	$22,364
2 Returns and allowances	2	0
3 Subtract line 2 from line 1	3	$22,364
4 Cost of goods sold (from line 40 on page 2)	4	2,008
5 Subtract line 4 from line 3 and enter the **gross profit** here	5	$20,356
6 Other income, including Federal and state gasoline or fuel tax credit or refund (see instructions)	6	0
7 Add lines 5 and 6. This is your **gross income** ►	7	$20,356

Part II   Expenses (Caution: Enter expenses for business use of your home on line 30.)

8 Advertising	8	$ 150	21 Repairs and maintenance	21	
9 Bad debts from sales or services (see instructions)	9		22 Supplies (not included in Part III)	22	218
10 Car and truck expenses (see instructions—also attach **Form 4562**)	10	480	23 Taxes and licenses	23	267
11 Commissions and fees	11	5,650	24 Travel, meals, and entertainment:		
12 Depletion	12		a Travel	24a	
13 Depreciation and section 179 expense deduction (not included in Part III) (see instructions)	13	136	b Meals and entertainment		
14 Employee benefit programs (other than on line 19)	14		c Enter 20% of line 24b subject to limitations (see instructions)		
15 Insurance (other than health)	15	650	d Subtract line 24c from line 24b	24d	
16 Interest:			25 Utilities	25	221
a Mortgage (paid to banks, etc.)	16a		26 Wages (less jobs credit)	26	
b Other	16b	637	27a Other expenses (list type and amount): Misc. $70		
17 Legal and professional services	17				
18 Office expense	18	78			
19 Pension and profit-sharing plans	19				
20 Rent or lease (see instructions):					
a Vehicles, machinery, and equipment	20a				
b Other business property	20b	1,200	27b Total other expenses	27b	70
28 Add amounts in columns for lines 8 through 27b. These are your **total expenses** before expenses for business use of your home ►	28	$9,757
29 Tentative profit (loss). Subtract line 28 from line 7	29	$10,599
30 Expenses for business use of your home (attach **Form 8829**)	30	
31 **Net profit or (loss).** Subtract line 30 from line 29. If a profit, enter here and on Form 1040, line 12. Also enter the net profit on Schedule SE, line 2 (statutory employees, see instructions). If a loss, you MUST go on to line 32 (fiduciaries, see instructions)	31	$10,599

32 If you have a loss, you MUST check the box that describes your investment in this activity (see instructions)	32a ☐ All investment is at risk.	
If you checked 32a, enter the loss on Form 1040, line 12, and Schedule SE, line 2 (statutory employees, see instructions). If you checked 32b, you MUST attach **Form 6198**.	32b ☐ Some investment is not at risk.	

Part III   Cost of Goods Sold (See instructions.)

33 Inventory at beginning of year. (If different from last year's closing inventory, attach explanation.)	33	$ 100
34 Purchases less cost of items withdrawn for personal use	34	1,958
35 Cost of labor. (Do not include salary paid to yourself.)	35	
36 Materials and supplies	36	
37 Other costs	37	
38 Add lines 33 through 37	38	$ 2,058
39 Inventory at end of year	39	50
40 **Cost of goods sold.** Subtract line 39 from line 38. Enter the result here and on page 1, line 4	40	$ 2,008

Minor repairs (10)
*Moving expenses (10)
Night watch service (10)
*Office furnishings (see Depr.) (Y/E)
*Office in home (see discussion)
Office supplies (2)
Passport fees for business trip (10)
Payroll and withheld payroll taxes (4)
Periodicals (2)
Permit fees (8)
Postage (2)
Professional fees (10)
Professional journals (2)
Professional organizations (10)

Property taxes (8)
Publications (2)
Reference books (useful life 1 yr. or less) (2)
Rent (6)
*Repairs (subject to certain requirements) (10)
Research and experimentation (10)
*Robbery (see Casualty losses)
Safe deposit box (2)
Salaries (4)
Sales tax (8)
Service charges (2)
*Shipping (see Freight) (1 or 2)
*Shoplifting (see Casualty losses)
Small tools (useful life of 1 yr. or less) (2)

State income tax (not deductible on the state
  return) (8)
Stationery (2)
Supplies (2)
*Telephone (7)
*Theft (see Casualty losses)
*Theft insurance (see Insurance) (10)
This book (2)
Tools (useful life one year or less) (2)
*Travel away from home (10)
Uniforms (2)
Unincorporated business tax (8)
Union dues (10)
Utilities (7)
*Vandalism (see Casualty losses)
*Vehicles (see Automobile) 9 or Y/E
Wages (4)
Water (see Utilities) (7)
*Worthless inventory (see Cost of goods sold)

Car and Truck Expenses

All expenses for operating a vehicle for business
are deductible except regular commuting expenses
between your home and your usual place of business, which the IRS considers personal and not
deductible. There are two ways of figuring vehicle
expenses. As in so many other situations, one is
difficult and one is easy.

Method One: You can keep itemized records of
all your vehicle expenses. These include gasoline,
oil, lubrication, maintenance, repairs, insurance,
parking and tolls, garage rents, license and registration fees, even auto club dues. The purchase
price of the vehicle and the cost of major repairs
such as an engine overhaul may have to be depreciated over several years. See the Depreciation
chapter in this section of the book.

Vehicle expenses must be prorated between
personal use (not deductible) and business use
(fully deductible). The most common method of
proration is based on the miles driven. For example, let's say you drove 10,000 miles last year of
which 2,500 miles was in connection with business. Twenty-five percent of all your vehicle expenses are deductible, and twenty-five percent of
the cost of your vehicle can be depreciated.

Keeping itemized records of all your vehicle
expenses is tedious work. The Internal Revenue
Service realizes this also. In one of their rare helpful moods they have come up with...

Method Two: An optional Standard Mileage Allowance. Instead of recording each fill up and
every oil change, you may take a standard flat rate

for every business mile driven. The IRS sets this
rate every year; the 1992 rate is 28¢ per mile. The
standard mileage allowance is in lieu of depreciation and all vehicle expenses except parking, tolls,
interest and state and local taxes, which are deductible in addition to the mileage allowance.

Using the standard mileage rate reduces the
cost basis of your vehicle (for determining profit or
loss when the vehicle is sold). You must reduce the
basis by 11 cents for each business mile driven.

Corporations: Owner-employees of small corporations who use the standard mileage allowance
are not allowed a business deduction for interest
paid on the vehicle.

Vehicle expenses are reported on Form #4562
which must be attached to your income tax return.

The Fine Print

You may not use the standard mileage allowance if you lease the vehicle, if your business operates more than one vehicle at a time, or if you use
the vehicle for hire such as a taxi. Business vehicles that do not qualify for the standard mileage
allowance may still make use of Method One,
itemizing actual expenses.

The method you choose the first year you use
your vehicle for business determines what methods you can use in future years (for that particular
vehicle). If you use Method One (itemizing) the
first year, you must stay with that method as long
as you use that vehicle. If you use the mileage
allowance the first year, you can switch back and
forth if you want, itemizing some years and using
the mileage allowance other years. If you do switch
from the mileage allowance to itemizing, you must
use straight line depreciation.

Depreciation is limited if the vehicle costs over
a certain dollar amount or if the vehicle is used
50% or less for business. This is covered in the
Depreciation chapter.

Interest Expense

Interest paid on business debts is deductible,
with a few important exceptions.

Interest on loans to purchase, improve or construct real estate must usually be capitalized—
that is, added to the cost of the property.

Interest paid on back taxes and any tax penalties is not deductible.

If you borrow money to purchase part or all of

an existing business, the laws can get complicated. If the business is a sole proprietorship, partnership or S corporation, part of the interest may be deductible as a current business expense, but part may have to be capitalized. Generally, the interest on the part of the loan that applies to actual business assets (equipment, inventory, etc) is deductible. The interest that applies to intangibles (goodwill, trademarks, etc) must be capitalized. If you are purchasing a regular C corporation (not an S corporation), you are actually buying stock, and the interest comes under a different set of rules (investment income and expense) and is not deductible as a regular business expense. Obviously, this is an area where you will probably need the help of a good tax accountant.

One more situation, for corporations: If you are an employee of your own corporation, and you get a personal loan to purchase business assets, the interest is not deductible as a business expense. If the corporation itself borrows the money, the interest would be deductible. As you can see, how you structure corporate finances can have a major effect on how much you pay in taxes. Be sure to get some professional tax help.

Bad Debts

Business bad debts—bounced checks and other uncollectible accounts—are fully deductible. The bookkeeping section, under the headings "Return Checks" and "Uncollectible Accounts," tells how to set up a bad debts folder.

Businesses using the cash method of accounting cannot take a bad debt expense for unpaid and uncollectible accounts, because the income was not recorded in the first place. Bounced checks, however, are deductible bad debts, because they were

posted to the income ledgers.

A few businesses that anticipate large bad debts sometimes set aside money in a bad debt reserve fund, sort of like self-insurance. Such reserves are not really business expenses and are not tax deductible.

Business Gifts

Tax deductions for business gifts are limited to $25 per recipient in any one year. Keep records of who the gifts were given to, how much and why.

Samples of your merchandise, given to prospective buyers or to people who might review or publicize your products, are not considered gifts and are not subject to these gift limitations. You write off the cost of the free samples (not the retail or market value) as part of cost-of-goods-sold. See the chapter on Inventory.

Casualty Losses/Theft Losses

Business losses from fire, storm or other casualty, or from theft, shoplifting or vandalism are fully deductible to the extent they are not covered by insurance. There is no limitation as in the case of non-business losses.

Inventory that is stolen or destroyed should not be shown as a casualty loss. The inventory loss is part of your cost-of-goods-sold (discussed in this section) and cannot be deducted a second time. Stolen or destroyed depreciable property can be deducted as a casualty loss, but only to the extent of the undepreciated balance. For example, let's say your box of tools was stolen. You paid $200 for it two years ago and have already taken $40 depreciation on it. You may show a theft loss of only $160 ($200 less the $40).

The IRS says that business losses are not deductible if covered by insurance even if no claim is filed with the insurance company.

Education Expenses

Here is a good opportunity to get some additional education and charge the cost to your business—*if* you are careful in selecting your courses of study. The cost of education and any related expenses are deductible only if the education maintains or improves a skill required in your business. Education expenses are *not* allowed if the education is required to meet minimum educational requirements of your present business or if the education will qualify you for a new trade or business.

A welder in business for himself who takes a course in a new welding method can charge the expense to his business. A self-employed dance teacher who also takes dance lessons can charge the cost of the lessons to the dance business. On the other hand, a leather craftsperson who takes a course in massage cannot deduct the expenses. The education must be directly related to the business you have already begun to operate. Taking a course in pottery *before* opening your pottery shop is not deductible. By the way, any self-employed person can take a course in bookkeeping and deduct the cost as a business expense.

Education expenses include tuition, course fees, books, laboratory fees, and travel expenses while away from home overnight. Overnight travel is subject to special limitations. See the chapter "Travel Away From Home."

Entertainment

Generally, only 80% of entertainment expenses are deductible on your tax return.

In some cases there is a fine line as to what is entertainment (subject to the 80% limit) and what is something else such as advertising (not subject to the limit). Entertainment is more likely to get an IRS second look than other miscellaneous expenses.

For more information, see IRS publication #463, "Travel, Entertainment and Gift Expenses."

Meals

Regular meals at work are generally not deductible. For some business meals, however, 80% of their costs are deductible.

The famous business lunch, wining and dining a current or prospective customer, is 80% deductible but only if business is specifically discussed at the meal and if the cost is not "lavish or extravagant." You must have a receipt and write on it who you took out and why.

Meals while traveling away from home on business are also deductible, subject to the 80% maximum. See the chapter "Travel Away From Home."

There are a host of exceptions to the 80% rule. Food samples made available to the general public are fully deductible. Cost of the annual company picnic or the Thanksgiving turkeys you give your employees every year are fully deductible. Meals provided to employees on the business premises are sometimes fully deductible, sometimes subject to the 80% limit, and sometimes not deductible at all. The IRS's "Tax Guide for Small Business" (Publication 334) has more detailed information.

Freight

"Freight" refers to all shipping charges. "Freight-in" is shipping to you; "freight-out" is shipping of goods you sell. Freight-in on inventory purchased for resale must be included as part of the cost of the inventory. Freight-in on depreciable fixed assets (equipment, furniture and fixtures, etc.) should be added to the cost of the asset. Freight-out and shipping charges on goods you sell are fully deductible expenses.

Insurance

Most current business-related insurance premiums are deductible, including fire, extended coverage, liability, theft, vehicle (but see "Car and Truck Expenses"), worker's compensation, group insurance premiums for employees, unemployment, surety and fidelity bonds. Personal life insurance premiums are not deductible. Health insurance premiums are partly deductible and are covered in a separate chapter, Health Insurance.

If you pay an insurance premium covering more than one year, you may deduct only the current year's portion. Even if you use the cash method of accounting and paid the cash this year, the IRS will not allow a deduction for prepaid insurance extending beyond one year.

Special note regarding "business interruption insurance": The insurance premiums may or may not be deductible, depending on what the insurance actually covers. This is explained thoroughly in the Insurance chapter in the Getting Started section.

Health Insurance

You, as sole proprietor, partner in a partnership, or owner of an S corporation are allowed an income tax deduction of 25% of the cost of health insurance for yourself, your spouse and your dependents. The deduction is not allowed if you are eligible for employee health insurance through your own employer (if you are also holding down another job) or through your spouse's employer. The deduction may not exceed the net profit from your business.

The deduction does not apply when computing self-employment tax. You pay self-employment tax based upon your net profit before the 25% health insurance deduction.

If you have employees, the deduction is allowed only if you provide health insurance for all your employees. The cost of such employee health insurance is 100% deductible (for both income tax and self-employment tax); only the insurance for yourself and your family is subject to the 25% limitation. The IRS has a detailed set of "nondiscrimination requirements," defining who is and isn't an employee for this particular law.

Unlike most tax deductions, the health insurance deduction has an expiration date—sometime during 1992. Congress may extend the date to the end of the year or longer.

If you are an employee of your own corporation, the rules are quite different. In a regular corporation (not an S corporation), you are fully eligible for tax-free employee health insurance, and your corporation is allowed a full deduction for the cost of the insurance. There is no 25% limitation. But the insurance must be available to other employees, under the same non-discrimination requirements.

If you are the owner of an S corporation or a partner in a partnership, the business can purchase health insurance for you and deduct it as a business expense, but it is not tax-free to you. It becomes part of your W-2 wage or part of your taxable partnership income. So, the net tax effect is a wash—no tax savings. But since some insurance companies give better rates to businesses, particularly when you are purchasing insurance for your employees as well as yourself, this option may be worth considering. Sole proprietorships are not allowed this option.

Regardless of the legal structure of your business, any health insurance you purchase for your employees (not yourself) is fully tax deductible.

Moving Expenses

You may deduct all the expenses of moving your business from one location to another. This is an ordinary business expense. There are no special requirements.

The costs of moving to a new home may also be deductible on your personal tax return (not as a business expense) if you meet certain requirements. The move must coincide with a move to a new business location where you plan to stay and work for at least 78 weeks. There is also a distance requirement: the distance between your *new business* and your *old home* must be at least 35 miles greater than the distance between your *old business* and your *old home*. (Better read that again.)

If your old workshop, for example, was five miles from your old home, in order to deduct the cost of moving to your new home, your new shop must be at least 40 miles from your old home. It does not matter where your new home is located.

When home and business are combined, the move must be at least 35 miles to qualify for a home moving expense deduction. If the move is less than 35 miles, you may still prorate the expenses, home versus business, and deduct the business portion as a business expense.

Try it this way:
(a) What is the distance from your *former* residence to your *new* business location? _____ miles.
(b) What is the distance from your *former* residence to your *former* business location? _____ miles.

If the distance in (a) is 35 or more miles *farther than* the distance in (b), you will be eligible for a moving expense deduction. If the distance is *less than* 35 miles, you are not eligible.

If you move to a new home but keep the same place of business, you may not deduct any moving expense no matter how far you move.

The allowable deductions for a move to a new home include:

1. Transportation for you, your family, furniture and all your possessions. If you drive your car, you may deduct either the actual out-of-pocket expenses (gas, oil, repairs, etc.; but not depreciation or any portion of auto insurance) or a standard mileage allowance. This is a different mileage allowance than the Standard Mileage Allowance. Consult the IRS for the current rate.

2. Lodging and 80% of the cost of meals in route.

There are also allowable deductions for temporary living expenses up to thirty days, travel in search of a new residence (*after* you have located your new shop), and incidental expenses connected with the sale, purchase or lease of your residence.

Moving expense deductions are subject to specific limitations in scope and in amount. The Internal Revenue Service publishes a free pamphlet, #521, "Tax Information on Moving Expenses," which explains the entire law in detail.

Repairs

Minor repairs on any of your business property, tools and equipment are fully deductible as a current expense.

Major repairs, however, that either add to the value or extend the useful life of an asset must be treated as a permanent investment and handled in the same manner as the purchase of a depreciable asset. See "Depreciation."

Travel Away From Home

Charge the expense of your vacation to your business? Many small business people plan to take that long-dreamed-of tour of the Far East, make a few business "contacts" along the way, and deduct the entire trip as a business expense. The IRS says "NO!" Legitimate business travel expenses are deductible, but the rules are very specific.

If the reason for your trip is *primarily* personal, NONE of the traveling expenses to and from your destination are deductible. Only expenses directly related to your business may be deducted.

If your trip is primarily for business and it is within the United States, the cost of travel is entirely deductible even if some of the trip is for pleasure. Two important exceptions: only 80% of the cost of food and beverages is deductible; deductions for travel on luxury boats, ocean liners and cruise ships are limited (check with the IRS for maximums—they can change annually).

More stringent rules apply to travel outside the U.S. You must allocate travel expenses between the business portion of your trip and the personal portion. If, however, the trip is no more than one week *or* the time spent for pleasure is less than 25 percent, the entire cost of travel is deductible (with the same exceptions on food and beverages, and on luxury water transportation).

There are special rules if you attend overseas conventions, seminars or other business meetings outside North America. A tax deduction is allowed only if the meeting is directly related to your business and if, in the IRS's opinion, there is a valid business reason for holding the meeting overseas.

Additional, more stringent rules apply to business conventions held aboard cruise ships. Some of these expenses are partly deductible, some are not deductible at all. Check with the IRS for this year's rules.

Local business travel, when not going somewhere overnight, is limited to transportation expenses only. Regular commuting expenses, home to work and back, are not deductible. Side trips to customers or to suppliers are deductible.

You are allowed deductions for food and lodging and miscellaneous expenses only if you are away from home overnight. "Home" is defined as your regular place of business. For years, the IRS has been in and out of tax court with people, arguing the definition of "home". Self-employed itinerant workers, traveling contractors, and salespeople are continually challenged by the IRS on travel deductions, the IRS claiming that the road is home, so no deductions allowed. The courts lately have been siding with the travelers and overruling the IRS. If your business is of this nature and if travel expenses are substantial, I'd advise consulting a good tax accountant. Just having a small home-base office, where you pick up your mail and telephone messages, do your billing, post your books, etc. might be enough to satisfy the IRS.

Travel expenses typically include:

1. Cost of transportation for yourself and your luggage to and from your destination.

2. Meals and lodging (must not be "lavish or extravagant"). Meals are subject to the 80% limit.

3. Cost of transportation while away from home (taxi fares, auto rentals, etc.).

4. Business entertainment, subject to the 80% limit.

5. Personal services such as laundry and dry cleaning, barbering, etc.

For meals, lodging and incidental expenses, you can keep a record of actual expenses or, at your option, you can use a standard "per diem" rate—so much per day. The standard rate, set by the IRS, varies from city to city. For rates and details, ask the IRS for a free copy of Publication 1542, "Per Diem Rates." The IRS offers yet another option: you can figure your actual lodging and incidental expenses, and then add a "standard meal allowance" (which also varies from city to city).

The Internal Revenue Service is forever suspicious of business travel expenses, particularly sole proprietorships where the owner is accountable to no one else: you feel like taking a business trip (and you can afford it), you take it. The IRS wants to be sure it's not a vacation in disguise. You want to be sure you can prove, if audited, that the trip wasn't a vacation. A log of daily activities and business contacts is not required by law, but it may well help convince a skeptical IRS auditor that your trip to the Bahamas really was for business.

One tax client of mine who owned a retail coffee shop took an expensive trip to Scandinavia and wrote it off as a business deduction. When she was audited, which didn't surprise either of us, she was able to show the IRS auditor photos she took of coffee shops she visited throughout her travels. She showed the auditor Scandinavian coffee mugs she's now importing. She got through the audit successfully.

For more information on travel deductions (including Standard Meal Allowances) see IRS publication 463, "Travel, Entertainment, and Gift Expenses."

Inventory, and Something Very Important Called Cost-Of-Goods-Sold

"Inventory" refers to merchandise held for sale in the normal course of business. It is the sale of inventory that normally provides a business (unless it is a service business) with its main source of revenue. Inventory includes finished products, work in process, raw materials and any materials that will go into the making of a finished product. Inventory does *not* include your tools, equipment, office supplies or anything else purchased for reasons other than resale.

Not all of your inventory purchases can be deducted as current year expenses. Only the cost of those goods actually sold is deductible. This is a very important distinction, and you should understand it completely. The cost of inventory *un*sold at year-end is an asset owned by you and will not be a deductible expense until sold (or until it becomes worthless, which will be covered later in the chapter).

Let's first use a simple example of cost-of-goods-sold. My friends John and Karen Resykle buy antiques, junk and old clothes at garage and rummage sales and then resell the merchandise at a profit at flea markets. Last year, John and Karen purchased a total of $4,200 worth of merchandise (cost to them). At year-end, they still had $300

worth of merchandise on hand and unsold. John and Karen's deductible cost-of-goods-sold is $3,900 ($4,200 purchased, less $300 unsold). Note that the selling price of the inventory has no bearing on the calculation of cost-of-goods-sold.

The above example assumes that there was no inventory on hand at the beginning of the year. Let's now say there was $400 on hand (their cost) at January 1. John and Karen's cost-of-goods-sold is now $4,300:

Inventory on hand at January 1	$400
Add: Inventory purchased during the year	4,200
Total inventory available for sale	$4,600
Subtract: Inventory on hand at December 31	(300)
Cost-of-goods-sold	$4,300

If you are starting a new business and already have inventory on hand that you will be putting into the business, inventory you purchased before going into business, you can add the cost of that inventory (or the market value if less than cost) to the current year's purchases—even though you didn't buy it this year—and include it in your cost-of-goods-sold calculations. You can record this inventory in your expenditure ledger as "Inventory on hand at start of business" and post to Column One.

Taking Inventory

As you can see, at the end of the year you will need to make a list of inventory on hand. This is called "taking inventory" or "taking a physical inventory." (Business folk use the word "inventory" to refer both to the goods and to the procedure of counting the goods.) *Do not value the inventory at sale price.* The inventory should be valued at your cost.

If you are a manufacturer, computing the cost of your inventory will be a difficult task, for two reasons. First, you must calculate the cost not only of your raw materials but of your finished and partially finished goods as well. This will require a lot of educated guesswork—it always does. Remember, value your inventory at its dollars-and-cents cost to you. That cost includes materials, supplies and paid labor. It does not, however, include the value of your own labor (unless you are an employee of your own corporation).

The other complication in computing cost-of-goods-sold, for all manufacturers (and for retailers and wholesalers with gross receipts over $10 million a year), is a nasty law called "full absorption accounting" (also known as "uniform capitalization rules"). The cost of a manufacturer's inventory must include the cost of overhead attributable to the manufacturing operation. Such manufacturing overhead becomes part of the cost of the manufactured product and cannot be deducted as an expense until the product is sold. "Overhead" in this context is very broad and refers to almost everything related to inventory: repairs, maintenance, utilities, rent, indirect labor and production supervisory wages, indirect materials, tools and equipment, quality control costs, warehousing costs, general administrative costs, insurance, taxes, employees' fringe benefits, you name it.

I'll try a "simple" example: let's say that the space in your shop is divided, half for manufacturing and half for sales. Your expenses for the year included $1,200 for rent and utilities, and $5,000 for inventory. At the beginning of the year, there was no inventory. At year-end, there was $500 (cost) on hand. Your cost-of-goods-sold must be computed as follows:

Inventory on hand January 1		$0
Inventory purchased during year		5,000
One-half rent and utilities		
(manufacturing portion)		600
Cost of goods available for sale	$5,600	
Subtract: inventory on hand Dec. 31		(500)
$500 is ten percent of the inventory purchased during the year; therefore, you must assume that ten percent of the overhead is also still "on hand". So you must subtract ten percent of the manufacturing portion of rent and utilities		(60)
Cost-of-goods-sold		$5,040

This $560 inventory (goods and overhead) "on hand" at year-end will become the inventory on hand January 1 of next year. This example assumes no other overhead expenses related to the inventory, no paid salaries in the manufacturing, no inventory stored in the sales area. These costs would have to be included in computing cost-of-goods-sold.

There is an important distinction here between inventory that has not yet been used (the parts or raw materials), and finished or partly finished products. The untouched inventory has little or no manufacturing overhead associated with it, and it can be valued at its purchase cost without adding these overhead costs. Only finished and partly finished inventory must include a percent of the overhead.

In the above example, the entire $500 inventory on hand at year-end is finished goods. Had it instead been untouched parts or materials, the entire $600 in manufacturing overhead could have been deducted instead of only $540 (the $60 still "on hand" would no longer be "on hand"); the cost-of-goods-sold would increase from $5,040 to $5,100. If the $500 inventory was some of both— some manufactured goods, some untouched goods—well, as you probably already figured, the computations get all the more complicated (but you can relax—we are not going to go through them).

Very small and custom-order manufacturers can avoid the uniform capitalization rules by trying to have no finished or partly finished inventory on hand at December 31. If everything you manufactured is sold by year-end, the overhead is also "sold" and can be deducted 100%.

Inventory Loss of Value

In computing cost-of-goods-sold, inventory on hand at year-end is usually valued at its cost to you and not at its sales price which, in normal circumstances, is higher than its cost. If for any reason your year-end inventory is *worth less* than what you paid, the inventory should be valued at this lesser amount. "Worth" refers to its retail value—what you can sell it for. Clothes that are no longer in fashion, damaged or destroyed goods, goods unsalable for any reason—all such items should be reduced to their market (sales) value. If year-end inventory is totally worthless, it should be valued at zero. This inventory valuation method is known as "lower of cost or market."

You may have figured out by now that reducing the value of your inventory—"writing it off" as a loss—increases your expenses, thereby decreasing your profits and your taxes. Let's look again at our first example, John and Karen Resykle, the flea market entrepreneurs. Their purchases during the year were $4,200; cost of inventory on hand at year-end was $300. Originally, their cost-of-goods-sold was $3,900 ($4,200 less the $300 on hand).

Karen finds, however, that she made some bad purchases, and the inventory on hand at year-end for which she paid $300 cannot be sold for more than $200. Year-end inventory is therefore reduced to $200, that being the lower of cost or market. The cost-of-goods-sold, instead of being $3,900, is now $4,000 ($4,200 purchased, less $200). The additional $100 cost-of-goods-sold increases deductible expense by $100. Since John and Karen's income is unchanged, the additional expense reduces their profits by $100 and, therefore, reduces their taxes also.

When you value inventory below cost, the IRS requires you to prove your figures by offering the devalued inventory for sale within 30 days after the end of the year. *Excess inventory* (also called "overstock"—more goods on hand than you can sell) must be valued at original cost or replacement cost—not market value—whichever is lower.

Inventory Lost, Stolen or Given Away

The cost of stolen or missing inventory and the cost of samples given away are deductible as part of cost-of-goods-sold. This inventory is not on hand at year end, so it is not included in your year-end inventory count. Therefore, it automatically becomes part of your cost-of-goods-sold (even though it really wasn't sold—the term "cost-of-goods-sold" really should be "cost of goods sold, lost, stolen, given away, damaged, unsalable, etc.). No additional expense is allowed. By the way, "free samples" given to friends and relatives (not business related) or kept for your own personal use are not deductible, period. Their cost must be excluded from your inventory purchase expenses.

Cost-of-goods-sold is your most important and usually your largest item of expense. The federal income tax form has two main categories of expense: (1) cost-of-goods-sold, and (2) all other. You will be required to show on your tax return how you calculated your cost-of-goods-sold.

Inventory Valuation—LIFO & FIFO

Businesses may value inventory using the first-in, first-out method (FIFO), which is calculated as though the oldest inventory is sold first and the newest inventory is on the shelves; or the last-in, first-out method (LIFO), which is calculated as though the newly purchased inventory is sold before the older inventory. The actual inventory on hand doesn't have to actually correspond to the method you choose. You can sell your inventory first-in, first-out yet account for it using the LIFO method, and vice-versa.

The tax consequences of FIFO versus LIFO can be significant. Remember, inventory on hand and unsold is an asset owned by you and cannot be written off as an expense until sold. In times of inflation, the inventory purchased last week might be much more expensive than the same inventory purchased a year ago. If the old inventory sold first, and the new more expensive inventory is unsold—which is what the FIFO, first-in, first-out method assumes—your cost-of-goods-sold expense is the older, less expensive inventory. If, on the other hand, the newer inventory sold first, and the older, less expensive inventory is unsold—LIFO, last-in, first-out—the more expensive inventory gets written off as a cost-of-goods-sold expense. Under LIFO the result is a lower dollar value of inventory on hand (the older inventory), a higher dollar value of inventory sold (the newer inventory), a higher cost-of-goods-sold expense, and—this is where we're heading—lower taxes.

Despite LIFO tax savings, many businesses prefer the FIFO method because it is easier to figure the cost of year-end inventory. You simply look up the most recent bills from your suppliers. Hunting up old bills to figure LIFO can take more time than it's worth, particularly if you have a large or varied inventory. The IRS has lent a sympathetic ear to this problem. They have a standard formula you can use to convert FIFO figures to LIFO.

Still, many businesses use FIFO because the IRS's LIFO rules are a good deal more complex than the FIFO rules. Also, switching from one method to the other requires a special adjustment. Contact the IRS for more information.

Depreciation

Assets that will be useful to you over a period of years are treated differently than other business expenses. Some of these assets can be written off (deducted as a business expense) the year of purchase. Some, however, may have to be "depreciated". This is a tax term and means that the cost of an asset is spread out over several years; each year, a portion of the cost is deducted. The assets are variously called "fixed" or "capital" or "depreciable" assets. The same rules apply to both new and used assets.

A mechanic's tools and equipment, a contractor's machinery, a writer's typewriter are examples of depreciable assets. So are display cases, furniture and fixtures, and major improvements to your shop. Major repairs that increase the value or extend the life of an asset are considered depreciable assets. Your car or truck can be depreciated if you do not take the optional standard mileage allowance (see "Car and Truck Expenses").

All materials and supplies and all inventory, regardless of cost, are not capital assets and may not be depreciated. Stationery, business cards, small and inexpensive tools, anything that will be consumed in a year should be deducted as an expense the year it is purchased.

If your business is located in a building that you own, you can depreciate the portion of the building being used for business (including your own home if you meet the home office requirements). If you rent, your rent is a direct expense, and there is no need to compute building depreciation. A special note: the land apart from the improvements cannot be depreciated. Land is considered a permanent asset that cannot be expensed until sold.

Certain assets are specifically excluded from regular depreciation and write-off rules, and must be treated under a completely different set of rules not covered in this chapter (inquire of the IRS): motion picture films, video tapes, and sound recordings (originals, not mass-produced duplicates for sale or rent, which are in fact inventory and not depreciable assets); and patents, copyrights, and trademarks. Valuable antiques and art treasures may not be depreciated or written off until sold.

Warning: The Rules Change All The Time

Depreciation rules change almost every year, sometimes dramatically. And with every change, I swear, the rules get more lengthy and more complex. Generally, whatever rule was in effect when you purchased an asset (or when you first used it in business if you purchased it before going into business) is the rule you must use for that asset for as long as you own the asset. So if you've been in business and buying depreciable assets for several years, you'll be calculating depreciation using several different sets of rules!

The depreciation rules explained below are only for newly-acquired assets, under IRS laws in effect when this edition of *Small-Time Operator* was published. These are federal rules only. For state income taxes, some states use the same depreciation rules and some require entirely different depreciation calculations.

Writing Off Assets The Year Of Purchase

Don't panic yet. You may be able to avoid depreciation calculations entirely. At your option, up to $10,000 of depreciable assets can be written off to expense the year of purchase (or the year first used in business). If you choose this option which is called, in IRS jargon, "the Section 179 Deduction"—you simply deduct the cost of these assets on your tax return just as you would deduct any other current business expense. Use Form #4562.

There are restrictions and limitations:

1. Buildings cannot be written off under these rules. Buildings must be depreciated. Only depreciable assets other than real estate (the IRS calls it "Section 1245 Property") can be written off. Two exceptions to this rule: single-purpose livestock and horticultural structures *can* be written off under these rules.

2. The maximum write-off is reduced to $5,000 for married couples filing separate returns.

3. If you purchase more than $200,000 in depreciable assets in any one year, the $10,000 maximum is reduced, dollar for dollar, by the amount in excess of $200,000. So if you spend $202,000 on depreciable assets this year, the maximum you can write off is $8,000. If you spend $210,000 or more, you are allowed no write-off.

4. The write-off cannot exceed the total taxable income from the business for the year. Any write-off disallowed because of this income limitation can be carried forward to the next year—and future years if necessary, if the next year's income is again less than the remaining balance—until fully written off.

5. If you sell assets you've previously written off, or if you convert them to non-business use, you may have to "recapture" the amount you wrote off (add it back into income) the year of sale or conversion, depending on how many years you own the asset. The same recapture rules that apply to depreciation also apply here (explained below).

6. Reduced dollar limits may apply to vehicles, cellular phones and computers if used only partly for business. Consult the IRS.

Depreciable assets in excess of the above maximums must be depreciated.

Why would anyone choose complex, multi-year

depreciation over this simple, write-it-off-now deduction? In the early days of a business, expenses are often high and income low. Many businesses lose money the first year or two or three. You may owe little or no income tax and therefore have no real use for the additional tax savings the write-off offers. It might be better for you to depreciate those assets, deducting the bulk of the expense in future years when you could use it to reduce taxes.

You can write off some assets and depreciate others. It is not an all-one-way or all-the-other law.

How Much Can Be Depreciated Or Written Off?

You are allowed to depreciate the cost of your depreciable asset. "Cost" is defined as the actual purchase price and includes sales tax, freight charges and any installation charges. If you bought your equipment very inexpensively, your cost is what you paid, not what the equipment is "worth". When equipment is purchased in installments (on time) the cost is the total purchase price as if you had paid cash for it. Any finance or interest charges—a bank loan, or credit terms from the supplier—can usually be written off as a regular business expense the year paid, completely separate from the cost of the asset itself. One exception to this rule: for buildings or equipment that you construct yourself or have custom made for you, if they take more than two years to build or if they are depreciated over 20 years or more, the finance or interest charges must be added to the cost of the asset and treated as part of the asset.

Depreciable assets used in your business that were purchased before going into business can be depreciated (or written off) regardless of when acquired. Such assets must be valued at their cost or at their market value at the time the assets are first used in your business, whichever is less. If your old box of hand tools, which cost you $200 eight years ago, was only worth $50 (market value) when you first used those tools in your business, you may only depreciate $50.

Depreciable assets used partly for business and partly for pleasure can be depreciated (or written off) to the extent used for business. For example, if you use your tools 50% for business and 50% for personal use, you can depreciate (or write off) 50% of the cost.

Write Off Period

There are several categories of assets, each with a different write off period (also called a "recovery period")—how many years the assets are to be depreciated. The categories most used by small businesses and farmers are:

3-Year Property: on-road tractor units, hogs, race horses over two years old, all horses over 12 years old.

5-Year Property: cars, light general-purpose trucks, most equipment used for research and experimentation, computers and peripheral equipment, typewriters, calculators, and similar office equipment, semi-conductor manufacturing equipment, solar, wind and some other alternative-energy property, heavy trucks, trailers, aircraft, buses, some electronic equipment, cattle, sheep, goats.

7-Year Property: most machinery, equipment, furniture, fixtures, display cases, signs, etc., railroad track, horses other than those listed as 3-year Property.

10-Year Property: most boats, barges, tugs, single-purpose agricultural and horticultural structures, fruit and nut trees and vines.

20-Year Property: general purpose farm buildings.

27½ Year-Property: residential rental real estate, including built-in elevators and escalators.

31½ Year-Property: all real estate (including built-in elevators and escalators) other than residential rental property and farm buildings.

Methods of Computing Depreciation

There are four methods of depreciation. For most assets other than buildings and farm equipment, you can choose from any of the four methods. All four methods result in the same tax write-off eventually, but each method involves different amounts that can be written off in any given year:

1. *Modified ACRS.* ACRS stands for Accelerated Cost Recovery System. "Cost recovery" is the government's term for depreciation. "Accelerated" means that this method of depreciation allows faster write-offs than other methods—larger write-offs in the first few years, smaller write-offs in later years. "Modified" refers to the fact that it is different than an older, out-of-date ACRS method. Most business assets other than buildings

and farm equipment can, at your option, be depreciated under this method (see below for the exceptions). For people who know standard depreciation formulas, this method is based on 200% declining balance with a switch to straight-line when that maximizes the deduction. For people who don't know what the last sentence said, the Depreciation Table will help you compute Modified ACRS depreciation quickly and easily.

2. *150% ACRS*. This method is similar to Modified ACRS above, but with somewhat smaller depreciation in the earlier years. At your option, equipment eligible for Modified ACRS above can be depreciated using this method. This method is required for farm equipment.

3. *Straight-Line*. The straight-line method distributes the depreciation equally over the write-off period. Each year, the same amount is depreciated (except the first year, when only part of a year's depreciation is allowed; more on this later). Straight-line spreads depreciation over the same number of years as the above ACRS methods but with a smaller write-off in the earlier years. Buildings (and built-in elevators and escalators) and fruit and nut trees and vines must use this straight-line method. At your option, you may use straight-line instead of Modified ACRS for other assets as well (except for assets that must be depreciated under #4 below).

4. *Alternative ACRS*. This is really regular straight-line depreciation but over a longer write-off period than that used in the two above methods. Alternative ACRS must be used for luxury cars (unless you take the Standard Mileage Allowance, in which case you take no depreciation at all); assets financed with tax-exempt bonds; assets used predominantly outside the United States; assets imported from certain trade-restricted countries; the following assets if used 50% or less for business: vehicles (again, unless you take the Standard Mileage Allowance), airplanes, computers, cellular phones, and entertainment or recreational property. At your option, this Alternative ACRS method can be used for any of your other depreciable assets.

Under Alternative ACRS, there is a large variety of write-off periods. Generally, cars, light trucks and computers are written off over five years; furniture, fixtures, display cases, office equipment, signs, retail and wholesale equipment, agricultural equipment, and recreation and amusement equipment are written off over ten years; manufacturing equipment varies depending on the type of manufacturing, ranging from five to fifteen years (ask the IRS); buildings are written off over 40 years.

Which of the four methods should you choose? If you want faster write-offs, higher deductions right away, Method #1 Modified ACRS is the best choice. If you already have reduced your taxes down to nothing and don't need any more deductions, Methods #2, #3 or #4 will bring larger deductions in future years.

First Year Depreciation

Under all of the above depreciation methods, you are not allowed a full year's depreciation the first year. For assets other than buildings, you are allowed only a half year's depreciation. If you compute your own depreciation, just divide the first year's depreciation in half. At the end of the write-off period, you add the remaining half year's depreciation. So, in effect, this "half-year convention" adds an extra year to the write-off period. A seven year asset, for example, will be depreciated over an 8 year period—½ year the first year, a full year the second through seventh years, ½ year the eighth year. If you use the Depreciation Table, the half year is already figured into it.

There is an important exception to the half-year rule. If more than 40% of your depreciable assets (other than real estate) are purchased in the last three months of the year, you do not use the half-year calculation. You must instead group the assets according to which quarter of the year they were purchased (assets purchased January through March, April through June, July through September, October through December). You then make four separate depreciation computations. Those assets purchased in the first three months of the year are depreciated as though they were all purchased half way through the first quarter. That is, they get 10½ months depreciation, which figures to 87.5% of the full first-year depreciation. Those assets purchased in the second quarter of the year (April through June) likewise are depreciated as though they were all purchased half way through the second quarter. They get 7½ months depreciation, or 62.5% of the full first-year depreciation. Assets purchased July through September get 4½ months depreciation, or 37.5%. Assets purchased October through December get 1½ months

DEPRECIATION TABLE

Year	3 Yr. Assets			5 Yr. Assets			7 Yr. Assets		
	Meth. 1 Mod. ACRS	Meth. 2 150% ACRS	Meth. 3 St. Line	Meth. 1 Mod. ACRS	Meth. 2 150% ACRS	Meth. 3 St. Line	Meth. 1 Mod. ACRS	Meth. 2 150% ACRS	Meth. 3 St. Line
1	33%	25%	17%	20%	15%	10%	14%	11%	7%
2	45	38	33	32	26	20	25	19	15
3	15	25	33	19	18	20	17	15	15
4	7	12	17	12	17	20	13	13	14
5				11	16	20	9	12	14
6				6	8	10	9	12	14
7							9	12	14
8							4	6	7

depreciation, or 12.5%. This wonderful set of calculations is called "the mid-quarter convention". You can't use a simple table to compute this depreciation. You'll have to calculate depreciation yourself, quarter by quarter the first year. And every subsequent year, the assets from each quarter will have different annual calculations as well. You can be sure that the congressman who dreamed this up doesn't own a small business or prepare his own tax returns. (Go back and read "Writing Off Assets The Year Of Purchase").

First year depreciation on buildings is calculated building by building using what's called a "mid-month convention". Whatever month a building is acquired for business (or first used for business, such as a new office in your home), you are allowed ½ month's depreciation that month and then full depreciation for the remaining months of the year. So if you purchased a building in April, you are allowed 8½ months depreciation the first year, or 70.8% of the full year's depreciation. Then at the end of the depreciation period, you get an additional 3½ month's depreciation.

Note that the "year" in all the above methods refers to the calendar year, not to the first twelve months you own an asset.

Depreciation Table

This table will help you compute depreciation using Modified ACRS, 150% ACRS, or Straight-Line. You can also use it to compare the three methods, giving you some idea how different the systems are. The fourth method, Alternative ACRS, can't be included in a simple table because there are too many asset categories. "Year" refers the calendar year, not to the first twelve months you own the asset. Percentage is the percentage of cost you can write off that year.

WARNING: This table is only for assets qualifying for the half-year convention (see "First Year Depreciation"). Do not use for assets requiring "mid-quarter" calculations.

Part Business, Part Personal

Depreciation may be computed only for the business portion of a depreciable asset. If your tools are used half for work and half for pleasure, you may compute depreciation only on half the cost. Likewise, if you opt to write off an asset the first year rather than take depreciation, you can write off only the portion applicable to business.

Special limitations apply to certain assets used 50% or less for business, as previously mentioned under the Alternative ACRS method above. Small businesses should be particularly aware of vehicle and computer use, try to keep it above 50% for business (or for vehicles, use the Standard Mileage Allowance and forget these rules). Keep detailed records—dates and hours for the computer, dates and mileage for the car—to verify business use.

Limitations on Automobiles

Regardless of the percent used for business or

the depreciation method used, automobile depreciation is limited to a maximum of $2,660 the first year, $4,300 the second year, $2,550 the third year, and $1,575 each succeeding year. (Dollar limits change from year to year; verify amounts with the IRS.) Due to this limitation, expensive cars cannot be fully depreciated in the five years normally allowed. The depreciation will have to be spread out over a longer period. The above maximum amounts can change from year to year; check with the IRS for current figures.

Selling An Asset

When you sell an asset that has been written off, or fully or partly depreciated, there may be a taxable profit on the sale. These are known as "recapture rules"and are somewhat complex and depend on how many years you've had the asset, how much depreciation or write-off you've taken, and what method of depreciation you've used. The basic concept: The cost of the asset is reduced by the total amount of depreciation or write-off taken, to come up with what's called the "adjusted cost" (also called the "cost basis"). If the selling price is higher than the adjusted cost, you have a taxable profit. If the selling price is lower, you have a tax-deductible loss.

For example, let's say you bought a piece of equipment a few years ago for $4,000, and you already deducted $3,000 of depreciation. Your adjusted cost is $1,000 ($4,000 original cost less $3,000 depreciation). Let's say you sell the asset for $2,500. You will have a $1,500 taxable profit:

Original cost	$4,000
Accumulated depreciation	(3,000)
Adjusted cost	$1,000
Sale price	(2,500)
Profit	$1500

Now, let's change the example and say you sold the same asset for $600. You will have a $400 deductible loss:

Original cost	$4,000
Accumulated depreciation	(3,000)
Adjusted cost	$1,000
Sale price	(600)
Loss	$400

Sale of a depreciable asset should be recorded on your income ledger the month of sale, but below the regular sales figures for the month. Although the sale may be subject to tax, it is not a regular business sale and should be shown separately. You should also note the sale on your equipment ledger.

Discarding or Junking an Asset

It's the ninth time you've tried to fix the dang thing, it's breathed its last...

If an asset is fully depreciated or fully written off when it becomes worthless/useless/unsalable junk, that's as far as the taxes and bookkeeping go—there is no profit and there is no loss. But if the asset is only partly depreciated, you can write off the balance of the cost (the undepreciated part of the cost) in full the year the asset becomes worthless.

For example, a piece of equipment cost you $3,000 a year ago, and so far you've deducted only $800 in depreciation. The thing burns up. This year you can write off $2,200, the undepreciated balance ($3,000 cost less $800 depreciation). This example assumes, besides no selling price, no insurance. If the asset is insured, any insurance payment is treated the same as income from the sale of an asset, explained above under "Selling an Asset".

When you junk an asset, no entry should be made to your income ledger, but you should note it on your equipment ledger.

IRS Reporting

IRS Form #4562, "Depreciation & Amortization" can be used to figure depreciation. You must use the form if your business is a regular corporation (not an S corporation); or if you are depreciating (or writing off) newly acquired assets; or if you are depreciating a vehicle, airplane, computer, cellular phone, or recreation/entertainment equipment. Otherwise, the form is optional.

I hold in my hand 1,379 pages of tax simplification.
—U.S. Congressman D. Latta

When it comes to law, why, I have nothing to say. For laws were never meant to be understood, and it is foolish to make the attempt.
—the Tin Woodsman of Oz

1	2	3	4	5	6	7	8	9	10	11	12	13	14	15	16	17	18
DATE	DESCRIPTION	METH.	WRITE OFF PERIOD	NEW OR USED	%	COST	REDUCTION FOR INV. CREDIT	WRITE OFF	BAL. TO BE DEPR.	DEPR. 19___	BAL. TO BE DEPR.	DEPR. 19___	BAL. TO BE DEPR.	DEPR. 19___	BAL. TO BE DEPR.	DEPR. 19___	BAL. TO BE DEPR.

EQUIPMENT LEDGER AND DEPRECIATION WORKSHEETS

The Depreciation Worksheet

The combination Equipment Ledger and Depreciation Worksheet in the Ledger section will help you keep track of your equipment and other depreciable assets and the depreciation on them. If you use Form #4562 (see above), this worksheet will help you prepare that form. Some people simply photocopy the worksheet and attach it to the IRS form.

Use a separate line on the worksheet for each depreciable asset. Fill out all the columns when you purchase an asset and you will never have to hunt up the information a second time. Even if you hire an accountant to prepare your taxes, you will save the accountant time—and save yourself money—if you fill out Columns 1, 2, 5, 6 and 7 (the basic information) so that it will be readily available.

Enter the information as follows:

Column 1, Date. Date purchased or date first used in business.

Column 2, Description. Be specific enough to distinguish this particular asset from all others. If the asset is your one and only welding torch, the description "welding torch" is sufficient. If, however, you have four welding torches, "welding torch, serial no. 34-15" or some other specific designation is needed.

Column 3, Method. The depreciation method you've selected from those currently available (see the discussion in this chapter), or an older depreciation method for older assets you've been depreciating under previous years' rules.

Column 4, Write Off Period. How many years the asset is being depreciated. Discussed above, under "Write-Off Period."

Column 5, New or Used.

Column 6, Percent Used for Business. One hundred percent if the asset is used solely for business; a smaller percent if partly personal.

Column 7, Cost. See the discussion of cost in this chapter.

Column 8, Reduction for Investment Credit. This column is only for people already depreciating assets acquired before 1986. For newly acquired assets, this column should be zero.

Column 9, Write-Off. If you take the option of writing off rather than depreciating some of your assets (see the discussion in this chapter), fill out the amount in this column. This column is not for depreciation.

Column 10, Balance to be Depreciated. Column 6 x Column 7 - Column 8 - Column 9 = Column 10. This column is actually the cost adjusted for the percentage used for business, investment credit and first-year write-off. The amount you arrive at here is commonly called the "cost basis." This is the amount that is actually depreciated.

The four sets of paired columns, 11 and 12, 13 and 14, 15 and 16, and 17 and 18, provide four years of depreciation scheduling for each asset. The first column in a pair is the depreciation for the year, and the following column is the remaining undepreciated balance. Column 10 less Column 11 equals Column 12, and so on.

A Last Word on Depreciation

If you are totally dismayed by this chapter, you are not alone. Depreciation is vastly complex, a real struggle to compute correctly. Few business owners are willing and able to make these calculations, and they usually turn to tax accountants for help. Many accountants now own computer programs that can automatically compute depreciation under all of the different methods, select the correct method for you, compare methods to find the biggest tax savings.

Depreciation shouldn't have to be so complicated. In fact, until a few years ago when a massive new tax law took effect, depreciation was a fairly simple, easy-to-understand calculation. But some people in Congress, ignorant of how tax laws translate into actual calculations on paper, tried to rectify some perceived inequities in the old law; and this is the monster they produced. The irony is that the final outcome, the bottom line deduction for depreciation (for small businesses anyway), is little different than the old, simpler system. I suspect that if enough Congressmen and Congresswomen heard from enough angry business owners, we might see a simpler law again.

Office in the Home

The term "office" refers to any home business space—shop, storefront, warehouse, office, etc.— and expenses directly related to the space such as utilities, insurance, property taxes, etc.

You will not be able to deduct any expenses for a home office unless it is used on a regular basis as your principal place of business or a place of business that is used by your patients, clients or customers in the normal course of business.

"Principal place of business" is usually defined as where you actually generate your income, where you do your income-producing work. The tax courts have also allowed a home office deduction when the home was the only actual office or "place of business" even though income was actually earned away from home—as was the case of a self-employed surgeon who earned all his income in operating rooms but had his only office at home. He was allowed a home office deduction. If this situation applies to you, I suggest you discuss it with a knowledgeable tax accountant.

If your business is also operated out of another location such as a storefront, you cannot deduct the cost of a home office unless your customers normally come to your home.

Joe Campbell, who owns Resistance Repair, does his repair work in a rented repair shop but does all his bookkeeping at home because there is no extra space in the shop and because the bookkeeping requires quiet, uninterrupted thinking time which is impossible at the shop. All legitimate, for sure, but his home office is not deductible. Another friend of mine who is an attorney has her office in downtown San Francisco but also sees her clients on a regular basis in her home. Her home office is deductible.

If you work a day job and run your home business in the evenings or if you have a regular business away from home and a second business in the home, you are allowed the home office deduction for the home business as long as it meets the other requirements.

To be eligible for the home office deduction, a specific part of your home must be used exclusively for business. It can be a separate room or even part of a room as long as it is used for the home business and nothing else.

There are two exceptions to the exclusive rule. If your home is your sole fixed location for a retail sales business and if you regularly store your merchandise in your home, the expense of maintaining the storage area is deductible. If you operate a licensed child care business at your home, you also do not have to meet the exclusive test.

As already discussed in the Bookkeeping section under "Rent" and "Utilities" and in this Tax section under "Depreciation", expenses related to office in the home include a percentage of your rent if you rent your home or a percentage of the depreciation if you own your home, and an equal percentage of home utilities, property taxes, mortgage interest and insurance.

If your home business shows a loss, part of your home office expenses are not deductible this year. A home business may deduct any regular business expenses (other than expenses attributable to the office itself) and may deduct interest and property taxes on the home office, regardless of profit or loss. But the remaining home office expenses— rent or depreciation, insurance, utilities—may be deducted this year only to the extent there is no loss.

For example, assume your home business generated $20,000 in sales this year. Your expenses, not including the home office, were $18,000. The home office portion of rent (or depreciation), insurance and utilities came to $4,000. Home office portion of interest and property taxes was $800. Your allowable deductions are computed this way:

Total sales	$20,000
Expenses (other than office expenses)	(18,000)
	$ 2,000
Home office portion of interest and property taxes	(800)
	$ 1,200

This means that only $1,200 of the additional $4,000 in office expenses are deductible this year. The remaining $2,800 can be carried to a future year and deducted then, again as long as there is no business loss.

A second example: Let's say sales were $20,000, non-office expenses were $18,000, home office portion of property taxes and interest came to $3,000, all other home office expenses were $4,000. Now the calculations look this way:

Total sales	$20,000
Expenses (other than office expenses)	(18,000)
	$ 2,000
Home office portion of interest and property taxes	(3,000)
LOSS	$(1,000)

Since you are already showing a loss, none of the additional $4,000 in home office expenses are deductible this year. The entire $4,000 must be carried to a future year. Note that the interest and property taxes are deductible even though they result in a loss.

If you own your own home and are depreciating a part of it as a business office, you will run into tax complications when you sell the house. In computing the profit on the sale, you are required to reduce your cost basis by the amount of the depreciation, which has the effect of increasing your profit and taxes on the sale.

To claim a home office expense, you must fill out a lengthy form that attaches to your Schedule C, Form 8829, "Expenses for Business Use of Your Home." For more information, ask the IRS for a free copy of Publication #587, "Business Use of Your Home."

If you are not eligible for the home office deduction, you still may deduct all other allowable expenses associated with your home business. Remember, however, that part of your home telephone may not be deductible. The basic charge for the first telephone line into the house is not deductible. You may deduct business-related long distance charges, extra services, special equipment, and the full cost of any additional business lines into the house. The Appendix includes a lengthy chapter covering home businesses.

Non-Deductible Expenses

Certain expenses are specifically disallowed by law and cannot be deducted on your income tax return, no way, no how:

1. Expenses not related to your business, and business expenses not meeting the "ordinary and necessary" or the "reasonable" test.

2. Federal income tax, any tax penalties, or interest on back taxes. State income tax is deductible on your federal return but not on your state return.

3. Any fines for violation of the law. Even though you were parked on business, you cannot deduct that parking ticket.

4. Payments to yourself. The profit from your business is not an expense of running your business; and when you pay yourself, it is not deductible. The only way you may pay yourself a wage and deduct it as an expense is to incorporate (see the chapter on corporations.)

5. Loan repayments. The loan was not income when received and is not expense when paid. Any interest on the loan, however, is often deductible, but there are exceptions. See the Interest chapter.

6. Clothing, unless used exclusively for work and unsuitable for street wear.

7. Regular meals at work—but see the Meals chapter for exceptions.

8. Regular commuting expenses between your home and usual place of business.

9. Cost of land, until you sell it. Only the structure on the land may be depreciated.

10. Certain start-up expenses as explained in the Start-Up chapter.

Self-Employment Tax (SECA)

Self-employment tax, also known as SECA (Self Employment Contributions Act), is social security-Medicare tax for self-employed individuals. Independent business people pay the highest social security and Medicare rates of all, and they go up every year. Self-employment tax is based on your net profit, the taxable net income of your business.

Sole proprietors (including independent outside contractors and freelancers) and partners in partnerships are subject to self-employment tax. The tax is not imposed on corporate stockholders; if you own a small corporation, you are an employee of your business and pay regular social security and

---

Owner of a small factory in New Orleans offered a $25 bonus to employees for money-saving ideas. First winner paid was the man who suggested the bonus be cut to $10.

—reported in the San Francisco Chronicle

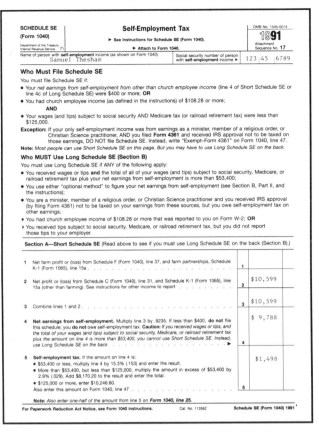

Medicare instead of self-employment tax. (Any director's fees not included as part of a regular salary—no social security or Medicare withholding—are subject to self-employment tax.) Rental income, earned interest, and other non-business income are not subject to self-employment tax.

Self-employment tax is apart from and in addition to federal income tax. You may owe no income tax but still be liable for self-employment tax. Retirement deductions, deductions for health insurance, and the regular personal deductions and exemptions, which reduce income tax, cannot be used to reduce self-employment tax. Very often this tax comes as quite a shock to new and very small businesses. People, particularly in part-time and sideline businesses, are not making enough profit to worry about income taxes, but they never realize they may have a substantial self-employment tax bill.

Special note, if you business profits are $400 or less: You do not have to pay any self-employment tax and can skip this entire chapter (if you net $401, you pay self-employment tax on the entire $401, not just the one dollar over the $400 minimum). If you made $400 or less but want to pay self-employment tax—to increase your social security account—the IRS provides an optional method whereby you can pay into social security and Medicare. It is explained on the SE tax form.

Figuring The Tax

For 1992, the self-employment tax rate is 15.3% (combining 12.4% social security tax and 2.9% Medicare tax) on profits up to $55,500. Above $55,500, the tax rate is 2.9% on profits from $55,501 to $130,200. Your actual tax, however, will be lower than these figures indicate because of two deductions.

The first deduction reduces the self-employment tax itself. You figure the tax not on your full profit, but on a reduced amount. You reduce your profit by 7.65% (which is half the self-employment tax rate) and figure the tax on the reduced profit. You accomplish this by multiplying your profit by .9235.

For example, if your taxable profit was $30,000, multiply the $30,000 by .9235, which comes to $27,705. The self-employment tax will be 15.3% of $27,705, which comes to $4,239 (pennies rounded). Warning: if your business made more than $55,500, the formula is different; see below.

The second deduction is an income tax deduction, taken on your 1040 tax form. Whatever your self-employment tax figures to be, you reduce your business profit by half the self-employment tax before figuring your income tax.

Using the same example—a business with a $30,000 profit—the self-employment tax is $4,239 (see above if you don't remember how we got the $4,239). Half the $4,239 if $2,120 (rounded). So you reduce your $30,000 profit by $2,120, to get $27,880, and figure your income taxes on the $27,880.

It is important to understand that the two deductions are completely separate calculations, using different figures. In the example—a business with a $30,000 profit—self-employment tax is figured on $27,705 (the first deduction), and income tax is figured on $27,880 (the second deduction).

Self-employment tax is computed on your regular federal income tax return, using Form #1040-SE.

The best thing Congress can do is go home for a couple of years.

—Will Rogers

Special note, only for businesses with profits in excess of $55,500: You compute your self-employment tax and the two deductions differently, because your profit is taxed at two different rates: 15.3% on the first $55,500, and 2.9% on $55,501 up to $130,200. You follow the same basic procedures, but using two different tax rates.

Husband and Wife Businesses

If a husband and wife operate a business together, who pays self-employment tax depends on how the business is set up. If the business is a partnership, formally set up as such and filing partnership tax returns, both spouses pay self-employment tax. If the business is a sole proprietorship, only one spouse pays self-employment tax—the one who is the primary operator of the business. This is covered in more detail in a chapter in the Appendix, "Husband and Wife Partnerships."

Outside Employment (If You Also Hold a Job)

Self-employed people who are also holding down jobs where social security and Medicare is withheld from their pay should combine the two incomes to arrive at the self-employment tax maximum. You will be in one of these situations (only one of the following three situations will apply to you):

1. If the combined incomes, outside job and business profit, are **under $55,500,** nothing changes. You figure self-employment tax (and the two deductions) exactly as described above—but only, of course, on your business profit. Your outside wages are subject to social security and Medicare taxes; you do not pay self-employment tax on them.

2. If by chance your outside job paid **more than $130,200,** well, congratulations to you. You will owe no self-employment tax on your business profits no matter how much the business makes. You can skip the rest of this chapter.

3. If the combined incomes, outside job and business profit, are **over $55,500,** you pay a reduced self-employment tax. How you figure the tax depends on several factors:

(a) If your outside job pays **more than $55,500** but combined earnings are under $130,200, all of your business profits are subject to the lower 2.9%, less the two deductions.

(b) If your outside job pays **more than $55,000** and combined earnings are over $130,200 (after reducing your self-employment income by the first deduction), make this calculation: Subtract the outside job's salary from $130,000. Multiply the answer by 2.9%. This is your self-employment tax (but don't forget the second deduction).

If your outside job pays **less than $55,500** (but combined earnings, job and business, are over $55,500), you first subtract the outside job wages from $55,500. The result is how much of your business profit is subject to the higher 15.3% self-employment tax. For example, let's say you have a job paying you a $25,000 annual wage. $55,500 minus the $25,000 comes to $30,500. So the first $30,500 of business profit is subject to the 15.3% tax (less the deductions). Any business profit above $30,500 is subject to the lower 2.9% tax (again, less the deductions), but only until combined wage and profit hit $130,200, after which there is no self-employment tax.

Although the calculations under situation #3 sound confusing, you will find them much easier to do than to explain.

Please keep in mind that all the above limits and percentages—the $55,000, the $130,200, the 15.3%, and the 2.9%—change from year to year. Find out from the IRS if these figures (and procedures) have changed before relying on them.

Special note: Remember that if your business profit is $400 or less, you owe no self-employment tax regardless of the maximum combined incomes.

For more information, request a free copy of IRS Publication #553, "Information on Self-Employment Tax."

Retirement Deductions

You may invest a portion of your business profit in a special retirement plan and pay no income taxes on the money invested or the interest earned until you retire and withdraw the funds.

There are three different tax-deferred retirement plans available to business owners: The "Self Employed Retirement Plan," commonly called a "Keogh" or "H.R. 10" plan (named for the congressman who sponsored it and his bill number); the "SEP," or "Simplified Employee Pension Plan"; the "Individual Retirement Account" or "IRA." Each plan has different options, different maximum contributions, different deadlines for making contributions, and—most important to employers—

	IRA	SEP (regular plan)	KEOGH (profit sharing)	KEOGH (money purchase)
Maximum contribution	$2,000	13.04% or $30,000	13.04% or $30,000	20% or $30,000
Minimum contribution	none—discretionary	none—discretionary	none—discretionary	fixed–same % each year
Deadline	set up and contribute by tax return filing date (no extensions)	set up and contribute by tax return filing date (including any extensions)	set up by last day of year, contribute by tax return filing date (including any extensions)	set up by last day of year, contribute by tax return filing date (including any extensions)
Employees that must be included	none	all over 21 and service in 3 of last 5 years.	over 21 & 2 years service and 1,000 or more hours a year	over 21 & 2 years service and 1,000 or more hours a year
Paperwork	minimal	minimal	forms and special tax returns	forms and special tax returns

different requirements for including your employees in the plans.

IRA

The simplest plan is the IRA. Any business owner or wage earner can set up an IRA. The maximum annual contribution is only $2,000 or your taxable earnings, whichever is less. If you or your spouse has an outside job that includes a retirement plan, the allowable IRA deduction may be reduced. With an IRA, you have no obligation to cover any of your employees. You can set up or contribute to an IRA anytime up to the date your tax return is due (April 15 of the next year for calendar year taxpayers).

SEP

A SEP is also easy to set up. You can invest up to 13.04% of your earnings every year, up to a maximum investment of $30,000 a year. The law actually says that the maximum is 15%, but the convoluted way of computing the contribution works out to 13.04%. You can set up or contribute to a SEP right up to the due date of your tax return (April 15 of the next year, or later if you file an extension), applying the deduction to the previous year's income. With a SEP, however, you must include all employees over 21 years old who have worked for you for three of the last five years, including part-time and occasional employees.

Who actually pays for the employees SEP plan depends on how your SEP is set up. Under the regular SEP plan, the employer pays the full cost of the plan. Whatever you, the employer, contribute for yourself, you must contribute an equal percentage for each eligible employee. However, under a different SEP plan called the Salary Reduction Arrangement, employees can choose to take a cut in pay and have the employer put that money instead in an SEP plan. Such an arrangement obviously costs the employer nothing (other than the extra paperwork). Only businesses with 25 or fewer employees are eligible for the Salary Reduction Arrangement. This Salary Reduction SEP has other requirements and dollar limits different from the regular SEP; your bank should have full details. Any money an employer invests in an SEP on behalf of employees is a tax-deductible business expense.

Keogh

The Keogh plans (there are several versions) are much more complicated, more paperwork, more government forms to file—so much so that many bankers will actually try to talk you out of setting up a Keogh; they hate the paperwork. But the Keogh plans offer larger contributions and different requirements for including employees. For some businesses, a Keogh plan will be more than worth the extra trouble.

Under the most common Keogh arrangement, the "defined contribution plan," you can choose what's called a "profit sharing plan" or a "money purchase plan." The profit sharing plan allows a maximum annual contribution of 13.04% of earnings, up to a maximum annual investment of $30,000, the same as the SEP. The money purchase plan allows a maximum contribution of 20% of earnings, up to $30,000 (the law says 25%, but the calculation works out to 20%). The money purchase plan, however, requires that you make the same percentage contribution every year; whatever percentage you decide on when you open the plan, you're stuck with it. Under the profit sharing plan (and also under IRA's and SEP's) you can change the contribution, or make no contribution at all, each year. Under both Keogh plans, you must set up the plan by December 31 (or end of fiscal year for fiscal year taxpayers) but you have until the due date of your tax return, including extensions, to make your contribution.

Keogh plans have a different set of requirements for including your employees. You must include and pay for employees over 21 years old who have worked for you two or more years, but only if they work 1,000 or more hours per year. So any employee who works less than half-time doesn't have to be covered under a Keogh plan. Under a SEP, you'll recall, *all* employees who've worked for you three or more years must be covered. This is a major factor for many small businesses with only part-time help. As with the SEP, any Keogh contributions made for employees are tax deductible business expenses.

There is yet another type of Keogh plan, called a "defined benefit plan." You decide what pension you want to receive after you retire; the contributions are then based on the pension amount. Defined benefit plans usually allow larger contributions and bigger taxs deductions than defined contribuiton plans. But most business owners shy away from the defined benefit plan because it is much more complicated and expensive to set up than a defined contribution plan. Many banks, in fact, don't even offer it. There is no easy formula or percentage to figure how much to contribute each year. People who are close to retirement age and just setting up a new retirement plan may find a defined benefit plan very attractive, however, because it allows them to make much larger contributions than the other plans. In effect, it allows them to catch up for lost time.

Rules & Restrictions: All Three Plans

Under all the above retirement plans—IRA, SEP and Keogh—the income figure you use to calculate retirement contributions is not the full profit from your business. You must reduce the profit by the special income tax deduction of one-half your self-employment tax (this is the "second deduction" as explained in the "Self-Employment Tax" chapter). You also have to include your non-business income and losses in determining total income for IRAs, SEPs and Keoghs.

Self-employment tax: Retirement contributions for yourself are not deductible for computing self-employment tax. You base your self-employment tax on your business profit before the retirement contributions. If, however, you are making retirement contributions for employees as well as yourself, the contributions made on behalf of the employees are deductible business expenses, and they reduce your profit and all your taxes including self-employment tax.

Withdraws: Under all the above retirement plans, you cannot withdraw your money without penalty until age 59½.

State taxes: Not all states allow the retirement deduction in calculating state income tax. You may still owe state income tax on the full amount of your profit.

Corporations: IRAs are for individuals, sole proprietors and partners in partnerships. SEPs and Keoghs are available to all businesses, including corporations, but the maximum deductions, limitations, etc. for corporations may be different than those described above. There are also special corporate retirement plans you can set up, quite different than those described here.

A final word for employers: If you want to set up a retirement plan just for yourself, without having to pay for your employees' retirement, many insurance companies offer "non-qualifying plans" of all types. But under those "non-qualifying plans" (so called because they do not qualify for an income tax deduction) you must pay regular income taxes on your entire business profit. You are not allowed any tax deduction.

More Information

Most banks offer IRA's, SEP's and Keogh plans. Each plan will be different, and the earned interest will vary with the bank and the amount invested. Shop around.

The IRS publishes two free booklets, Publication #590, "Individual Retirement Accounts" (which also covers SEP's), and #560, "Self Employed Regirement Plans" (Keoghs).

Estimated Tax Payments

If your federal tax for the current year, income and self-employment combined, is estimated to be $500 or more, you are required to pay your tax in quarterly installments. The government wants your tax money just like the taxes withheld from employees' paychecks. The four quarterly installments are due April 15, June 15, September 15, and the following January 15. You do not have to pay the fourth estimate if you file your tax return by January 31 and pay the balance due.

How do you estimate your taxes? You can base your estimate on your prior year's taxes, even if you were not in business then. Whatever your total tax came to last year, divide it by four and send the IRS four equal installments. If your total tax last year (including self-employment) was less than $500, you are not required to make any estimated tax payments.

Special note to people already in business and who were required to file estimated taxes in any of the last three years: You cannot use the above method to estimate taxes if your adjusted gross income (bottom of page one on the 1040 form), excluding any profit from a sale of your home, increased by $40,000 or more from the previous year *and* totals at least $75,000. You must use the method explained in the next paragraph.

You also have the option to estimate your taxes based on your current year's income. Four times a year, you figure your taxable income for that quarter and send in the correct tax. As you can imagine, this is not an easy task. Under this method you may be hit with an interest penalty if you underestimate by more than 10 percent.

When you compute your actual tax at year-end, any overpayment of estimated taxes will, at your option, either be refunded or applied to the following year's estimates.

If you pay very low estimated tax or none at all, and if you are having a profitable year, be prepared when April 15 rolls around. You may have to come up with a lot of cash to pay all of this year's taxes *and* to pay next year's first quarterly estimate; both are due the same day. You may want to make voluntary estimated payments or set some money aside in a separate bank account to cushion the blow.

Estimated taxes are filed on a four-part form, #1040-ES. For more information, see IRS Publication #505, "Tax Withholding and Estimated Taxes."

The above rules apply to sole proprietors and partners. There is a different set of rules for corporations and a third set of rules for farmers and fishermen. If you base your estimates on the prior year's taxes, you must have been a U.S. citizen or resident for the entire previous year. If you are hit with an underpayment penalty, talk to the IRS or your accountant about it; there are several situations where the IRS will waive the penalty.

Operating Losses

If your business suffers a loss this year, you will owe no income taxes on the business, which I'm sure you know. But did you know that you can use this year's loss to offset profits from other years? You are allowed to carry back what the IRS calls a "Net Operating Loss" from a trade or business to apply against prior income and receive a refund of prior years' taxes, even if you were not in business then. The loss can be carried back three years. And if your taxable income for the three prior years is not sufficient to absorb the entire loss, you may carry the balance forward to apply to as many as fifteen future years. At your option, you can forego the three-year carryback period and apply your Net Operating Loss entirely to the 15 future years. An NOL, like any other tax deduction, is worth more in a high income year. If the three preceding years generated little or no income tax, you probably will do better to forego the carryback, and apply the entire NOL to future years.

Net Operating Loss is not simply the business loss shown on your tax return. It is a complicated combination of business and non-business income and deductions. I do not include the NOL calculations in *Small Time Operator* because they'd go on for several pages, and there's really no way to simplify the procedure. The step-by-step calculations are explained in detail in the IRS's *Tax Guide for Small Business* (Publication 334), free from any IRS office. Don't be put off by their complexity—the Net Operating Loss deduction may save you a bundle in income taxes.

Tax Credits

Tax credits are special tax deductions created by Congress to stimulate the economy or to encourage businesses to act in socially responsible ways.

In the past, there have been credits for hiring disadvantaged and handicapped people, for using solar, wind and renewable energy sources, for rehabilitating old buildings, for doing research and development, for investing in equipment.

Some credits appear on Schedule C or on your partnership or corporation return, reducing your taxable profit. Other credits are on the first page of your 1040 return, directly reducing your taxes.

Unfortunately, the credits come and go, available one year and not the next. If you fail to take a tax credit you are entitled to, the IRS will not tell you. The IRS's Publication 334 *Tax Guide for Small Business* and Publication 17 *Your Federal Income Tax* (both free from any IRS office) list the current credits.

The Internal Revenue Service and You

Small-Time Operator is not a manual for beating the IRS at their own game nor is it intended to be another "101 Ways to Reduce Your Taxes." Still, a general knowledge of the Internal Revenue Service and its inner workings may benefit you in your dealings with the agency and may even add to your peace of mind.

Most people, including most small businesses, file their tax returns and never get audited. The IRS audits less than 2 percent of all tax returns. IRS agents have to earn their keep and they are not going to be nickel-and-diming every little business that files a return. In almost all instances, returns selected for audit are those obviously out of line with Internal Revenue's idea of the "norm." The IRS does audit a random sample of tax returns every year, but the number is very small.

All tax returns, big and small, are automatically checked on the computer for errors—addition, multiplication, tax computation. If there is an arithmetical error, you will be notified of the error and any change in your taxes due to it. This is not an audit; and if you make an error, it does not increase your chances of being audited.

Many income tax returns are checked against other documents sent to the IRS, particularly W-2s, 1099 forms, and other "information returns." If your tax return does not include income that was reported to the IRS on a W-2 or 1099 form, you may get an inquiry, or even a tax bill, from the IRS.

All federal income tax returns are entered into computers at the regional IRS Service Centers and sent to the National Computer Center in Martinsburg, West Virginia. There, the returns are inspected and compared to what is known as the "Discriminate Input Function Formula," a computer program of the average American's financial profile. If your return falls within the "DIF" formula, you will be deemed An Honest Taxpayer. Your return will be filed away in the deep recesses of computer storage and will probably never be seen again. If, on the other hand, the computer "kicks out" your return—flags it for a possible audit—it will be sent back to your local IRS district office. An agent in the local office will review the return and decide whether or not to initiate an audit. Not every tax return rejected by the computer is audited; only those the agent feels are potential "money makers" for the IRS are selected.

It is hard to specify those items the IRS will be

looking for when examining the return of a small business, but generally, you can expect them to look for the following:

1. A reasonable profit, comparing total expenses to total sales. If your sales are $10,000 and your expenses $9,990, you may arouse suspicion that all is not right.

2. Consistency from one year to the next. Large fluctuations or unusual changes from year to year might invite an audit.

3. Unusual or unreasonable expenses. Large expenses not usually found in your type of business will be suspect. Large deductions for entertainment, conventions or travel away from home often invite audits.

If you have been audited in the past and wound up owing more tax, your chances of being audited again are increased. On the other hand, if prior audits did not result in more tax, you probably will not get audited again even if the computer does "kick out" your return.

Another possible audit situation comes about due to an undertaking known as the State Income Tax Information Exchange Program. The IRS has an agreement with most states to exchange tax information including information about audits. If your state income tax return was audited, the state may notify the IRS about your audit: the year involved, the reason for the audit and the results. The exchange program works both ways. The IRS may also notify the participating states about the results of IRS audits. The IRS can also provide tax information to city governments, for any city with a local income tax and a population over two million.

Business Loss

A business loss on your tax return is by no means a sure cause for audit, though your return is more likely to be examined than one showing a healthy profit. It is not uncommon for a new business to sustain a loss the first year, with all the start-up costs combined with early, slow business. A warning, however, to people who manage to show a loss year after year: if you do not show a profit for at least three out of five consecutive years, the IRS can declare your business to be a hobby ("an activity not engaged in for profit") and disallow any losses. If you breed, train, race, or show horses, the IRS hobby loss test is two out of seven years instead of three out of five. These are

not firm rules, however. A business can deduct losses for several years in a row without ever being challenged by the IRS. In the event of an audit, the IRS will allow the ongoing losses if they are convinced that you are operating a real business and trying, though unsuccessfully, to make a profit.

If your business is showing losses in the first year or two, you can keep the IRS from invoking the hobby-loss rule until the full five year period is up, by filing Form 5213, Election to Postpone Determination. The form must be filed within three years of the due date of your first business tax return (for most businesses, April 15 of the fourth year in business). If you don't file this form, it doesn't mean the IRS will be auditing you or challenging your loss deduction—they'll probably accept your return as is, and you'll probably never hear from them. The form is just extra insurance and may be totally unnecessary.

Notice of An Audit

Your first notice of an audit will be a letter from the IRS informing you of the audit and the year or years to be examined. You may be asked to come in person to a meeting with an agent or merely to send in certain written information. They may request to see a specific bill to support a specific item of expense, or they may request your entire set of ledgers. And you may be asked to bring or mail in copies of your tax returns for other years that are still open to audit.

If your books are in order and your bills are available, there is no need to fear an audit, and there is no real reason to hire an accountant or a tax lawyer to escort you to the meeting. And if you know you've been "caught," there is not much you can do but pay up and go home to lick your

"MOST PEOPLE BRING THEIR ACCOUNTANT."

wounds. There is probably little or nothing even the most expensive accountant can do for you. Should you, however, find yourself in legitimate disagreement with the IRS, or you feel that matters are getting too complicated, it may be time to seek professional help (see the chapter in the Appendix, "Seeking Professional Help"). The IRS code is extremely complex, and IRS agents have been known to make mistakes. Do not accept a ruling you disagree with. The IRS provides all taxpayers an elaborate system of appeals, starting with informal meetings with agents and going right up to the Supreme Court.

Generally, no penalties are assessed where there is an honest mistake on a tax return. You will owe only the back taxes and interest—as long as you pay up when the IRS says pay up.

There *are* a large variety of IRS penalties, some mild and some severe, for various offenses: failure to file (the penalty increases significantly after 60 days); failure to pay (the more you owe, the bigger the penalty); "negligence"; "intentional disregard of rules and regulations without intent to defraud"; "willful attempt to evade or defeat taxes"— i.e., fraud. Where fraud is involved, the IRS can impose both "civil" penalties and "criminal" penalties. Civil penalties (fines) can be imposed in the normal course of an audit. Criminal penalties (very large fines and/or jail) may only be imposed after full due-process of law, a trial, etc.

If you cannot afford to pay the taxes when your tax return is due, file the return on time anyway. The penalties will probably be less. Quite often, the IRS will waive penalties where failure to file a return or failure to pay the tax is due to "reasonable cause."

Except for special situations, the general statute of limitations—the length of time the IRS has to audit a return and assess back taxes—is three years from the time the return is filed. If you omit from your return more than twenty-five percent of your gross income, the statute of limitations is increased to six years. There is no time limit if your return is "false or fraudulent" or if no return is filed. Most IRS audits, however, are initiated within twenty months of filing the return. So, if you haven't heard from them by then, you probably won't.

This chapter is full of vague words: "reasonable cause," "without intent to defraud," "intentional disregard of rules and regulations," "willful attempt to evade," "unusual" this and "unreason-

able" that. Many people make their livings arguing over these and other godawful terms. As with so many other legal situations, the words often wind up meaning whatever the agent or the judge wants them to mean. This is not an area for amateurs. If you are caught up in an audit involving these issues, your philosophy and your finances will have to dictate your reactions. Good luck.

Failure to File a Tax Return

I would like to cover briefly an area about which I have received a surprisingly large number of questions over the years: what if someone has been in business a few years and never filed a tax return? It's rarely a case of intentional dishonesty. A typical example is a craftsperson who starts out with a hobby. At Christmas, he sells a couple hundred dollars worth of merchandise, and he never thinks of his craft as a business. But now, two or three years have passed, and he realizes that $5,000 or $10,000 a year is going through his bank account, and he's never filed a tax return. Now what?

Contrary to what many people think, the Internal Revenue Service is not all-powerful nor all-seeing. Their computers are not set up for Big Brother snooping—not yet, anyway. The IRS will not know you have earned money unless you or someone else reports it to them. For most Americans, this information comes to the IRS on a Form W-2, report of income of employees. All employers are required to prepare a W-2 for each employee each year.

A self-employed person is most likely to be known to the IRS via something called a Form 1099, report of income paid an individual other than an employee. If you sell your services to another business (not goods, just services) and that business paid you $600 or more during one year, they are required to file a Form 1099, notifying the IRS that you have received this money. Also, if you are an independent sales agent and you purchase $5,000 or more in goods for resale (from one company in one year) that company will report the purchase to the IRS on a 1099 form. In both of the above situations, the business that files the 1099 must also send you a copy of the form. If your bank account is in your business name, the

---

People will do silly things to avoid taxes
    —J. C. Small, tax attorney, Counsel to the
    Director, N.J. Division of Taxation

"You're saying that as a professional writer, your expenses totaled $22,000 more than your income? What kind of way is that to make a living?"

interest the account earns will be reported to the IRS on a Form 1099. The bank is required to report any interest payment of $10 or more to the IRS.

If you receive a copy of Form 1099 or a W-2, the feds have your name. If the amounts paid exceed the minimum requirements for filing, you are likely to get a letter of inquiry or possibly even a tax bill from the IRS. Government forms you yourself file might also alert the IRS to your existence, such as employment reports, sales tax reports, even state tax returns. On the other hand, if no one reports you, and if you file no reports or other documents, the IRS will probably not know of your existence. Probably. But you are breaking the law, and there is no statute of limitations on how many years later they can come after you.

The law says, and I recommend, that you file returns for all those prior years, pay the back taxes, interest and penalties. Some people will just go on their merry way and never file and never be found; we've all heard of someone with that kind of experience. Other delinquent folk may decide that this is the year to file their first return, and let the prior years lie, hopefully, unnoticed.

The penalty for failure to file an income tax return, as I mentioned above, depends on several factors including how long it's been, how much you owe and the reasons why you haven't filed. There is no penalty if you can show that failure to file was due to some reasonable cause and not to willful neglect.

If you find yourself summoned by the IRS to discuss those tax returns you never filed, I suggest you get some professional help. Maybe, get yourself a stiff drink first.

Amending Old Tax Returns

There may be gold in old income tax returns. Two interesting facts few people know: One, most income tax returns—especially small business returns—have errors no one, including the IRS, discovered; and two, you may amend prior year's tax returns and get refunds of overpaid taxes.

The IRS catches glaring and obvious errors on tax returns: mistakes in addition or tax computation, missing forms, entries on the wrong line, improper procedures. Beyond the obvious, unless you get audited—and less than two percent of small business tax returns are audited—your return will be accepted as is, errors and all.

Whenever I get a new tax client, I have a look at the prior year's tax return before I prepare the current one. Over the years, I've found errors and omissions on over half the returns prepared by professionals and on close to 100% of the returns prepared by the taxpayers who do their own returns. In many of the cases, more tax was paid than required by law.

Amended tax returns must be filed within three years from the date you filed your original return or within two years from the time you paid your tax, whichever is later. A return filed early is considered filed on the due date. So for 1992 tax returns filed and paid on time (April 15, 1993) or ahead of time, you have until April 15, 1996 to amend the return.

How do you know if there is an error or omission on your tax return? If you prepared the return yourself, there's probably an error. The tax laws are so vast and complex, even the experts don't know it all. Unless you've studied the tax laws thoroughly, you've probably missed something. If you took your taxes to one of those tax chains or storefront tax operations, your return was probably prepared by someone with little experience and brief training. These people do not take the time to delve into your business finances looking for tax savings. If the tax preparer took your numbers and asked few or no questions, chances are good your return is not all it could be.

The most common omissions and errors I've found on business tax returns are: not taking tax credits you are entitled to; failing to accrue expenses at year-end (see the chapter Accrual Accounting); overlooking legitimate business expenses that didn't get into your ledgers or your business checkbook, such as out-of-pocket cash payments, business expenses paid out of your personal checking account, automobile expenses, home office expenses, purchases that are partly personal and partly business, bank service charges, equipment and furniture used in your business but purchased prior to starting your business; incorrectly computing depreciation or choosing the wrong depreciation method; miscalculating cost-of-goods-sold.

If you find or suspect an error or omission, ask your accountant about it. If you prepared your own return or if it was prepared by someone of questionable competence, locate an experienced tax accountant (see the chapter "Seeking Professional Help" in the Appendix) and ask her to look over your return. Most accountants will give it at least a glance. Some will catch and correct an error. Others will want to do the entire return over from scratch: they're less likely to make a mistake if they are not working from someone else's mistake.

Tax returns are amended on form 1040-X for unincorporated businesses, 1120-X for regular corporations, 1120-S (marked "Amended") for S corporations, and 1065 (marked "Amended") for partnerships. Refunds are fairly prompt.

An amended return is more likely to get the once over from an IRS agent, and amending the return starts the standard three year statute of limitations on audits over again: the statute runs from the date the amended return was filed instead of the date the original was filed. My experience, however, is that amended returns are not more likely to be audited than original returns.

If your federal return was in error, your state return was probably also in error. States have similar procedures for amending returns. Some states require you to amend the state return (within a specified time deadline) if you amend your federal return.

Federal Information Returns

The government requires that certain business transactions be reported to the IRS on special "information returns." These reports are not tax returns, and no taxes are paid with them. In most cases, you must also give a copy of the information return to all parties involved in the transactions. Some information returns are covered in other sections of the book, several more are covered here. But the IRS has been adding new requirements almost every year, so it's best to check with them

to see what else you have to report.

Large cash transactions. Businesses that receive $10,000 or more in cash (currency), money orders or cashier's checks (but not personal or business checks) in a single transaction or in two or more related transactions, must report the information to the IRS on Form #8300.

Real estate transactions. The person responsible for closing real estate transactions (usually the title company but sometimes the broker) must report the information to the IRS on Form #1099-S.

Royalty payments. If you pay $10 or more in royalties to one person in any calendar year, you must report the payment to the IRS on Form #1099-MISC.

Dividend payments. Corporations paying $10 or more in dividends must report each payment to the IRS on Form #1099-DIV.

Interest payments. If you pay $600 or more in interest in any calendar year on a business debt, you must report the payment on Form #1099-INT.

Owners or operators of fishing boats report all payments to crew members on proceeds from sale of catch, on Form #1099-MISC.

Interest received. If, in the course of your trade or business, you receive $600 or more of mortgage interest from an individual in a calendar year, you must report the income to the IRS on Form #1098.

Lenders. If you lend money in connection with your business, and in full or partial satisfaction of the debt, you acquire an interest in property secured for the debt, you must file form 1099-A.

Stock brokers. Report sales of stocks, bonds commodities, etc. on Form 1099-B.

Barter. Barter exchanges file Form 1099-B.

Rent. Businesses paying $600 or more a year in rent (for business premises, machinery or equipment, farm land) must file Form 1099-MISC.

Tips. Large restaurants must report tips on Form 8027.

Outside services. Businesses paying $600 or more a year in fees, commissions or prizes to nonemployees and outside contractors, must file Form 1099-MISC. This is covered in detail in the Growing Up section of the book.

Independent sales agents. If you make direct sales of $5,000 or more of consumer products to outside sales agents in any one year, you must file Form 1099-MISC.

Employers give all employees W-2 earnings statements every year. See the chapters on becoming an employer in the Growing Up section.

Federal Excise Tax

Most small businesses are not liable for federal excise taxes. Businesses that are required to file excise tax returns must have a Federal Employer Identification Number (EIN) even if you are not an employer. Use IRS Form SS-4 to request a number.

Regular excise taxes are imposed on manufacturers of trucks, truck trailers, truck parts, tires, inner tubes, fishing equipment, outboard motors, bows, arrows, firearms, ammunition, coal, gasoline and gasohol, lubricating oils, and cars that do not meet fuel economy standards; on businesses operating aircraft; on businesses using fuel in inland waterways; on retailers of heavy trucks and trailers; on retailers of diesel, gasoline substitutes, noncommercial aviation and marine fuels; and on retail sales of furs, jewelry and watches over $10,000, automobiles over $30,000, boats over $100,000, and airplanes over $250,000—new items only (used items escape the tax). The excise tax is payable quarterly on Form #720, "Quarterly Federal Excise Tax Return." Excise taxes are also imposed on brewers; on wholesale and retail beer, wine and liquor dealers; on manufacturers of stills; on tobacco; and on importers and dealers in firearms. These excise taxes are paid on Form #11.For more information on the above taxes, ask the IRS for a free copy of Publication #510, "Excise Taxes."

A highway motor vehicle Federal Use Tax is imposed on owners of large highway trucks, truck trailers and buses. Form 2290 must be filed annually. For more information, see IRS publication #349, "Federal Highway Use Tax."

State Income Taxes

As of last year, every state had some form of income tax on resident unincorporated businesses except Alaska, Florida, Nevada, New Hampshire, New Mexico, South Dakota, Tennessee, Texas, Wyoming and Washington, though Washington has a "gross receipts tax" and New Hampshire has a "business profits tax" (more on that later). The states that do levy income taxes have procedures and rules similar to the federal ones. Most states simply compute state tax either as a percentage of your federal income tax or based on a percentage of the income shown on your federal return. Five of the more ambitious—maybe I should say ornery—states have their own separate set of income tax rules just different enough from the federal rules to require separate calculations. The Royal Pain In The Butt Award to Alabama, Arkansas, Mississippi, New Jersey, and Pennsylvania.

State income taxes, like federal income taxes, are based on your net income or net profit. Income less deductible expenses gives you net income. Generally, states allow businesses to deduct the same expenses as the feds allow with a few important exceptions: you may deduct state income tax on your federal return but not on your state return; you may not deduct federal income taxes on your federal tax return, but several states allow a deduction for federal income taxes; several states do not make allowances for Net Operating Loss carryback and carryforward; many states have varying numbers of years allowed for NOL carryback and carryforward; self-employment tax is a federal tax only, although some states allow a deduction for it; and remember, not all states allow the same nontaxable retirement contributions the feds allow.

Most state income tax returns for calendar-year taxpayers are due April 15, the same due date as the federal returns. Six states have later due dates: Arkansas—May 15; Delaware—April 30; Hawaii—April 20; Iowa—April 30; Louisiana—May 15; Virginia—May 1.

The above state income tax information does not apply to corporations. Corporate income tax laws and filing dates vary considerably from state to state.

State Gross Receipts Taxes

A gross receipts tax is a tax on total business receipts—sales, income—before any deductions for expenses. The tax is in addition to any income or sales tax. Some states call their sales tax a gross receipts tax, but the tax referred to here is not a sales tax. Sales tax is collected from your customers. Gross receipts taxes are paid out of your own pocket.

Hawaii, Indiana and Washington have some form of gross receipts tax on small businesses. Indiana calls theirs a "gross income tax." Delaware has a gross receipts tax but only after a very large deductible (between $20,000 and $35,000 a month). Alabama authorizes counties to impose a "license tax" that, at a county's option, can take the form of a gross receipts tax. South Dakota has a 2% gross receipts tax on building contractors. Alaska and Washington have a gross receipts tax on fishing businesses. Several states impose a gross receipts tax on logging operations.

Michigan has a special state Single Business Tax, 2.35% of net profits, but only after a $44,000 deductible. This tax is in addition to the sales and income tax.

New Hampshire has a state Business Profits Tax equal to 8% of the profits on your federal tax return if your business grossed more than $12,000.

Other States Taxes

The list of state taxes on businesses is virtually endless. Many states tax either the manufacturers, wholesalers or retailers (and sometimes all three) of alcoholic beverages, fuel oils, gasolines, tobacco products, motor vehicles and airplanes. Mining operations, financial institutions, utilities, insurance companies and real estate dealings are taxed in most states. Many states have an admissions tax on theatres, amusement parks, etc. Many states tax freight, express and private car companies. Several states tax logging, timber and forest land. Some states have a special chain store tax for businesses with more than one location. Some states tax hotel rooms and restaurant meals. Some states have special state business licenses.

You should make an effort to find out about your state's tax laws on small businesses. Call state offices, ask other business owners, ask your accountant. You don't want to be caught by surprise or hit with some whopping penalty for failure to file a tax return you didn't know about.

County, City And Other Local Taxes

Counties almost always impose property taxes on real estate. In some states, counties also impose a property tax on business assets other than real estate, such as equipment, furniture and tools.

Some counties impose an inventory tax (sometimes called a "floor" tax), a property tax on business inventory on hand at a given date. Where inventory tax is collected, many retail stores hold big sales just before tax time to bring their inventories down in order to reduce the tax.

Some large cities impose income taxes, gross receipts taxes, and/or sales taxes on businesses. These taxes are usually in addition to any similar state tax. A few large cities impose a flat "Business Tax" or "Business Registration Fee," which is in addition to the regular business license.

You can contact your county or city offices to inquire about business taxes. Chances are, if any business taxes are levied locally, they'll be contacting you! With the exception of some income taxes, business taxes are a deductible business expense.

He says we're free.

Section Five
APPENDIX

"Mercy!" Scrooge said. "Dreadful apparition, why do you trouble me?"

The same face; the very same. Marley in his pigtail, usual waistcoat, tights and boots. The chain he drew was clasped about his middle. It was long, and wound about him like a tail; and it was made of cashboxes, keys, padlocks, ledgers, deeds, and heavy purses wrought with steel. His body was transparent; so that Scrooge, observing him, and looking through his waistcoat, could see the two buttons on his coat behind.

"You are fettered," said Scrooge, trembling. "Tell me why?"

"I wear the chain I forged in life," replied the Ghost; "I made it link by link and yard by yard; I girded it on of my own free will, and of my own free will I wore it. Is its pattern strange to you?"

Scrooge trembled more and more. "But you were always a good man of business, Jacob," faltered Scrooge.

"Business!" cried the Ghost, wringing its hands again. "Mankind was my business. The common welfare was my business; charity, mercy, forbearance, and benevolence, were all my business. The dealing of my trade were but a drop of water in the comprehensive ocean of my business."

Excerpted from **A Christmas Carol**
by Charles Dickens

How to Balance a Bank Account

The balance on your bank statement will rarely agree with the balance in your checkbook. But you know that. What you probably don't know, if you've never balanced a bank account, is that the difference is almost always easy to locate and reconcile. The difference is due to one or more of the following:

1. Checks you have written but which have not yet cleared the bank; called "outstanding checks."

2. Deposits not yet posted by the bank; called "deposits in transit."

3. Interest earned or bank service charges you have not recorded in your checkbook and any return (bounced) checks that you still show as deposits; called "reconciling items."

4. Someone's error, usually yours; called "oops."

If you follow these procedures, balancing your bank account will take only a few minutes each month (hopefully):

1. Sort the canceled checks returned with the bank statement into numerical order.

2. Match each canceled check with the corresponding entry in your checkbook. Put a checkmark next to your checkbook entry so you'll know the check has been canceled. It is also a good idea to compare the amount on the canceled check with the amount you wrote in your checkbook. Too many of you speedy checkwriters will write a check for $15.16 and post it in your checkbook as $16.15. It is known as "transposition" and is an occupational disease of even the best bookkeepers. There will most likely be several checks you have written that have not cleared the bank yet. Don't worry: people are often slow in cashing checks, or the checks may have to travel back and forth across the country, from bank to bank.

3. If the bank returns copies of your deposit slips with the statement, match these to the deposits in your checkbook. The banks, however, are getting lazier in their old age, and many will not return duplicate deposits slips to you. You will have to match your checkbook record of deposits with those recorded on the bank statement. Again, check off the deposits in your checkbook. And again beware of transposition errors. Unlike checks, deposits should clear the bank immediately. Mailed deposits should clear within a few days. Any real lag in a bank recording of deposits may mean a lost or misplaced deposit, which can be disastrous for you; contact the bank at once.

4. Look for any unusual items returned with the bank statement: notice of a bounced check or a check printing charge or some other bank charge. Also examine the statement itself for any bank charges or service fees. They will be listed along with the checks with a reference number or letter next to the amount. Somewhere on the statement is an explanation of what it means. By the way, if they hit you for a bank charge you don't think is proper, call the bank and complain. Quite often, the bank will cancel the charge. They would rather keep your business and your good will than get a $2 fee out of you. If your account pays interest, the amount is usually shown as the last item on your bank statement.

Now that you've checked off everything and marveled at all the little entries buried here and there on the bank statement, you are ready to reconcile. With pencil in hand and a blank piece of paper, or the back of the bank statement if there is enough room:

1. Write down your checkbook balance.

2. Total all the checks you have written that have *not* cleared the bank, the ones without a checkmark next to them. These are your outstanding checks. *Add* this total to your checkbook balance.

3. *Subtract* from your balance any deposits you have recorded that have *not* cleared the bank. These are your deposits in transit.

4. *Subtract* from your balance any of those extra charges the bank included in the statement.

5. *Add* to your balance any interest paid.

6. If you made any errors recording check or

deposit amounts adjust your balance.

The final figure you come up with should equal the bank balance on the statement. It doesn't? Damn. Let's try to isolate the problem.

Repeat the reconciliation, and check your addition. If you don't have an adding machine, this may be a good time to read the chapter on adding machines and calculators at the end of the bookkeeping section; at least it will be a good excuse to get away from these numbers for a little while. Still computes the same? When you checked off the canceled checks and the deposits, did the amounts all agree? Are you sure?

At this point, the error is 99 percent certain to be in your running checkbook balance. Sometime during the month, you wrote a check and recorded the correct amount but subtracted it incorrectly from the balance. Go back and re-subtract each check from the balance, check by check. You are bound to find the error.

No luck? Did you lose one of the canceled checks? Add up the number of canceled checks and compare with the total number of checks listed on the bank statement.

Still can't find the difference? There *may* be a bank error but it's not very likely. Examine the bank statement: the beginning balance should be the same as last month's ending balance. Was there a reconciling item on last month's statement you forgot to post to your checkbook? Did you balance last month's bank statement? (I'm still trying.) Check the addition on the bank statement. If you do find something amiss on the statement, notify the bank.

I think that it is impossible to go through all these procedures and not locate the error. But if you've done the impossible, I'd suggest two more things: (1) Cool it for a few days. Just put it all away and forget it. Later, when you're in a better mood, repeat the procedures outlined here, from scratch: don't look at your old calculations; if they're wrong they will throw you off. *AND IF THAT DOES NOT WORK*, then (2) take your checkbook and the statement and the canceled checks and all down to the bank and get them to help you.

The one solution I failed to mention is the easiest: forget it. Assume you've made a mistake somewhere, correct your balance to agree with the reconciliation, and forget it. But that's just not my nature, so...

If you do have an error or if there are reconciling items such as bank charges, you must correct your books accordingly:

Error in addition: Adjust the most recent checkbook balance up or down to correct the error. Make a note in the checkbook as to exactly what you are doing.

Error in check or deposit amount: Adjust the most recent checkbook balance and write a note of explanation. If you recorded a check incorrectly, make sure you haven't made the same mistake on your expenditure ledger.

Bank charges: Record them on your checkbook the same way you record a check, reducing your bank balance accordingly. Remember also to post the charge to your expenditure ledger in Column Two—*Supplies, Postage, Etc.*

Balance Sheets

A balance sheet, also known as a "statement of assets and liabilities," is a listing of your assets, liabilities, and net worth or equity at any given point in time. Balance sheets are sometimes required on partnership and corporation income tax returns. Most banks will ask to see a balance sheet (as well as a statement of income and expense; see the "Financial Management" chapter in the bookkeeping section) when considering business loans. Audited corporate financial statements must include comparative (current year and prior year) balance sheets.

All balance sheets are made up of three sections: assets—the property you own; liabilities—money you owe; and equity—the net worth of your business, the difference between the assets and the liabilities.

Assets are broken down into two categories:

Current: Cash, and assets that will be used or sold in the normal course of business within a year. Current assets usually include accounts receivable—your customers' unpaid credit accounts—less an allowance for uncollectible bad debts; notes and loans receivable—money owed to you other than regular credit accounts—due within one year; inventory—finished goods, work in process and raw materials—valued at cost or market, whichever is less; prepaid expenses (beyond 12 months) such as next year's insurance. Current prepaid expenses such as rent or this year's insurance are not included.

Other Assets: Cost of depreciable fixed assets such as equipment, vehicles, furniture and build-

```
                 BALANCE SHEET
             Bear Soft Pretzel Co.
              as of December 31

                    ASSETS

Current Assets
   Cash                              $ 375
   Accounts Receivable      $140
      Less allowance for
         bad debts          (20)
                            ____      120
   Prepaid insurance                  150
   Inventory (at lower of cost
      or market):
      Pretzels--hot         $ 25
      Pretzels--stale          1
      Flour, sugar, salt      75
                            ____      101
Other Assets
   Equipment, at cost      $2,300
      Less accumulated
         depreciation       (450)
                            _____   1,850
   Total Assets                    $2,596
                                   ======

                  LIABILITIES

Current Liabilities
   Accounts Payable                 $ 120
   Loan payable, portion due
      within one year                 250
Long-Term Liabilities
   Balance of loan payable            750
   Total Liabilities               $1,120
NET WORTH (owner's equity)          1,476

                                   $2,596
                                   ======
```

ings less the accumulated depreciation; cost of land; intangible long-term assets such as patents and capitalized incorporation fees; notes and loans receivable that will not be collected within one year.

Long-term notes and loans receivable that are payable to you in installments over several years should be split between "current" and "other." The amount coming due within one year should be shown as "current"; the balance should be listed under "other assets."

Liabilities are also divided into similar categories:

Current: Notes and loans payable due within one year; unpaid taxes and tax penalties; unpaid wages.

Long-term: Any loans or other liabilities due after one year. Like long-term receivables, notes and long-term loans payable in installments over several years should be split between "current" for the amount due within twelve months and "long-term" for the balance.

You should also include under liabilities any "contingent" liabilities you know about. Contingent liabilities are crystal-ball suppositions about the future: liabilities that may or may not materialize. If the IRS is auditing you or you are being sued, for example, and there is a possibility you will owe money, some dollar estimate of the liability must be included on the balance sheet. Contingent liability estimates should be clearly labeled as such and should be explained fully.

Balance sheets can be simple or quite complicated. A balance sheet prepared for your bank when requesting a loan need not be elaborate. The audited financial statements required of corporations that sell stock to the public, however, include fully detailed and footnoted balance sheets. Any basic accounting textbook will include a chapter on balance sheets. The best way to learn about balance sheets, I have found, is to study the published financial statements that most corporations put out. You usually can get them free on request.

Seeking Professional Help: How to Locate a Good Accountant

This book should help you with most aspects of beginning and operating a small business and successfully steer you through the common obstacles without need of an accountant. But the time may come when your finances are getting a bit too complicated, or you may need help incorporating your business. And then there's income taxes. It's a rare business owner who has the time and inclination to study and understand tax laws. So how do you find a good accountant?

Locating a good accountant is like trying to find a reliable doctor; you have to ask around. The best people to ask are those like you, in business for themselves. If you do not know an accountant and cannot get a reliable recommendation, here are a few suggestions to help in your search:

1. Picking a name at random from the telephone book is probably the biggest mistake you could make. There is no way to know what kind of person you will get or how qualified he or she may be.

2. Stay away from the storefront tax operations, the ones that open shop every January and promptly disappear April 15. Most of the people who work for these chains have little experience, brief training, and are usually familiar only with Mr. and Mrs. Nine-to-Five and their typical tax problems. These part-time accountants are not trained to handle complex problems nor do they take the time to delve into your business finances looking for tax savings.

3. Choose an experienced tax accountant, preferably one who specializes in small business. It's not necessary to hire a certified public accountant; CPA's are probably the best qualified, but most of them specialize in complex transactions and big business. Expect to pay professional prices.

4. Talk to the accountant personally before you commit yourself. If he or she will not talk to you on the phone other than in vague generalities, call someone else. Does the accountant seem familiar with your situation and your problems? Is the man too "grey flannel suit" and big business oriented to relate to you? Most important, does he make sense to you? Beware of the accountant who talks Advanced Sanskrit or IRS code sections. You need an accountant to answer questions, not show off the glories of his trade.

It is important to understand what a tax accountant can do for you and, just as important, what the accountant cannot and will not do for you.

A good accountant will prepare your tax return faster than you thought humanly possible. A good tax accountant will know the different tax options you have, such as different ways to compute depreciation, and help you make the best choice. A good accountant will show you ways you might reduce taxes by restructuring your business, changing your bookkeeping, timing certain purchases and payments, or making other changes that will help you better deal with tax laws. This is the accountant's area of expertise, and you should make the most of it—you're paying for it.

Tax professionals are held accountable for the work they do and the advice they give. They are not going to tell you how to break the law, and they don't want to hear about any illegal tax maneuvers. Certainly you can and should ask honest questions—Is this legal? Is this deductible? Must this be reported?—but expect honest answers. Don't put the accountant in a situation he shouldn't be in; you may be causing trouble for yourself and for the accountant.

These warnings don't mean that you and your accountant shouldn't explore questionable areas of the law if you are so willing, and if the accountant feels you have legal ground to stand on. Some tax laws are very straightforward; but many are ambiguous, subject to interpretation, honest disagreement, what we call "gray areas". Some laws are so new and convoluted, no one is quite sure how to interpret them. The best tax accountants know, from experience and from studying tax manuals and court decisions, how to handle those "gray areas" of tax law.

A Special Chapter for Farmers

Federal income tax rules for small-time farmers are somewhat different from those for other small businesses. Some of the differences are outlined in this chapter but for complete information farmers should obtain a free copy of IRS Publication #225, "Farmer's Tax Guide." It is revised annually.

Farmers do not report their profit or loss on schedule 1040C. Farmers should use schedule 1040F, "Farm Income and Expenses."

Purchased breeding stock and dairy stock must be treated as depreciable property, just like a tractor or a piece of machinery. One exception to this rule: the cost of egg laying stock—chicks, pullets and hens—can be written off to expense the year of purchase. Livestock born on your farm cannot be depreciated because there is no purchase cost to depreciate.

The cost of feed, fertilizer, seeds and young plants (except cost of seeds and young plants for tree farms, orchards and timber operations) can sometimes be deducted the year of purchase even if they are purchased for future years' use, but only if they do not exceed 50% of current expenses.

The cost of clearing, leveling and conditioning land, purchasing and planting trees (other than certain young plants), building irrigation canals and ditches, laying irrigation pipes, constructing dams and building roads must, in most cases, be depreciated. Some soil and water conservation expenditures that meet government approved con-

SCHEDULE F (Form 1040)

Department of the Treasury
Internal Revenue Service (T)

Profit or Loss From Farming

▶ Attach to Form 1040, Form 1041, or Form 1065.

▶ See Instructions for Schedule F (Form 1040).

OMB No. 1545-0074

1992

Attachment Sequence No. **14**

Name of proprietor	Social security number (SSN)
Frank & Fay F Jones	123 : 34 : 4566

A Principal product (Describe in one or two words your principal crop or activity for the current tax year.)
Eggs and poultry

B Enter principal agricultural activity code (from page 2) ▶ | 2 | 5 | 0 |

D Employer ID number (Not SSN)
9 | 4 : 5 | 6 | 7 | 8 | 9 | 0 | 1 |

C Accounting method: (1) [X] Cash (2) [ ] Accrual

E Did you make an election in a prior year to include Commodity Credit Corporation loan proceeds as income in that year? . . [ ] Yes [X] No

F Did you "materially participate" in the operation of this business during 1991? (If "No," see instructions for limitations on losses.) [X] Yes [ ] No

G Do you elect, or did you previously elect, to currently deduct certain preproductive period expenses? (See instructions.) [ ] Does not apply [ ] Yes [X] No

Part I Farm Income—Cash Method—Complete Parts I and II (Accrual method taxpayers complete Parts II and III, and line 11 of Part I.)
Do not include sales of livestock held for draft, breeding, sport, or dairy purposes; report these sales on Form 4797.

1	Sales of livestock and other items you bought for resale	1	
2	Cost or other basis of livestock and other items reported on line 1 . . .	2	
3	Subtract line 2 from line 1	3	
4	Sales of livestock, produce, grains, and other products you raised	4	$7,526
5a	Total cooperative distributions (Form(s) 1099-PATR) 5a	5b Taxable amount	5b
6a	Agricultural program payments (see instructions) 6a	6b Taxable amount	6b
7	Commodity Credit Corporation (CCC) loans:		
a	CCC loans reported under election (see instructions)	7a	
b	CCC loans forfeited or repaid with certificates 7b	7c Taxable amount	7c
8	Crop insurance proceeds and certain disaster payments (see instructions):		
a	Amount received in 1991 8a	8b Taxable amount	8b
c	If election to defer to 1992 is attached, check here ▶ [ ]	8d Amount deferred from 1990 .	8d
9	Custom hire (machine work) income	9	65
10	Other income, including Federal and state gasoline or fuel tax credit or refund (see instructions) . . .	10	10
11	Add amounts in the right column for lines 3 through 10. If accrual method taxpayer, enter the amount from page 2, line 52. This is your **gross income** . . . . ▶	11	$7,601

Part II Farm Expenses—Cash and Accrual Method (Do not include personal or living expenses such as taxes, insurance, repairs, etc., on your home.)

12	Breeding fees	12		25	Labor hired (less jobs credit) .	25	860
13	Car and truck expenses (see instructions—also attach **Form 4562**).	13	$ 71	26	Pension and profit-sharing plans	26	
14	Chemicals	14		27	Rent or lease (see instructions):		
15	Conservation expenses (attach **Form 8645**)	15		a	Vehicles, machinery, and equipment	27a	
16	Custom hire (machine work) .	16		b	Other (land, animals, etc.) . .	27b	
17	Depreciation and section 179 expense deduction not claimed elsewhere (see instructions) . .	17	801	28	Repairs and maintenance . .	28	90
				29	Seeds and plants purchased .	29	
				30	Storage and warehousing . .	30	
18	Employee benefit programs other than on line 26	18		31	Supplies purchased	31	221
				32	Taxes	32	38
19	Feed purchased	19	482	33	Utilities	33	100
20	Fertilizers and lime	20		34	Veterinary fees and medicine .	34	50
21	Freight and trucking	21	40	35	Other expenses (specify):		
22	Gasoline, fuel, and oil . . .	22	80	a	....	35a	
23	Insurance (other than health) .	23		b	....	35b	
24	Interest:			c	....	35c	
a	Mortgage (paid to banks, etc.) .	24a		d	....	35d	
b	Other	24b		e	....	35e	
				f	....	35f	
36	Add lines 12 through 35f. These are your **total expenses** . . . . ▶					36	$2,883
37	**Net farm profit or (loss).** Subtract line 36 from line 11. If a profit, enter on Form 1040, line 19, and on Schedule SE, line 1. If a loss, you MUST go on to line 38 (fiduciaries and partnerships, see instructions)					37	$4,768
38	If you have a loss, you MUST check the box that describes your investment in this activity (see instructions). } If you checked 38a, enter the loss on Form 1040, line 19, and Schedule SE, line 1. If you checked 38b, you MUST attach **Form 6198**.				38a [ ] All investment is at risk. 38b [ ] Some investment is not at risk.		

---

servation requirements can, at your option, be deducted as an expense the year incurred instead of being depreciated. The specific requirements and dollar limitations are explained in the IRS's *Farmer's Tax Guide*. All expenditures for citrus and almond grove development must be depreciated.

Farmers—and fishermen, too—do not have to make quarterly estimated tax payments if your gross income from farming (or fishing) is at least two-thirds of your total estimated gross income from all sources. One estimated tax payment for the entire prior year's taxes is required of farmers, due on January 15. And you don't have to make that estimated tax payment if you file your regular income tax return by the last day in February.

Farmers can use the ledgers in this book, but you will probably need to make some alterations. Generally, most farm sales are not subject to sales tax, so you probably do not need a sales tax column in your income ledger. I suggest that you delete the headings on columns three, four, five and six in your income ledger and re-title them to suit your needs. Use a different column for each different type in income, such as livestock sales, produce sales, milk sales, patronage dividends, etc. The columns in the expenditure ledger can also be re-titled to make them more useful to a farmer. Column One-*Inventory* can certainly be deleted, probably Column Five-*Advertising*, and possibly one or two other columns. In their place, you may want columns for livestock purchases, repairs, feed, fertilizer, veterinary fees or other typical farm expenses.

A few words from the Internal Revenue Service to part-time and "weekend" farmers: "A farmer who operates a farm for profit may deduct all the ordinary and necessary expenses of carrying on the business of farming. The farm must be operated for profit. Whether a farm is being operated for profit must be determined from all the facts and circumstances in each case. However, you will not ordinarily be considered as operating a farm for profit if you raise crops or livestock mainly for use of your family, but derive some income from incidental sales." Such "incidental sales" are subject to income tax, but deductions are limited and cannot exceed income (that is, no losses allowed).

Husband & Wife Partnerships

When a husband and wife operate a business together, the business may be a corporation, a partnership or a sole proprietorship. Each of the three legal forms requires different paperwork, and each can result in differences, possibly major differences, in income taxes, social security, Medicare and fringe benefits.

For an unincorporated business, the business may be a partnership or it may be a sole proprietorship. If the couple execute a written partnership agreement and file partnership tax returns (Form 1065), the business is definitely a general partnership. Beyond this one clear distinction, the law is not cut-and-dried. The IRS has ruled that, generally, if one spouse (let's say the wife) is the main operator of the business, the wife is a sole proprietor. The husband, with a lesser interest in the business, is either an employee or has no "official" designation (more on this below). Some criteria the IRS uses in determining the status of a husband-and-wife business are (1) does one spouse spend more time than the other operating the business? (2) are the business licenses in one spouse's name? (3) does one spouse have other employment? Generally, the IRS will accept whatever you tell them.

A sole proprietorship is easier and less expensive to set up than a partnership. For starters, a husband-and-wife partnership will require a written partnership agreement. A partnership must also prepare a separate tax return (Form 1065) in addition to the couple's 1040 return. Some partnership tax returns must include a balance sheet and a schedule of each partner's contributions and withdrawals (family farms and family-owned wholesale and retail stores are usually exempt from this requirement). Sole proprietorship tax returns do not include balance sheets or schedules of owner's draw.

In a sole proprietorship, the owner can hire his/her spouse as an employee and deduct the wage as a business expense. Of course, the wage paid the spouse is taxable income to the couple. Assuming the couple files a joint tax return, their income tax is the same whether the couple operate as a partnership or as employer-employee.

You will recall that partners in a partnership, and sole proprietors, pay self-employment tax, which is combined social security and Medicare for the self-employed. Employees, including spouse-employees, are subject to regular social security and Medicare taxes. So a husband and wife who set up a partnership will each pay self-employment tax on his and her share of the profits. A wife

who sets up a sole proprietorship and hires her husband as an employee will deduct social security and Medicare tax from his paycheck and pay an additional employer's portion. She will also pay self-employment tax on her own share of the business profit.

An example will help. A husband and wife set up a 50-50 partnership. The business earns a profit (before any draw or wage paid the partners) of $20,000 for the year. Each partner's share is $10,000. The partners file a joint return and pay income tax on the combined $20,000. Each partner is also subject to self-employment tax on $10,000; together they pay self-employment tax on $20,000.

Now we'll change the example. The same business is instead structured as a sole proprietorship with the wife as owner and husband as employee. The husband is hired at a salary of $10,000 a year. The sole proprietorship also earned the wife a profit of $10,000 (after paying her husband his wages). The couple file a joint return and pay income taxes on the combined $20,000—the exact same amount of income taxes paid on the above partnership. The social security and Medicare taxes, however, will be different. The husband's $10,000 wage is subject to regular social security and Medicare taxes, both employer and employee; the wife's $10,000 profit is subject to self-employment tax. These are different taxes (the husband's social security and Medicare, and the wife's self-employment), both change every year, and there may be different rates.

If the husband is an official employee of his wife's business, the business must keep complete payroll records on the husband, issue regular payroll checks, file payroll tax returns, issue a W-2 at year-end, and comply with state regulations as well.

Things can be a whole lot simpler than this. The wife can set up a one-person sole proprietorship. The husband can work in the business but not be on the payroll nor otherwise officially included in the business. There is nothing wrong with this arrangement; it is perfectly legal. Under such an arrangement, the husband is not subject to any federal or state payroll taxes, and he pays no social security or Medicare taxes. No paperwork is required. Any "wage" the husband might take under this arrangement would not be taxable, and the wife would not be allowed a business deduction. Her business profit and her taxes would be figured as if the husband earned no wage. This arrange-

ment is by far the least expensive way to set up a husband and wife business. The money the couple saves in payroll costs, social security and Medicare taxes, and accounting fees can be substantial. The drawback is that the husband receives no social security credit in his own name and is not eligible for employee fringe benefits.

Another consideration, for businesses that are making a large profit, in excess of the $55,500 social security and self-employment tax maximums. If one spouse is a sole proprietor and the other spouse is not on the payroll, the first $55,500 is subject to the maximum self-employment tax rate (15.3%). Any profit in excess of $55,500, up to $130,200, is subject to a much lower rate (2.9%). If both spouses are officially part of the business, either as partners or as employer-employee, both spouses are subject to social security and/or self-employment taxes, each spouse to the $55,500 maximum. Together, they will pay a great deal more in Social Security taxes than if only one of them earned all the business income. Again, this applies only to businesses with profits in excess of $55,500.

A similar social security tax situation exists if one spouse has a high paying outside job and is also the sole proprietor and the only official person in the business. The business profit subject to self-employment tax will be reduced by the amount of outside income (as explained in the Tax section under Self-Employment Tax), reducing the self-employment tax substantially. Again, this savings can only be realized if only one spouse has an outside job and also runs the business alone.

How about one spouse hiring the other as an outside contractor? For starters, you have to meet the IRS criteria for outside contractors. If you do, in effect what you've created are two separate sole proprietorships requiring two separate Schedule C tax returns. Both spouses will be required to pay self-employment tax, and both will be eligible for all sole proprietorship benefits.

The IRS says you should determine whether you are a partnership or a sole proprietorship based on the facts, based on how the business is set up and operated, and not based on the tax consequences.

Regardless of whether the business is a sole proprietorship or a partnership or whether a spouse is on the payroll on not, neither spouse is subject to federal unemployment taxes and neither is eligible for federal unemployment benefits. Most states also exempt husband and wife businesses from state unemployment insurance. Both spouses can participate in a Keogh or SEP retirement plan and, if they meet certain income restrictions, an IRA (Individual Retirement Account) as well.

If you incorporate your husband-and-wife business, the rules are different. Both spouses as owner-employees of a corporation are subject to the same payroll taxes as regular employees. You are eligible for company-paid fringe benefits, and you can set up a corporate retirement plan for yourselves (which is different from a Keogh plan).

In determining how to set up a husband-and-wife operation, much more than the taxes and the paperwork needs to be considered. The structure of the business itself can affect the feelings the couple have toward each other, how well they work together, and (alas) how hard and how fair a divorce might turn out. This is a particular problem in the situation where one spouse is not on the payroll or otherwise "officially" part of the business. One very astute woman pointed out to me, "An unpaid worker is generally an unappreciated worker, causing resentment and possibly a great deal of difficulty in a marriage. Tax savings should not be the number one priority in a husband/wife business arrangement. Mutual respect, sense of responsibility, appreciation, and cooperation are far more important than saving tax dollars. The old saying, 'Penny wise and pound foolish', could very possibly apply to a business arranged just to save a few tax dollars." What's more, if the unpaid spouse had to look for another job, it might be difficult to establish a work history or job worth without a corresponding salary history.

Two Separate Businesses

If a husband and wife each operate their own businesses, where two complete and separate businesses exist (possibly side by side), each spouse is a sole proprietor, each with his and her own set of ledgers, permits and licenses, and Schedule C tax returns. The husband pays self-employment tax on the profits from his business, and the wife pays self-employment tax on the profits from hers. If the couple files a joint tax return, the profit or loss from the two businesses are combined for figuring income tax.

If the two businesses share any assets, share an offic or other business space, or share any other business expenses, the expenses and depreciation should be divided between the two businesses, 50-50 if owned equally by both. It is not important which business actually writes the check or which has the equipment or lease or invoice in its name. Just be sure that each business records its share of the expense in its own ledgers.

Filing Your Business Records

I read somewhere that 85 percent of all business papers that get stuck in the filing cabinet are never looked at again. From my own experience, I can believe it. But it is the other 15 percent of the paperwork that you want or need to locate, and it is the outside chance of an audit, or a lawsuit involving someone who worked for you eight years ago, that makes an organized filing system a necessity for all businesses.

A Northern California business that provides typesetting and graphic design for many small press publishers is owned and operated by a husband and wife, but the business is in the wife's name only. When I inquired why they structured it that way, the wife answered, "Many of our clients, both men and women, seem to prefer to patronize businesses owned by women. I think it brings us more work."

Complete records and a good filing system are as important as a complete bookkeeping system. Every business and financial transaction, every meeting, every action involving employees should be documented and kept for future reference or for proof if you get audited. If all documents—or groups of documents such as sales invoices for the month of March—have their own *labeled* file folder or their own *labeled* envelope, locating them at a later date will be an easy job.

Here is a list of documents you should keep:

1. Articles, by-laws, partnership agreements and other documents that establish and define the business. Keep as long as the business exists.

2. Names, addresses, social security numbers and other pertinent data for all owners and stockholders including date joined and date departed. Keep as long as the business exists.

3. Record of owners' contributions and withdrawals and all other financial transactions between owners and the business. Keep as long as the business exists.

4. Minutes of board meetings. Keep as long as the business exists. You'll find yourself going back to the old minutes many times. If owners ever get in a dispute, old minutes will often provide ready answers.

5. Permits, licenses, insurance policies and leases. Keep as long as they are in force but, for IRS purposes, keep at least three years.

6. Loan papers. Keep as long as the loan is outstanding but, for IRS purposes, keep at least three years. Actually it's a good idea to keep loan papers for as long as the business exists. Though a loan may have been paid off several years ago, you may want to show a bank a record of the old loan when you apply for a new one.

7. Invoices, bills, sales receipts, cash receipts, credit memos and other day-to-day business documents. For IRS purposes, keep at least three years. If your sales documents include customers' names and addresses, you may want to keep them longer should you decide to do a mailing or other promotion.

8. Complete data on all current and past employees: names, addresses, social security numbers, date hired, wage rates and dates of raises, payroll withholding, W-4 exemptions, injuries and workers' compensation claims, evaluations, date employment ended and why. Keep as long as the business exists. It is rare but it does happen that some government agency or court will ask you to produce 15-year-old employment records. If this happens, be sure you are legally required to produce the records and be sure you are not violating a law or an agreement of confidentiality by provid-

ing the records. Either get a written statement from the employee or get some professional advice.

9. Bank deposits, canceled checks and bank statements. For IRS purposes, keep at least three years.

10. Annual profit and loss and other annual financial statements. Keep as long as the business exists. Monthly, periodic or sporadic financial statements probably should be kept two or three years. It is useful to compare monthly profit and loss statements for two or three consecutive years to see if there is a pattern—a cycle—of business activity.

11. Tax returns. Keep a copy of each year's income tax return for as long as the business exists. Assuming payroll tax information is also recorded on individual employee's permanent records, keep payroll tax returns at least three years for IRS purposes. Keep property tax returns for as long as the business exists. Keep all other tax returns, such as sales tax, excise tax, etc., at least three years.

12. Ledgers. Keep as long as the business exists.

HOME-BASED BUSINESSES

I'd guess that on every city block and on every rural road in the United States, someone is operating a business out of a home. Home-based businesses have their own unique problems and rewards, and they are subject to some legal and tax restrictions not imposed on other businesses. Just about everything in this book applies to a home business the same as any other business.

Some businesses are naturally suited to being operated out of a home, and others, of course, are not. Ideal home businesses are those where the location of the business is not a significant factor in the success of the business; businesses that require little physical space; and businesses that do not intrude on neighbors and the character of the neighborhood. So, retail stores, manufacturing operations, restaurants, auto repair shops, and businesses where a lot of customers come to the business premises are usually not suitable for operating out of the home.

The "ideal" home businesses include:

1. Mail-order, unless you must have some huge inventory of goods.

2. Publishing, again depending on the inventory.

"One of the main things that drove me into business was ignorance. I hadn't the faintest idea how the world worked. Bargaining, distribution, mark-up, profit, bankruptcy, lease, invoice, fiscal year, inventory—it was all mystery to me, and usually depicted as sordid.

"I noticed that great lengths were gone to in order to prevent 'consumers' from knowing that part of purchase price went to the retailer. It seemed exquisitely insane to me. You sell deception and buy mistrust, to no advantage. The retailer in fact earns his 25-40 percent by tiresome work, but the prevailing attitude makes him out a clever crook.

"As Buckminster Fuller advises: Always promise less than you deliver, and let customers, business associates, staff come to their own conclusions about you. Small business is based on earned trust. Send cash-with-order in your first dealings with another firm. Pay bills on time. Small businessmen respond faster to honesty than any other kind of person: Most of them don't care what you wear, smoke, or think if you're straight with them and don't care what they wear, smoke, or think.

—Steward Brand in the Whole Earth Catalog

3. Secretarial, typing, bookkeeping, accounting, typesetting, design, computer programming, or similar office services.

4. Any service business where you go to your customers instead of having them come to you, such as cleaning, home repairs, sales agent.

5. Small crafts, as long as the workshop isn't too noisy or smelly, and assuming you deliver your goods to your customers as opposed to having a retail shop or showroom at home.

A home-based business is a good way to get started for a small investment, compared to the cost of leasing, furnishing and maintaining a business premises. It's also an excellent way to test your untested business ideas. I always recommend, whenever possible, that people start a new business with as little money as possible, out of the home, in your spare time, without quitting your regular job. Find out if that business will work, find out if you are cut out to run a business. Some people think they have the world's greatest idea, and maybe they do—but maybe they don't. Some people think they will love being their own boss and find out later they hate it. And everyone makes mistakes, particularly when getting started. A $200 mistake and a $20,000 mistake could be the same mistake. If you start part-time, as cheaply as possible, out of your home, your disasters will always be small ones. You'll also be able to learn your trade and learn business in general in a more relaxed, low-pressure environment.

Some people feel there is a stigma attached to home-based businesses, that such businesses are not well thought of by the public, that they have less credence than conventional businesses, that they're not to be taken as seriously, or they're more amateurish, or some other slight. Having run a business out of my home for over twelve years, I personally do not subscribe to these views, but I do realize that many people do, and that many home-based businesses might benefit by, if not out-and-out hiding the fact that the business is in the home, at least downplaying the fact. You also may just not want strangers, salesmen, and the like coming to your home and bothering the family or the neighbors.

Post Office Boxes

Some businesses use a post office box instead of their street address to hide their location. Unfortunately, this often backfires because a lot of peo-ple, particularly those who don't know you, are suspicious of businesses with P.O. box addresses. Is this a real business, or some scam or fly-by-night operation? It's too easy for you to close the box and disappear. A lot of suppliers ship by UPS (United Parcel Service); unless the UPS driver knows who you are and where you are located, you might not get your delivery. UPS and similar carriers cannot deliver to a post office box. Some magazines and newspapers will not accept advertising with P.O. box addresses.

Some businesses, particularly home mail-order businesses, find they must have a P.O. box. Mail left in a rural delivery box, or on your porch, can get stolen, damaged or blown away. And there are still many places in rural America where there is no house-to-house mail delivery available. In my hometown, everyone has a post office box; all the mail is delivered to the post office only.

Businesses that find they must have a P.O. box often list their street address as well as the box number on stationery, mailing labels, ads, brochures, listings, etc. You might want to discuss this with the local postmaster. The post office is more cooperative than you might think, particularly in rural areas and small post offices; there may be a simple solution to your problem. Also, the next time you see the local UPS driver, flag him (or her) down, introduce yourself, and tell the driver about your business and your location.

Deliveries

United Parcel Service (UPS) will make deliveries right to your door. You don't have to be signed up with UPS to get a delivery. If you want to ship out via UPS and you want UPS to come to your home for pick-ups, you will have to sign up with the company. For a flat-rate weekly charge, UPS will come to your business five days a week to see if you have anything to go out. Weekly, you will receive a bill for the flat-rate charge plus the charge for any packages you ship. The charge per package depends on its weight, how far it's going, whether you want ground or air service, how much it's insured (first $100 of insurance is included in the shipping charge), whether it's going C.O.D. If you only ship once in awhile, you can arrange with UPS to pick up only when you request it rather than every day. Under this arrangement, you call UPS when you have a package to ship, and they pick it up the next day. You pay the per-package charge plus the weekly flat-rate. You don't pay anything if you are not shipping that week.

Trucks will deliver freight to home businesses. If you are expecting a large or very heavy shipment, you should discuss the delivery with the trucking company ahead of time. Some trucks can make street-level deliveries—their doors are low to the ground or they have hydraulic lift gates. Many trucks, however, particularly highway semis, have very high doors requiring unloading at freight docks or with fork lifts. Some truck drivers will help unload freight, and some will expect you to do the unloading. Some trucks will deliver only to the curb or as close as they can drive to your door, and they will expect you to haul the stuff inside. Freight companies charge extra—sometimes quite a bit extra—for inside delivery. If the freight charge is coming C.O.D., find out ahead of time if you will need cash or if the trucker will take a check.

Zoning

Home businesses are often subject to restrictive zoning laws. Zoning laws vary considerably from one location to another. Some communities outlaw home businesses entirely (though I still stand by the first sentence in the introduction to this chapter!), some communities restrict the type and/or size of home businesses, some communities have no restrictions whatsoever. For specific zoning regulations, contact city hall if you are in city limits, or contact county offices if you are outside city limits. Don't tell them who you are; just ask if there are zoning restrictions on home businesses.

Before you get totally bogged down in zoning prohibitions, you should consider the reasons for zoning laws. People do not want a lot of noise, traffic, parking problems and strangers near their homes. They want quiet and peaceful residential neighborhoods. So they banish businesses, which often bring noise and traffic and strangers, to other areas of the community.

If you plan to start a home business where you will be operating noisy machinery in the garage, or where many people will be coming to your home, or where the sign in the window and the business "appearance" of your home detracts from the neighborhood image, you can expect complaints from your neighbors and problems with the zoning authorities.

But if you have some small office business or some quiet (and odorless) crafts business, and if very few if any customers come to your door, you are not likely to disturb your neighbors, and you are not likely to get in trouble with the zoning authorities, even if you are technically breaking the law. Zoning officials don't go snooping around looking for violations; they almost always act only when they receive a complaint.

The first and foremost zoning law, in my opinion, is: Be Considerate Of Your Neighbors. Put yourself in their situation. How would you feel if a neighbor started a business like the one you plan to start? If it seems appropriate to you, talk to your neighbors and tell them of your plans. Find out, before you start your business, if there will be opposition or bad feelings.

What happens if you are operating a home-based business and are suddenly visited by an official of the zoning board, advising you that you are breaking the law? Ask if a complaint has been filed, and if so, why? Are you causing a genuine nuisance? Will the zoning people allow you to alter your practices to eliminate the nuisance? Can you file some petition or request a waiver or variance that will allow you to continue in business? And if worst comes to worst, and you are forced to shut down, can you have 30 or 60 or 90 days to relocate? I am not suggesting that you may have to move in order to run a home business without zoning hassles, but you wouldn't be the first person who did. This is more true of someone who wanted to operate a retail shop or an intrusive workshop as opposed to some office or service-type business.

The town of Yellow Springs, Ohio, with a population of only a few thousand people, recently enacted a zoning ordinance restricting home businesses, limiting the number of employees and the number of "client visits per day," forbidding outdoor storage, and adding a host of other regulations the local newspaper described as, "at best useless, at worst potentially harmful to the community." The editor further stated, "I wrote that hesitantly, because the people who created the law are sound, smart people who intended to create nothing at all like this mess that we have. But when you get into the details of defining just what is a home business which does not unduly disturb a residential area, it becomes almost impossible to draw a fair line that will be applicable to all cases. The best defense of the new law is that it won't be enforced. But of course it will be—not equally against all home occupations but against some in some neighborhoods, where a neighbor demands it. Home businesses can exist, or not exist, according to their neighbors' preference, mood, personality or whim."

Landlords, Condominiums, Homeowners Associations

If you rent your home, live in a condo or co-op, or live in some type of restricted housing development, be sure the lease or ownership agreement does not prohibit a home business. Condominiums in particular often have strictly-enforced restrictions on home businesses.

Telephone

Telephone company rules for home-business phones vary from company to company and from state to state. The rules are set either by the company or by the state Public Utilities Commission. Generally, if you advertise your home phone as a business phone, you are required to have a business listing. If you print your home phone number on business cards, stationery, invoices, etc. (as your business phone, not as "home phone") you are required to have a business listing. And in some states, just using the phone for business requires a business listing.

Business listings are usually more expensive than personal listings, sometimes substantially more expensive. Many home businesses, particularly when getting started, do not get a business listing. If you are required to have a business listing and do not have one, and if the telephone company finds out, they will demand that you switch the phone to a business listing. In fact, the company may simply notify you that you are violating their rules and that they are switching your phone for you, effective immediately. There may or may not be a fine or some other penalty depending on your state's laws. You keep the same phone number.

How would the telephone company find out about you? They are not sleuthing around, looking for "bootleg" home business phones. This kind of rule-breaking is pretty low on their problem list. More often than not, the company finds out from the business owner himself, who, when talking to the company business office about some question or problem or incorrect call, lets it slip that it was a business call. Or, someone having trouble reaching you may contact the telephone company to report your business phone out of order, and the telephone company has no record of the business.

Regardless of telephone company rules, it often is useful and profitable to have a business listing, and for many home businesses, well worth the extra cost. The business listing includes a listing in the white pages and usually a free Yellow Pages entry (a one-line listing; an ad costs extra). Your business is also listed with the directory assistance operator. This is particularly valuable when people have heard of your company but don't know your phone number. If your business is not listed, a lot of these people will not be able to reach you. Often, people who are unfamiliar with your company will call directory assistance, just to find out if you are listed before they purchase something from you, or sell something to you on credit. The telephone listing is some assurance to people that you are most likely legitimate.

When you do list with the telephone company as a business phone, you can also list your personal name in the white pages (and with directory assistance) under the same number, for a small additional monthly fee. As you get more business (and more income) you may reach a point where you want two numbers, one for business and one for personal use; so you can answer one, "Hello," and the other, "Good morning, G.M. Aardvark Adding Machine Repair," or so you can decide not to answer the business phone in off hours, or so the kids can answer the phone without having to pretend they work for some business, or so you don't have the three-year-old answering the phone and frustrating some customer who is calling from the other side of the country. If you have teen-agers, you probably *have* to have a separate business phone; otherwise, no one will ever be able to reach you.

Funny as it may seem, one of the most difficult things to figure out is exactly how to answer a combination business-personal phone. Do you say, "Good afternoon, Aaaable Enterprises, first in service and first in the phone book, Mr. Thermelcrest speaking," only to hear your daughter's best friend giggling at you? Do you say, "Hello," and have a stranger at the other end hesitate and say, "Uh, is this, uh—is this a real business?" Some people answer using the business name during business hours and say hello on off hours, and the hell with the giggles. Some just say, "Good morning," or, "Good morning, Bob speaking." You will have to feel it out; pretty soon you will know what feels most comfortable to you and to the people calling.

You are not required to list an address for a business phone or for a personal phone. So if you don't want people to know where you are located, if you don't want strangers driving up to your home uninvited, you can request that your address be left off your listing.

If your phone is an important link to your customers, make the best use of it. If you will not be available to the phone during regular business hours, hire an answering service or at least get an answering machine: "This is Christopher's Crafts. No one is in the office right now, but if you'll leave your name and number..." Or, "This is Christopher's Crafts. Our regular business hours are Monday through Friday, 10 to 5..." By the way, if you want to encourage people to leave their names and numbers on your answering machine, keep your message brief. People, particularly when calling long distance, do not want to sit through a musical interlude, a recorded chat and a plug for your product. You may enjoy being the star of your own telephone recording, but to many people the telephone answering machine is irritating to start with. Long recorded messages just increase the irritation and make it more likely a prospective customer will simply hang up.

Once you have a business listing, it won't be long before a salesperson from the telephone company will call and try to sell you Yellow Pages advertising. A display ad in the Yellow Pages can be quite valuable to you if you are selling to the local public, particularly if you are trying to reach local people who don't know you. When people are looking for an item or service in the Yellow Pages, they are usually attracted first to the display ads. The tiniest business in the world can look big-time with a good Yellow Pages ad.

There is a real skill to designing effective Yellow Pages advertising. The phone company will be of some help, but you may want to consider getting a professional designer to help you (maybe you can find someone who will trade design help for your product or service). If you are designing your own ad, study other ads in the Yellow Pages. Note the ones you like, and emulate them. Note the ones you dislike, try to figure out what it is about them that you don't like, and avoid the same mistakes. Don't put too much writing in too little space.

Clutter is unattractive to the eye, and people will not take the time to read your ad. Don't waste valuable space with silly illustrations. Give brief, attention-grabbing information: "We stock all makes of geiger counters." "We are the only store in town where you can buy live giraffes." "We repair all brands and types of cameras." "Same day service." If you want people to come to your location, list the days and hours you are open. If the address is hard to locate, give brief directions: "One block west of Main between 6th and 7th."

Some businesses have no real use for Yellow Pages advertising. Many manufacturers and wholesalers, businesses that do specialized work for a limited number of customers, mail order businesses, businesses where you already know all your customers, and businesses that will not be seeking customers locally, have no reason to spend money on a Yellow Pages ad.

I just want a device to circumvent recorded phone messages. These gadgets may be fine (though I doubt it) for local business calls, but I do not see why I have to pay for a long distance call that is answered by a recording that informs me the person I am calling is not in. If no one answered the phone I would be smart enough to figure that out for free. I do not want the person I am calling to spend his money calling me, only to learn that I am not in either, even though I thought I would be. This kind of recorded non-communication has been known to go on for days.

Since it is impossible to convince businesspeople that recorded messages are bad business, why can't someone invent a gadget for a telephone that would prevent a long distance call from ringing when one is not in the office. A caller could hear that the phone is not ringing and hang up rather than having to pay to talk to someone who is not there. How many millions of dollars do we spend a year to find out we are not in? If common sense will not prevail, why not at least a service business which will make recordings sound natural, if that's possible. Normal human beings can't make a recording that says, "I am not here" without choking, giggling, gasping or sounding as if they had just witnessed Armageddon. The humanity in them simply revolts at such a stupid remark.

—Gene Logsdon, In Business *magazine*

Telephones and Tax Deductions

Tax deductions for your home telephone are limited. You may not deduct the basic monthly rate for the first telephone line into the home. Expenses beyond the basic rate, such as business-related long distance calls, optional services, and any special business equipment are deductible. Any additional business lines into the house after the first line are fully deductible if used exclusively for business. For tax purposes, it does not matter to the IRS how the phone is listed, business or personal. The first line into your home is not deductible even if it is listed as a business phone. A second line is fully deductible, regardless of its listing, as long as it is used 100% for business.

Home Offices and Tax Deductions

The Tax section of this book includes IRS rules on home offices, who may take a deduction and what the limits are. The term "home office" applies to any home business space—workshop, warehouse, retail store, etc.—not just an office, and expenses directly related to the space such as utilities and insurance. Failure to qualify for the home office deduction doesn't prohibit you from operating your business out of your home. It only means that one possibly large expense is not deductible on your federal income taxes. You will still be entitled to deduct all legitimate business expenses other than those directly related to the business space itself.

Federal & State Homework Laws

The U.S. Department of Labor, under the Fair Labor Standards Act, and several states, under various state "homework laws," restrict some businesses from hiring employees and outside contractors, if the employees work at their own homes. These laws do not usually apply to a sole proprietor, but only to people the proprietor hires. Contact the U.S. Department of Labor and your state's Department of Labor for details.

Insurance

Most homeowner and home-renter insurance policies specifically exclude home businesses from coverage. Many policies actually void coverage if the home is being used as a business without the insurance company's knowledge and approval. That is, if the house burns down, and if the insurance company finds out you were operating a business in the home, you may not get paid at all, even if the business had nothing to do with the fire. If a visitor, business or personal, is injured at your house, your liability coverage may be invalid because of the unreported business.

So don't keep your business a secret from the insurance company. Tell them your plans ahead of time and arrange for coverage. Most insurance companies will add business coverage as a rider on your regular homeowner's or renter's policy. How eager the insurance company is to insure you, and how much extra it will cost, will depend a lot on the type of business you plan to start, the risks involved, and the number of people—customers, employees, deliveries, etc.—involved. The cost of the insurance will also depend, of course, on how much and what type of insurance you want for the business. The various types of business insurance described in the separate Insurance chapter are usually also available to a home business. Generally, the additional cost of insuring a one-person office in the home—no employees, no manufacturing, few customers, little or no inventory—is very low when added as a rider on a homeowners policy.

"This Is A Business"

People who work in an office, at a store, at a warehouse, at any out-of-the-home business location, are working in an atmosphere that is totally business. It is totally a workplace. Its function is work and only work. For most of these people, the only other people they are in contact with during work hours are co-workers, customers and suppliers. It is an atmosphere conducive to work: you go to work, get your work done, and then you go home.

People who run their businesses out of their homes often do not have that clear-cut distinction of a work-space versus a home-space, and work hours versus personal hours. If you have a family, particularly if you have young children not yet in school, the distinction blurs even more. You may set up your separate office, put it in a spare room or the basement or garage, and you may say, "10 to 4 is work time, period," but you will find again and again that others are not cooperating as much as you'd like. "Keep an eye on the kids for an hour, will you, honey, while I run to the store." Friends call or stop by to visit during work hours. People who would never expect you to take a break in the middle of the day if you are at the office will think nothing of it if you are working at home.

What's the solution? Have firm rules that your workspace and your work hours are to be honored—and then be prepared to have those rules broken regularly. Ever try to explain rules to a three-year-old? Or to a tired spouse who needs a break from the kids for an hour? There has been more than one home business that relocated to a separate business location just to get away from the family and the constant interruptions.

Buying A Business

Buying a going business is certainly a fast way to jump right into the deep water. Instant business. Such a purchase will require a good deal of careful research. There will be legal and tax ramifications most likely requiring professional help. Get all the help you can, and take your time considering this major, major purchase.

How do you find out what businesses are for sale? Sometimes you'll see an ad in the paper, or you might just hear about one. More likely, you will have to ask around. Bankers, local business people, and people active in community affairs are likely to know who has a business for sale. Real estate agents and, if you live in a big city, professional business brokers will know about businesses for sale. But when an agent or broker helps put a deal together, they collect their fee—usually a percent of the sale price—and it will likely increase the price you will pay for the business.

There are three basic factors to consider when buying a going business: (1) Is the business worth buying? (2) Is the price right? (3) Are you the person to take over this business?

Let's consider the last factor first. If the business you want to buy is successful, busy, rolling down the track like a fast freight, are you—the new owner, manager, clerk, employer, bookkeeper, and trouble shooter—ready to handle such an enterprise? Do you have the experience and knowledge to jump right on and keep the business rolling smoothly? Or will your on-the-job training cause disruptions in the operation, possibly displeasing customers enough to lose them?

If the business depends a lot on the owner's personality, or on the owner's training and experi-

Tuli Kupferberg

ence (as in a repair shop or similar service business), taking over that business and keeping the customers might be difficult. Customers get used to certain stores. They expect a certain level of competence, service, convenience, courtesy, from a store they frequent. They expect certain merchandise to always be in stock—the former owner always had it in stock—or they expect a service to be performed within a certain time period they are accustomed to. If you can't get in sync with the way the business is already running, almost immediately, you may find that the customers have little patience for you.

Quite often, the buyer of a business will actually train with the seller, the two working in the store together for a period of time, so that the transition is smooth and easy. Discuss this during your negotiations with the seller, and whatever decision is made, include it in the written purchase agreement.

Once you've decided you are the man/the woman for the job, you must try to determine if this particular business is worth buying. Here are some important questions to ask:

1. Why does the owner want to sell? Is he simply tired out? A lot of business owners, particularly in retail businesses, wear themselves out after five or

six years, working every day. They just want to quit, take a rest, do something else. Is the owner old or ill, and wants or needs to retire? Is the owner in some sort of trouble and needs the cash? Make sure the trouble is not directly related to the business—and be sure to get legal help with this one. Is the business starting to fail? Does the owner "know something," troubling future prospects for the business—problems with the neighborhood, or a tough new competitor about to move in, or some other upcoming development that will be detrimental to the business—and wants to bail out?

2. How profitable is the business? Ask to see the ledgers and the tax returns for the last few years. Tax returns are an excellent source of information since no one tends to *overstate* income or profit on a tax return. If the owner declines to show you income and expense figures, something may be wrong, and you may want to move on. When you examine the ledgers and tax returns, if you don't understand the numbers, hire an accountant to help you. Are the profits on the increase, or on the decline? Is there enough income to provide you a living wage and to eventually pay off the cost of buying the business? Don't forget that the profit from a sole-proprietorship or a partnership will not include any salary for the owner. The profit *is* his salary. If it's a corporation, see how much of a salary the owner is taking. If the business has a hired manager or other employees who won't be needed if you buy the business, eliminating their salaries may improve the profit figure significantly.

3. Is the business in a good location? Can you assume the lease, and how many years are left on the lease? To buy a business with no lease means that the landlord can, on a whim, evict you, triple the rent, lord knows what. Be sure there are no city plans for rezoning that may affect your location.

4. What is the condition of the physical assets? Is the building in need of expensive repair or remodeling? Is the equipment in good shape, or will it need to be repaired or replaced soon? Will you have to sink a lot of money into the business to fix it up the way you want, or possibly to meet a building or health code requirement? Building inspectors sometimes tend to leave old businesses alone but suddenly notice all sorts of code violations when a new owner takes over.

5. What is the competition like? Is it growing? Are the competitors doing a lot more business than this store you want to buy? Can you determine why?

6. How reliable are your suppliers? Are any closing their doors, moving away or making other major changes?

The present owner of the business can probably answer all of these questions, though of course, you can't really expect unbiased answers. If you spend some time and study things closely, you will most likely find your own answers to the above questions. Observe the store, the customers, how much business is being conducted. Does what you see relate to the sales figures in the ledgers? Walk or drive around the area, see for yourself if there is any nearby competition, and how well they are doing. Talk to other business people in the area, particularly close neighbors. Tell them your plans, and ask their opinions. I can virtually guarantee you will get an earful of valuable information.

You should also become Sherlock Holmes with the present owner's figures. If this is a sales business, check month-to-month purchases as some indicator of how fast the inventory sells once it's in stock (called "turnover"). It also may indicate if the business has seasonal cycles—slow at one time of year, busy at others. And how well do the purchases relate to sales? There should be some correlation. Does the owner keep any of the purchases for himself, such as food in a grocery or restaurant? Check the inventory carefully. It may be much larger or smaller than the owner tells you, and it may be damaged or obsolete or simply unsalable. How much dust is on it? For any type of business, be suspicious of any recent high legal fees. What were they for? If you see loan or interest

---

When a certain elegant hotel first opened, guests complained frequently about the long wait for elevators in the lobby. A task force was called in to study the problem, and various solutions were proposed: a computer to run the elevators, doors that opened and shut faster, express service to the top floors. In the end, the hotel simply installed mirrors in the lobby. What with combing their hair, adjusting their ties, and checking their hems, patrons didn't notice the wait. Complaints ceased immediately. The point is, sometimes the problem isn't the problem at all.

—Ed Oleksiak, Innotech Corporation.

payments, find out what they were for. If you won't be assuming a loan, you won't be making those payments.

Finally you come to the most difficult question of all: How much should you pay for this business? Despite what the seller may tell you or what the textbooks may say, there are few real guidelines and no reliable formulas when it comes to such a huge, unique, emotion-laden transaction as the purchase of a going business. The bottom line, always, is that a business is worth no more than what a buyer will pay for it. The seller may *have* to sell this business; but you, the buyer, do not have to buy it. It is up to you to determine what you are willing to pay for it, and then find out if the seller will accept your offer.

You should realize that the seller has probably never sold a business before, certainly not this particular business. He probably knows what the business is worth, but he really has no idea what he can expect to get for it. A business is not like a used car, or even a house, when it comes to figuring out what price it will fetch. Comparisons are difficult, and prospective buyers are usually few. So, the seller is in the dark himself when setting a sale price. Quite often, the asking price is no indication at all of what the business will actually sell for. Businesses will often sell for half or even a third of the asking price.

The actual value of the inventory and equipment—what the present owner can sell it for if the business is closed and liquidated—is usually the bottom-dollar value of a business. A surprising number of successful businesses actually sell for close to this amount. So, first you must determine this value. The seller's original cost of inventory and equipment is a guideline, but you must consider age, wear, damage, and possible obsolescence.

Then, you can be sure the seller will want, on top of the value of the assets, additional money because the business is already successful, earning a profit, established. Some people call this intangible value "goodwill," and they attempt to put a price on it, some dollar figure they pull out of the air (which is probably why this is also called, in business jargon, "blue sky"). Often, the seller will ask for the equivalent of one or even two years' profits. Again, throw out the formulas. It is entirely up to you the buyer to decide if you want (and can afford) to pay for some or all of this "blue sky."

Keep in mind that the purchase price of the business is just a start. You will still need money for working capital (day to day expenditures, overhead, new inventory, etc.) and possibly for repairs, remodeling or sprucing up.

Whenever you consider buying a going business, you should also consider how much it would cost to set up, from scratch, a new, similar business at a different location. Why buy someone else's expensive business when you can start your own a lot cheaper?

Once the buyer and the seller of a business agree on the purchase price and payment terms, you will probably need professional help to draft a complete sales agreement. Everything regarding the sale should be in writing. The precise legal wording can have a major effect on how the sale is taxed, how the assets are valued for tax purposes, and how much of the purchase price will be deductible. The buyer should also be particularly careful that he will not unknowingly inherit old business debts, liabilities, lawsuits, or other problems he shouldn't be responsible for.

The costs of investigating businesses you are interested in buying come under a variety of IRS rules. General costs incurred before you actually pick a specific business you want to buy, such as travel expenses and general research, are usually not deductible at all. Once you are trying to purchase a specific business, the costs you incur are considered capital expenditures. (Whenever you see the word "capital" in tax law, it usually means you won't be able to write off your expenses right away.) If you do not finally buy the business, you have incurred a loss that may be deductible under the IRS's capital loss rules. If you do buy the business, the costs must be capitalized according to the "Start Up" rules explained in the Tax section of this book.

Freelance Writers, Photographers and Artists

Freelancers are in business for themselves, much like all other business people, no matter how reluctant they are to deal with it. Freelancers should read the chapter in the Growing Up section on "outside contractors." Many freelancers fall into

---

Business is easy. You buy low and sell high. Those accountants, marketing experts, engineers and all the rest are just confusing the issues.

—R. Farmer, Indiana Univ.

this category, responsible for their own business records, licenses, tax returns, and everything else covered in *Small-Time Operator*.

Freelancers sometimes get cash advances, deposits on work to be performed, advances on royalties. How are these handled? You should first read the chapter "Cash Vs. Accrual Accounting" in the Bookkeeping section. If you use cash accounting, as many freelancers do, the money is considered earned income, subject to taxes, when you receive it. If you refund all or part of it at a later date, you reduce your income at that time. This is similar to the "Sales Returns" described in the Bookkeeping section.

Accrual basis businesses recognize income when it is earned, not when cash changes hands. Any advance not yet earned is not considered taxable income until you do the work. This sometimes becomes a problem at year-end, if you have received an advance for work partially completed at December 31.You will have to report at least part of the advance, to the extent earned, on your tax return. This calculation may require an accountant's help. By the way, if a writer's advance on royalties is not refundable—you keep it whether the book sells or not—it is not considered an advance. It is current earned income, currently taxable.

Freelance artists, writers and photographers have been blessed with a special IRS exemption from the onerous "uniform capitalization rules" imposed on craftspeople and other manufacturers. The rules are covered at length in the Inventory chapter of the Tax section. Basically, producers of goods may not write off their production expenses until they've sold the goods they produced.

Self-employed artists, writers and photographers do not have to abide by the uniform capitalization rules. They may write off their expenses the year incurred. These rules apply to individuals who create literary manuscripts, musical compositions, dance scores, photographs, photographic negatives or transparencies, pictures, paintings, sculptures, statues, etchings, drawings, cartoons, graphic designs, or original print editions. The rules do *not* apply to craftspeople, cabinetmakers, potters, jewelers, print makers, film makers, and others in business providing similar products. Obviously, there is fine line here that must be carefully observed.

If you earn royalties, the income tax rules vary, depending upon your situation. If you are self-employed as a freelancer and royalties are a regular source of income, the IRS considers the royalties to be business income, handled the same as any other business income with regular business deductions, reported on Schedule C (if you are a sole proprietor), and subject to regular business taxes including self-employment tax. Everything in *Small-Time Operator* that applies to other small businesses also applies to you.

If, however, your royalties are only a secondary or minor part of your income—a little sideline source of income—the royalties are usually considered non-business income, reported on Schedule E of your 1040 tax return. You are entitled to deductions for some of your expenses, but your Schedule E income is not subject to self-employment tax and is not eligible for self-employed health insurance deductions nor self-employed retirement deductions.

Obviously, this can be a confusing area of law, particularly for sideline and part-time freelancers. Determining how to account for royalty income and expenses may require help from an experienced accountant. Quite a bit of tax money, particularly in self-employment taxes, may be at stake.

COMPUTERS

Some businesses will find computers virtually essential, a tremendous help and time saver. Other businesses will have little or no use for a computer.

As a bookkeeping tool, the computer can produce ledgers as simple as those described in Small-Time Operator or as elaborate as you want. If you find hand posting ledgers a tedious, lengthy, repetitious job, a computer can make the bookkeeping less time consuming and maybe even a little fun.

Financial analysis, such as comparative (month to month and year to year) sales or expense data, broken down into any categories you want, can be quick and easy on the computer. It might be a long job when done by hand. If you prepare regular profit-and-loss statements, balance sheets, cash flow projections, partners' capital accounts, or any other financial summaries, a good computer program can turn them out for you quickly.

As a day-to-day management tool, a computer can help a business keep all manner of inventory records, customer lists, and all kinds of needed files. Computers can prepare invoices for you, shipping documents, letters, brochures, and a pile of other documents you may find essential—or useless, or somewhere in between.

Computers cannot organize your business for you, generate sales, increase your profits or scare away the IRS. A computer will provide you with information (all of which is available without a computer). You still have to understand the information, and you still must make your own decisions.

A computer is not just another piece of office equipment like a typewriter or a copier. Mastering a business computer and getting it to provide accurate information the way you want it will require an initial commitment of time, learning how to use this machine.

Computers continue to get smaller and less expensive and capable of more and more functions. The needs of any small business, however, can easily be met by today's computers. So in that respect, a computer you buy now—as long as it can meet all your needs—will not become obsolete. But as newer computers are designed and marketed, the older models will probably be discontinued. Parts may be difficult to obtain. Will you have to junk your computer for lack of a $30 plastic gizmo?

Computers do occasionally malfunction, and the results can be anything from a nuisance to a disaster. A "glitch" is a computer term for a temporary malfunction, usually caused by overheating, static electricity or voltage fluctuations in the power lines. Such malfunctions can destroy programs and wipe out data. You can prevent disaster by making duplicate copies of your programs and records.

You should also be aware of the delicate nature of disks and the need to handle and store them carefully. Dust and dirt or fingerprints on disks can make them unreadable, and so can old age.

The computer itself may break down and require servicing (and how much will that cost you?). If your day-to-day operations are dependent upon your computer, a shut down computer means a shut down business. I personally know a wholesale business that actually had to close its doors for two weeks because its computer malfunctioned and wouldn't properly prepare sales invoices and shipping documents.

If a computer will be a great help to the actual day-to-day operation of your business, you may want to acquire one right away. But if you plan to use the computer only for bookkeeping, financial analysis, and the occasional letter or file, I suggest

you wait. You will have your hands full (and your bank account empty) just getting the business off the ground. After you've gotten to know your business, after it is running smoothly, once you know exactly what information you want and need, and especially once you know what you can and cannot afford, then you are ready to consider a computer.

Talk to other business owners who do use computers. Find out what the owners do with their computers, how useful they are, how expensive they are, how difficult they are to master.

Here is a list of considerations when you shop for a computer:

1. Can the computer handle all your needs for now and for the foreseeable future? Every computer is a little different and every one has different capabilities. Some computers are expandable—components can be purchased at a later date giving you additional functions and added capacity—and some computers cannot be expanded at all. For those that can be expanded, will the computer and its add-on components still be in production a few years later when you are ready to expand?

2. Is the equipment reliable? Well-built computers don't often break down, but every computer will eventually need maintenance or repair. How readily available and how expensive is computer repair? Some manufacturers and retailers offer maintenance contracts though many users find it less expensive to purchase repair work as needed.

3. Most computer manufacturers sell their own prepackaged programs. Many of the best commercially prepared programs, however, are designed and marketed by people who do not manufacture hardware. Can your computer handle these commonly used programs or will it require its own custom-written programs?

4. Every business operates a little differently, so every bookkeeping system is a little different. When you purchase software—a ledger program or an inventory control program—will it give you all you want or will it force you to make compromises you won't like? Can you alter the program to fit your needs? Some programs can be altered and some cannot.

5. Computers and software come with instruction manuals (called "documentation"). You will be referring to the manuals over and over again. It is essential that they make sense to you. Some manuals are well written but some are virtually impossible to understand. If the instructions are talking about "matrix input/output interface" when all you want to find out is how to get your monthly net profit, keep shopping around.

Many people already own small personal computers. Maybe you bought the kids a cheap computer for Christmas a few years ago, along with a dozen video games you hope you never have to see again. For a few months, it was *Pac Man* and *Galaxy Invaders* every evening. It was real cute to type in all your in-laws' birthdays and watch the computer type them back out at you, or to try to balance the family budget and find out that no matter what the computer told you, the real answer was still, Impossible. But now the kids have rediscovered softball, swimming and their ten-speeds, and the computer is buried in the closet, unused and forgotten. Well, that computer probably can perform some business functions, particularly simple bookkeeping. The popular, inexpensive spread-sheet programs can run on many very small computers. What's more, even though the computer was a non- business purchase, if you use it in your business you are entitled to a business tax write-off. For more information, see the Depreciation chapter in the Tax Section.

If you use your computer partly for business and partly for non-business use, you must keep a log (dates and hours) of the usage.

If you are not quite ready for a computer, you might want to consider a word processor. A word processor is a combination mini-computer and typewriter. You can compose letters on the video-display screen, correct and re-word them and get them just the way you want them; then push a key, and the word processor types out your finished letter. You can store the letter on a computer disk, and change it or retype it or use parts of it in another letter, any time you want. You can do the same thing with advertising copy, brochures, invoices and other business forms, mailing lists, and address files. The word processor can check your spelling and grammar for you, and help you format and lay out your documents. Some word processors have built-in spreadsheets that enable you to create simple ledgers, complete with calculations. A top quality word processor costs much less than a computer and requires very little time to learn how to use.

One of the best introductions I've seen, for using a computer, is a chapter in an excellent best-selling guidebook for landlords and landladies, *Landlording,* by Leigh Robinson. Leigh has been using computers for years, to keep track of the properties he manages, to keep his business records, to edit and typeset his excellent series of property management books, and to help him run his publishing company. (Anyone whose business will be landlording or property management should order a copy of *Landlording,* $24.95 postpaid, from Ex-Press, Box 1639, El Cerrito, CA 94530; or write for their catalog of related titles.) Leigh has given me permission to reprint part of his chapter, titled:

"Using A Computer"

Before you start thinking about using a computer, you really ought to learn a little computer jargon, "tech talk."

Jargon helps people engaged in similar pursuits understand each other quickly. Computer people use jargon just as you unwittingly do. They use so much of it that one group of computer people using one type of computer frequently cannot understand their colleagues who use another type of computer. Four words they all understand, though, are "hardware," "software," "programs," and "files," and you should understand what they mean, too. They're essential terms.

"Hardware" in computer jargon is anything you can see and touch. That includes the computer which sits on your desk, the keyboard your fingers tap on, the screen you look at, and the printer which gives you print on paper. "Hardware" also includes the disk drives which store information on disks much as videotape machines store information on tape cassettes.

"Software" in computer jargon is anything you can't see or touch. Computer programs which do word or number processing are "software" as are instructions which tell the computer where to find what's stored in its memory. Software is essential to making hardware work the way you want it to. A movie stored on a videocassette is software. You can't see it unless the videotape player interprets it for you. You can't touch it, yet you know the movie is there. The same is true with computer software. You know that something is in there interpreting your commands. You just can't see it. That's the software at work.

"Programs" are software. You can't see them or touch them. They're stored on magnetic disks, magnetic tape, or on computer memory "chips." They are very detailed instructions written by computer programmers to make computers act in certain ways in response to user commands. Programs turn computers into many different things. There are programs which make personal computers act like office calculators, flight simulators, electronic typewriters, speed reading machines, filing cabinets, telephone dialers, video arcade machines, drawing boards, musical instruments, utility usage monitors, photograph retouchers, and animation editors.

"Files" are software, too. They're what you, the computer user, save. When you write a letter on a computer or enter a whole series of numbers that you want to save, you save them on a magnetic disk as a file. Once they're stored on disk, you can retrieve them whenever you want.

Spreadsheet Programs:

Spreadsheet programs are not the only computer programs which process numbers, but they're the easiest for ordinary people like us to learn and use. Spreadsheets, along with word processing, do more to justify the use of a computer than any other programs because they're so versatile and powerful. They can do so much.

A computer spreadsheet program consists of what resembles a large piece of graph paper inside the computer. Each one of the graph paper's little boxes, or "cells," as they're called, may be labeled individually with a column and row designation, like every good seat in a college football stadium. The very first cell in the upper left-hand corner of a spreadsheet is A1 ("A" is the column and "1" is the row). The very last one in the bottom right-hand corner, depending on how many cells your spreadsheet program has, might be BK63 ("BK" is the column and "63" is the row.)

Now, if these carefully identified cells could hold only numbers, they'd be about as useful as a curl of calculator tape in a wastebasket. We'd have to keep asking ourselves what the numbers meant, just as we'd be asking ourselves what a radio sportscaster meant in announcing, "We have two great basketball scores for you, folks, 89 to 88 and 106 to 104!" You'd have to admit that those were great scores. But they wouldn't mean anything without team names attached to them.

So, spreadsheet programs allow you to put words into their cells as well as numbers, but what's more important, they allow you to put formulas (add up what's in cells A6 through AH6 and

---

Not so long ago, information was a place you called to get someone's phone number. Information was no big deal, just discreet bundles of data, sometimes useful, often not. But then information got redefined and became very important, became in fact the name of our age. We are, we are told, having an information explosion in an information society with an information economy in the midst of the Information Age. The important thing seems to be having lots and lots of data, regardless of content or meaning. A huge problem is that information has become synonymous with knowledge and intelligence, and computers have become synonymous with all these terms. There is a dangerous illusion that what a computer generates is scientific or objective.
—Bernard Zilbergeld, San Francisco Chronicle

put the sum in cell G6) and cell references (look at another cell and put its value or formula in this one) there, too. These formulas and cell references are what make spreadsheet programs versatile and powerful.

Because a blank computer spreadsheet has so many cells waiting to be filled and so many capabilities waiting to be used, it has tremendous potential in and of itself, but you won't see the true extent of that potential until you have filled some of those cells with a carefully prepared layout, which you can use over and over again. These cell layouts are called "templates." They're actually nothing more than words and formulas which you use frequently.

Rather than begin each computer spreadsheet session with a blank spreadsheet and put into it the same words and formulas you've used before and know you'll use again, you use a template, one you make up yourself or one you buy from someone else.

Except for one essential difference, a spreadsheet template is much like any of the bookkeeping forms in this book. The big difference is that the spreadsheet template has a "calculator" built right into it and that this calculator performs its mathematical calculations automatically.

Were you manually posting a series of numbers on a paper bookkeeping form, you'd first have to enter the numbers on the form and then you'd have to run a calculator tape to total them. You'd be entering every number twice and doubling your odds for making errors. Using a spreadsheet program and template, you'd be entering the numbers only once. The built-in calculator would take over from there, so you'd have fewer opportunities to make mistakes.

I would like to caution you here to examine closely every spreadsheet template you create. A simple formula error in one cell will be magnified whenever that formula affects any other cell. The error will just keep being repeated. Neither the computer nor the program knows any better. If, for example, you inadvertently tell the program to put the sum of every cell from H7 through H54 into cell H56, when you meant to include cell H6, too, you're going to have a problem. The problem may not surface for a while if you seldom enter a number in cell H6, and even when you do enter a number in H6, you may not notice what's wrong in H56. There won't be any bells blowing or error messages appearing on your viewing screen. The error will just creep in quietly, on little rat feet.

If that ever happens, you'll know why computer people are so mindful of the phrase, "Garbage in, garbage out!" Do be careful. Spreadsheets are powerful, but they're also unforgiving.

Data Base Management Programs:

Data base management programs are essentially filing programs but with math functions added. Your telephone book is a large data base, and all the names in it are filed alphabetically according to last names. If you wanted a list of all the people who have a certain telephone prefix or live on a certain street, you'd have to sit down and laboriously make a list of them. Ah, but if you have your whole telephone book entered into a data base management program, all you'd have to do to get a list of the people who live on Tewkesbury Street and have a 555 prefix is ask for it. The program would then sort through everyone looking for those two things in combination and it would print you a list.

Canned Programs:

So-called "canned programs" are different from word processing, spreadsheet, and data base management programs. Canned programs are not nearly so flexible as the others. They are not written to be flexible; they're written to perform specific tasks. In that, they might be said to resemble the combination of a spreadsheet program *and* a particular spreadsheet template. They do one thing and they should do it well because they can't be modified to do anything else.

Some canned programs are truly excellent. There are, however, a lot of canned business programs on the market which are, quite simply, terrible because they take a long time to learn or because they don't do very much of what you want them to.

Buyer of canned programs, beware!

Be wary, by all means, of the program which is sold as a complete software package. First, they're not going to be cheap. Second, they're not going to do all that you want them to do. And third, they're going to be difficult or impossible to change. They're set up one way and that's it.

If you are inclined to purchase any canned program for more than $200, make arrangements to try it out first before you buy. I have one which cost over $2,000 sitting on a shelf. It didn't work out for me, and I couldn't get my money back when I finally discovered that it wouldn't. That expensive lesson from Hard Knocks College you needn't learn the expensive way.

General Recommendations

Try to find someone who's using the hardware or software you're interested in acquiring and ask them how they like it. For contacts, try local business organizations, or call your area's high school or college computer department or attend a meeting of a local computer club.

Do not buy any piece of computer hardware or software until you can see an immediate need for it. There's not one computer or computer-related purchase I have ever made, whether it's been on sale or not when I bought it, which I couldn't buy today for less money that what I originally paid for it. Because you have to spend some time learning how to use each new piece of software for your computer, buying a whole batch of software which you can't use right away is foolish. By the time you get around to using all that you bought, there will be newer, improved versions available, and you'll have to pay extra for the updates.

To avoid many frustrations, buy a hardware configuration which comes with a mouse and works with "windowing" ("graphic user interface"—GUI) software. All Apple Macintoshes fit into this category and so do some IBM-PC's and PC compatibles. Windowing-GUI software takes little time to learn; that's why it's so desirable. Make sure that your system has two disk drives capable of storing at least 360K apiece. It should also have a printer capable of printing readable letters and reports.

Consider buying a used computer. Even the newer computer models appear for sale used, sold presumably by those who have to try the latest of everything without thinking about how they're going to use it. Used computers are available through your daily newspaper's classified ads and through computer flea markets. You may also find them listed on bulletin boards at computer stores and elsewhere. A used computer is much less expensive than new equipment, and the seller usually throws in some disks, accessories, and software at no extra charge. If you do acquire any used software, make sure that the seller gives you all the original diskettes and the documentation and agrees to help you get the software license transferred into your name.

Do not buy any used computer which lacks the manufacturer's serial number. Serial numbers on computer equipment are printed on adhesive labels which get peeled off when the equipment changes hands illegitimately. If you can't find a serial number on the equipment, it's probably stolen. The first thing a computer repairer looks for is that serial number, so it should be one of the first things you look for when you're contemplating the purchase of a used system; no serial number, no purchase.

Check your insurance policy to make sure it specifically includes your personal computer. Some don't. Some specifically exclude personal computers. If your insurance agent doesn't write computer insurance, ask other computer owners who writes theirs. It's inexpensive.

Always "back up" your work; that is, make duplicate copies of it on another disk. Power outages, magnetic fields, defective disks, operator error, disk drive problems, software worms, static electricity, and coffee spills all conspire now and then to cause you to lose the work which you spent hours on. The loony bins are full of people who didn't back up their work. Don't join them.

Trademarks

A trademark is a word, a name, a slogan or expression, a symbol, design or logo, or some combination of these, adopted by a business to identify its goods and distinguish them from goods manufactured or sold by others.

You acquire a basic trademark right, though with limited legal protection, simply by creating and using your trademark. You can acquire exclusive legal rights to a trademark by registering it with the U.S. Patent & Trademark Office. You may apply for and protect a trademark for up to

---

"Gato is a computer game that simulates World War II submarine warfare, but it has a feature that's made it incredibly popular with the office set. No matter where the user is in the game, all he or she has to do is hit the "delete" key, and bingo— away go the submarines and up pops a screen full of numbers. It looks like a real spreadsheet, and it has pulled the wool over the eyes of many a boss."
—reported in Inc. Magazine

three years before actually using it or any time after you start to use it. Generally, federal protection applies to trademarks that will be used in interstate commerce: you must be doing business across state lines or your product must cross state lines in the normal course of business.

The government charges a fee to register a trademark. The initial registration remains in force for ten years—but you must file a Declaration of Use statement between the fifth and sixth years. The trademark may then be renewed every ten years, for as long as you like. For more details, write the Patent & Trademark Office, U.S. Department of Commerce, Washington DC 20231.

The familiar ® symbol means that a trademark is officially registered with the U.S. Trademark Office, and full legal protection has been secured. The equally familiar ™ symbol (or "SM", for "service mark", if the mark identifies a service) is a formal notice that you are claiming ownership of a trademark but have not registered it. The ™ (or "SM") symbol can be used even if no federal trademark application is pending. Using this symbol, however, does not provide the full legal protection accorded a registered ® trademark.

Patents

A patent is a grant issued by the federal government giving an inventor the exclusive right to make, use and sell the invention in the United States. A patent may be granted to the inventor or discoverer of any new and useful process, machine, design or composition of matter, or any new and useful improvement of such. A patent will not be granted on a useless device (the government's definition of useless, not mine), on printed matter, on a method of doing business, on an improvement in a device that would be obvious to a skilled person or on a machine that will not operate. The government says it never has and never will issue a patent on a perpetual motion machine.

A patent will not be granted if the invention was in public use or on sale in the country for more than a year prior to filing your patent application. Also, an inventor is not entitled to a patent if the invention has been described in a publication more than a year before the patent application was filed.

Applying for and obtaining a patent is a lengthy and highly complex proceeding and usually requires help from a patent attorney or agent. Only attorneys and agents registered with the Patent & Trademark Office may handle patent applications.

Patents are usually expensive. The government charges filing fees, issuance fees, periodic maintenance fees, and sometimes fees for printing and claims work. Attorney fees can run into hundreds, and sometimes thousands of dollars.

A patent is good for 17 years—but only if you pay the government's required maintenance fees— and may not be renewed or extended. Anyone has free right to use an invention covered by an expired patent.

For more information, write the U.S. Patent & Trademark Office, U.S. Dept. of Commerce, Washington, D.C. 20231

Copyrights

A copyright protects the work of an author, illustrator or composer. Literary, dramatic, musical and artistic works can be protected by copyright. The owner of a copyright has exclusive rights to print, reprint and copy the work; to sell or distribute copies of the work; to dramatize, record or translate the work; and to perform the work publicly.

Writing and illustrations and musical compositions can be copyrighted. Ideas and concepts cannot, nor can names and titles, nor can *things*. A description of a machine could be copyrighted as a writing, but this would not prevent others from writing a description of their own or from making and using the machine.

Under the old copyright law, a copyright was obtained first by printing a copyright notice—the word "copyright" or the symbol "©", the year and your name—on the face or on the title page of the work, and then registering the work with the U.S. Copyright Office. To publish a work without a copyright notice automatically put it in the public domain; you permanently lost your exclusive rights to it.

U.S. law no longer requires a copyright notice. You own the copyright to your work whether it includes a copyright notice or not. But to avoid confusion, the Copyright Office strongly recommends that you print a copyright notice anyway. This will eliminate the possibility that someone will innocently reprint your work, thinking it isn't protected. This is known as "innocent infringement", and legal remedies are limited.

Copyright protection exists from the moment a

work is created. However, in order to receive full protection from the courts, including recovery of legal fees and a claim for statutory damages, a work and its updates must be registered with the Copyright Office of the Library of Congress. You fill out a simple form, pay a $20 fee and send the Copyright Office two copies of the work.

A copyright is good for your lifetime plus 50 years; it's not renewable. For more information and blank forms, write the Register of Copyrights, Library of Congress, Washington, D.C. 20540.

Artists: The Visual Artists Rights Act protects, in certain cases, original paintings, drawings, sculptures and some exhibition photographs from being altered or destroyed after the works are sold. Movies, books, posters and promotional materials are excluded.

Tax Deductions For Patents, Trademarks & Copyrights

Patents, trademarks and copyrights are considered "intangible assets." Their costs may not be written off when incurred. Patents and copyrights can be depreciated. Trademarks cannot be written off until disposed of.

Franchise Business

A franchise is an individually owned business operated as though it was part of a large chain. Midas Muffler, Kentucky Fried Chicken—KFC, McDonalds and H&R Block are examples of well known national franchises. Under a franchise operation, services and products are standardized; trade marks, advertising and store appearance are uniform. Your own freedom and initiative are obviously limited. But a well known franchise gives you "instant recognition"—the goods and services of the franchiser are proven and trusted. Or as an old Holiday Inn advertisement read, "No surprises here."

For a fee, the supplier (the franchiser) gives you (the franchisee) the right to use the franchiser's name and sell his product or service. The franchise agreement may require you to purchase your supplies or equipment from the franchiser; you may have to pay the franchiser a percentage of your gross sales. Franchise agreements are usually lengthy and full of requirements you must adhere to.

There are hundreds of franchise companies in the United States, some well known but some completely unknown, some with a good, profitable history, and some struggling like any other business. Their appeal to franchisees seems to be two-fold. One, they offer what they call a "turn-key" operation, a complete ready-to-run business (all you have to do is turn the key in the door) that includes training, management support and even some customer leads.

The second aspect is that franchisors often help with financing. Franchisors have their own loan sources; a few even own their own finance companies. But be warned: the franchisors will require you to put up a chunk of money of your own, and they may even want a second mortgage on your home to guarantee their loan to you. Just because it's a franchise, even a well-known franchise, there's no guarantee that it or you will be successful. If you can't make your payments, the franchisor will not hesitate to foreclose, and then re-sell the franchise to the next dreamer.

Before signing any franchise agreement, investigate the franchise thoroughly. The Federal Trade Commission requires franchisers to give prospective franchisees—before any agreement is signed—detailed and accurate information on the earnings franchisees can reasonably expect, the costs they will incur, the company's history and financial standing and terms of the agreement. Gasoline companies and auto manufacturers are exempt from this law.

Get a complete list of all franchisees and contact as many as you can. Find out how they are doing and what they think of the franchise. One expert on franchises, John deYoung of the National Business Association, suggests that you always ask franchisees, "If you had to do it over again, would you invest in this franchise?" Contact everyone who is suing the company and find out their side of the story.

Once you've done all the investigating you can do on your own, then be sure to have a lawyer and an accountant review the contract with you and explain to you *exactly* what you're getting into.

There are several thick books that list names and addresses and detailed information for individual franchises. Some of these books are updated every year. Your local library probably has a book listing franchises, or you can inquire at a Small Business Administration office.

How To Avoid Crooks:
Cost-Free and Common-Sense Procedures, Guidelines and Self-Warnings to Deal with New Accounts, Questionable Operations & Suspicious Strangers.

There are a lot of hustlers and con-artists in the world. Naive small business owners are particularly vulnerable, and every business, I suspect, gets "burned" once or twice. I am not talking about armed robbery or shoplifters or embezzlers. I'm referring to people who offer to buy from you or sell to you or some other business dealing. Pretty quickly, however, you start to recognize these kinds of people, and you learn how to deal—or not to deal—with people you are suspicious of.

In one business I helped set up and operate, which sold books wholesale and retail through the mail, I developed some systems and guidelines, safeguards for our business, that protected us from the rip-off artists as well as from people who struck us as suspicious but may in fact have been quite honorable. It is important that any procedures you set up appear to apply to everyone you deal with, so as not to offend people who may turn out to be valuable customers.

The first person who ever "took" us was a man who came by our booth at a book trade show. He was well dressed, in his fifties, and he handed me a nicely printed business card. He owned some distribution company in Arizona and asked us to ship him three cases of books with a bill. And, poof, he was gone. He got the books, and we got a "no such number" recording when I tried to call him to ask when our payment was forthcoming. Today, twelve years and many experiences later, I would be immediately suspicious of the man, the way he approached us, the look in his eye, the too casual dealing.

But suspicious or not suspicious, here is how I would suggest handling a new, untested and maybe untrustworthy account. The easiest way, of course, is Cash Up Front. We instituted a written sales policy, just a half-size sheet of paper we printed up and handed out to most prospective (and unknown to us) dealers and wholesalers. It stated, "We request that your first order be prepaid." As an extra incentive, we offered an additional 5% discount for prepayment. Some people offer free shipping for prepayment. This may sound like the end of your problems, period, but of course it isn't. All rules are made to be broken, and

you will always find yourself dealing with people who, for any of a thousand reasons, cannot or will not prepay (maybe they don't trust *you*)—and do you do business with them anyway? Do you take a chance? Sometimes that's what business is all about.

Minimize your risk. Like the cardinal rule of gambling, don't ship more than you can afford to lose. Tell them you will send them one case of whatever-it-is, so they can "try it out and see how it does"; and as soon as they use it up or sell it or whatever it is they're doing with it, *and pay for it,* you will be more than happy to ship some more. Emphasize that yours is a small business, and thanks to a lack of red tape and bureaucracy, you can ship reorders very quickly.

By the way, here is a little warning about shipping C.O.D. We once received an order for six cases of books from someone we did not know, and the guy said to send them C.O.D. We shipped six cases on the UPS, and put the C.O.D. tag—one bill for all six cases—on one of the cases. They were shipped as one lot, marked 1 of 6, 2 of 6, etc. Well, two weeks later, the case with the C.O.D. tag comes back refused, and Lo And Behold, the other five cases do not come back. No payment ever came either. If you ship C.O.D. to someone you do not know or trust, put a C.O.D. tag on every package.

One thing I suggest you do when you get an order (not prepaid) in the mail from a company you don't know, call Directory Assistance and ask them if they have a listing for the business. The telephone company charges a small fee for this now, but it is cheap insurance. No listing doesn't mean the company isn't legitimate (many home businesses are not listed) and, likewise, a business listing does not vouchsafe for it either, but it certainly is an indicator as to whether you're dealing with reputable people. Personally, I am immediately cautious of a company without a business listing; we usually stuck to the written policy and demanded prepayment.

If you do get the company's telephone number, and the order is big enough to warrant a long-distance call, call the company "to confirm the order," maybe inquire how they want it shipped, maybe tell them of your special prepayment offer, and definitely ask if you are going to get paid.

When dealing with someone for the first time and extending them credit, be very direct about being paid. Tell them you will be happy to extend credit, but you need their assurance that you will

be paid. If you are dealing face to face, look the person right in the eye. And get the person to say, "Yes, I will pay this bill." Sometimes they'll say, "Well, this and that corporation extend us credit, we have an AA#1 Dun & Bradstreet rating, we are an established business, member of the Chamber of Commerce" and various and sundry impressive stuff that is of absolutely no value to you. Just repeat that all you need is their assurance you will be paid. It's a powerful "Yes" when they say it. Even crooks have a hard time going back on their word.

If a bill goes past due, get on it right away. The longer you wait to try to collect it, the less likely you'll collect. Many people have little money, and they pay as they can until they just call it quits and disappear or file bankruptcy. You want to get paid before this happens, and squeaky wheels get greased. Write. Telephone once a week. Be friendly and understanding, but be persistent. Don't be hostile or threatening—it gets nowhere, and that's the truth—but be persistent. And if it finally becomes apparent that you aren't going to get your money, just drop it and forget it. It's bad enough not getting paid, no sense twisting the knife in your own wound with anger and ulcers and lost sleep.

Retail customers are easier to deal with. People don't usually expect to get credit, and they don't usually ask. When we received a retail order in the mail, "Please send one book and bill me," we almost always declined. Even if the person is honest (and most are) it's simply not worth the time, the invoices, the credit ledgers, writing for payment, etc. We sent an order form and a note saying that "We request prepayment on all retail orders." The word "all" is important because it implies no bias or suspicion towards one person. And try to help the customer, because lack of trust cuts both ways. Offer an unconditional guarantee. "Cash refund if you are not satisfied for any reason at all." No explanations required. Be simple and straightforward; it always sounds the most honest.

We handled retail telephone orders differently. We took VISA and Master Card, and most of the people who called had those cards. But a new business, particularly a home or mail order business, may have a hard time getting to be a credit card merchant. The banks, fearing fraud, are sometimes very selective as to who they will set up as credit card merchants.

For several years, we did not take credit cards and we did bill retail customers when we got telephone orders. A long distance telephone call is a lot more expensive (and a lot less anonymous) than a postage stamp, and therefore much less likely to be used by someone who's trying to rip you off. We told every customer that we would mail the merchandise and a bill, and all they had to do was agree to pay when it arrived. They agreed every time, and they paid *almost* every time. Non-payment was rare. If they didn't pay, we would send a reminder note in the mail and then kiss it off. Not worth the $10 or $12. Of course, if you take large dollar orders, you may want a less risky policy.

No credit policy should be cemented in concrete. Don't ask silly "will you pay" questions of huge and famous corporations that call to place an order. Send a bill with the order if you get a mail order from someone whose title or company suggests that they are likely to pay.

For many types of small businesses, the "credit crooks" are actually rare. And after a few experiences, I tell you, you can usually spot 'em a mile coming. Something about them always tips you off. Maybe it's their stationery; or the "hustle" in their voice; or their seeming lack of knowledge of how your particular type of business usually operates; or (always a "red flag" for us) some stranger talking large quantities and big dollars. In a strange way, it's kind of fun, too, sleuthing, feeling the people out—and what great dinner stories. Someday I'll tell you about the guy on the phone from Philadelphia, Mr. Cream Cheese my wife called him. He was a real *pro*.

Managing Your Business

Volumes have been written on the subject of small business "management." I put the word in quotes because it is such an all-encompassing term. Just about anything you, the owner, do is labeled "management."And just about every study made on small business failures blames over 90% of those failures on "Poor management."

"Poor management" refers to everything from sloppy bookkeeping to lousy business location. If you make or sell clothing, and the fashions suddenly change leaving you with unsalable merchandise, it's labeled "poor management": you should have been aware of the market trends and should have made advance preparations to anticipate them. If you expected your business to show a profit the first year, but you wound up with a loss and not enough reserve cash to keep things going, that's another situation they call "poor management."

Almost every library in the country has at least ten books on the subject of business management. Some of the books are excellent, some are shallow;

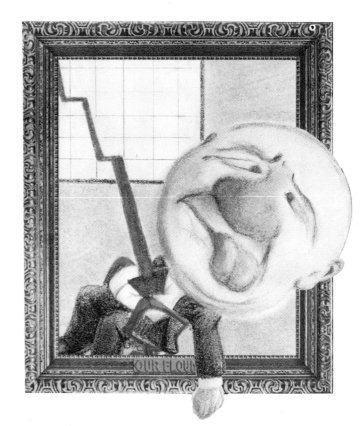

almost all of them go unread. An interesting Small Business Administration study of eighty-one small businesses showed that only one owner in eighty-one read any management literature. Most of those eighty-one businesses failed. There are thousands of defunct businesses, gone belly-up because of the same management errors repeated over and over again. I guess it's just human nature to want to learn from your own mistakes.

Management is an organic part of your business, interwoven into every aspect of business. It isn't like Step One—get a business license, Step Two—manage, Step Three—post the ledgers, etc. Management is something you can learn only by doing, but a few evenings spent with some good management reading certainly won't do you any harm. You will get the most value out of management books if you read them after you've had several months' experience in your new venture. You will understand much better what the books are discussing, and you will quickly spot the subjects most valuable to you.

Also, join the trade organizations for your particular type of business, and subscribe to the trade magazines. Many libraries have reference books listing dozens of trade organizations and journals.

The very best management advice you can get, however, is from other small business people.

Businessmen and women, I find, love to talk about business. Business is a large part of their lives, and they love to share their experiences and their ideas. You can't get better advice at any price. No accountant or lawyer or college professor knows half of what the person who's doing it every day knows. Strike up acquaintances, get to be friends with business people, find out about their local merchants organizations and attend their luncheons. Have a little fun, too.

Lara Stonebraker, Cunningham's Coffee: "It's important to keep your merchandise rotating in the store, to constantly change the position of things. You'd be surprised how many people will say, 'Gee, you've got something new in,' when you know it's been sitting there for two years; you've just moved it from this shelf to that shelf. It has to be displayed in a coherent manner. You can't have pepper grinders next to coffee pots; you have to have all those things that are related together. And you have to give your customers an incredible selection of things. If you have espresso pots, you have to have them in nine sizes because people will not be inclined to buy if there is only a choice of two or three. Even if you stock only one of these odd- sized items that you know will not be selling, you still have to have it just to fill up your shelf, to give the impression that you have a huge variety. People will come to your store because they know you have a large selection. A lot of times I know that it's purely psychological, because I know that I will never sell a twelve-cup pot and I know that I will never sell a one-cup. But I have to have them there just for the comparison, just so that people will feel that this is a store that has everything, that has all the choices they can possibly get, that they don't need to go anywhere else for it. I've seen a lot of coffee stores make this mistake, having only two sizes of something. It just doesn't give you confidence in the store.

"I do rotating displays on the very expensive things every other week. I try to create the kind of display that will make customers stop and look, but not so much that the background will overpower the item. You can't have too many plants, you can't have something that will distract from your merchandise. And you can't have a no-don't-touch atmosphere. You don't want things looking too pretty because then people will be afraid to touch them, they'll feel inhibited. Most important of all, you can't have any bare walls. There was a place in San Francisco that opened and the woman just didn't have enough money to buy another cabinet, so she had one wall, the prime wall for display, just blank. Mr. Peet came in and said, 'Oh, that's a lovely wall; are you selling walls?'"

No one dies wishing they had spent more time with their business.
—Arthur Lipper III, Venture Magazine

I never seen an armored car in a funeral yet.
—from the song, "Life's a One Way Ticklet"
by Cousin Joe

The Small-Time Operator Update Sheet

State and federal tax laws, Social Security rates, Federal Trade Commission regulations, federal requirements for employers, Small Business Administration loan information, and similar government rules change all the time. Most of the laws that do change, particularly tax laws, usually become effective January 1 of the new year.

Every January, I prepare a one-page *Update Sheet* for *Small-Time Operator*. The Update Sheet lists changes in tax laws and other government regulations, referenced to the corresponding pages in the book.

If you would like a copy of the *Update Sheet*, send a self-addressed, stamped No. 10 envelope and $1.00 to Small-Time Operator Update, P.O. Box 640, Laytonville, CA 95454.

With the *Update Sheet*, you can keep your edition of *Small-Time Operator* up to date, year after year.

The Future of Small Business

Even in our shaky economy, with giant corporations getting more and more of the consumer's dollars and with chain stores driving independents out of business, small businesses can and do survive and thrive. Small businesses attentive to local and neighborhood needs and small businesses attentive to customers' personal needs will always have an edge over large, faceless corporations. This is particularly true of service businesses where "the personal touch" is still very important.

Small business owners themselves can help foster this environment by patronizing other small businesses. We can purchase our food from local farmers markets and co-ops instead of huge supermarkets. We can buy locally made clothing and toys and furniture. We can patronize locally owned restaurants instead of national chains.

But we small business people, all of us, have a much greater problem. The future of small business is tied directly to the future of this planet and its inhabitants. Every person starting a business should consider along with profits, percentages and mark-ups, whether his or her actions are going to help or to damage this precious dwindling resource called Earth.

Even very small businesses must live within the framework of the big picture. We are part of an economy that is poisoning the earth, and both the earth and the economy are in obvious trouble. If corporations continue to pollute the earth with toxic chemicals, if logging companies continue to clear-cut forests, if agribusiness continues its chemical and erosion destruction of our farmlands, if the nuclear industry continues its mad fumbling with a technology it obviously does not understand and cannot control, we may not have a future worth talking about. And unless we can stop the lunatics in Washington from building more nuclear bombs, we may not have any future at all.

My hope is that our current ecological/economic upheaval will get just serious enough to force the Powers That Be to change course. And I hope they can make a buck at it, too, because, alas, that's what's driving them all.

"Small-scale operations, no matter how numerous, are always less likely to be harmful to the natural environment than large-scale ones, simply because their individual force is small in relation to the recuperative forces of nature. There is wisdom in smallness if only on account of the smallness and patchiness of human knowledge, which relies on experiment far more than on understanding. The greatest danger invariably arises from the ruthless application, on a vast scale, of partial knowledge such as we are currently witnessing in the application of nuclear energy, of the new chemistry in agriculture, of transportation technology, and countless other things.
"It is, moreover, obvious that men organized in small units will take better care of their bit of land or other natural resources than anonymous companies or megalomaniac governments which pretend to themselves that the whole universe is their legitimate quarry."

—E.F. Schumacher in Small Is Beautiful

When we try to pick out anything by itself, we find it hitched to everything else in the universe.

—John Muir

Section Six

THE LEDGERS

Ledgers

If you were able to examine a hundred different businesses you would probably see a hundred different bookkeeping systems. Every business has its own needs and its own idea how the ledgers should be set up. Some business owners enjoy bookkeeping and like to keep elaborate ledgers. Many owners simply hate the paperwork and keep books to the barest minimum.

I carefully designed these ledgers to be of use to the greatest number of small businesses, particularly new businesses with no bookkeeping experience. There is nothing elaborate about them. They are basic, but complete. You can use these ledgers as is or change them to fit your needs. I encourage you to experiment with your bookkeeping, to alter the ledgers in any way that will make them more useful to you and your particular business.

If you use a computer to help you with bookkeeping, these ledgers are an excellent prototype to use as a model and guide to how your computerized ledgers should look. As I mentioned in the text, I strongly recommend that, when first using a computer, you keep duplicate hand-posted ledgers for at least a month, just to be sure your computer program is error-free and producing correct information.

Your ledgers should be a permanent record. Keep them for as long as you own the business. They will help you prove your figures if you are ever audited. Comparing months and eventually comparing years will help you plan for the future. Lenders, investors and possible future buyers will want to see your old ledgers.

There are enough blank ledger pages to provide most small businesses with a full year's set of income and expenditure ledgers, year-end worksheets and summaries. There is, however, only one payroll ledger page, one partners' capital ledger, one inventory control sheet, and one petty cash ledger. You are welcome to make extra copies for your own personal use, or use the ledgers as prototypes to design your own.

INCOME LEDGER Month of _____

1	2	3	4	5	6	7
DATE	SALES PERIOD	TAXABLE SALES	SALES TAX	NON-TAXABLE SALES		TOTAL SALES
1						
2						
3						
4						
5						
6						
7						
8						
9						
10						
11						
12						
13						
14						
15						
16						
17						
18						
19						
20						
21						
22						
23						
24						
25						
26						
27						
28						
29						
30						
31						
	TOTALS FOR MONTH					

INCOME LEDGER Month of ———————

1	2	3	4	5	6	7
DATE	SALES PERIOD	TAXABLE SALES	SALES TAX	NON-TAXABLE SALES		TOTAL SALES
1						
2						
3						
4						
5						
6						
7						
8						
9						
10						
11						
12						
13						
14						
15						
16						
17						
18						
19						
20						
21						
22						
23						
24						
25						
26						
27						
28						
29						
30						
31						
	TOTALS FOR MONTH					
	2	3	4	5	6	7

INCOME LEDGER Month of _____

1	2	3	4	5	6	7
DATE	SALES PERIOD	TAXABLE SALES	SALES TAX	NON-TAXABLE SALES		TOTAL SALES
1						
2						
3						
4						
5						
6						
7						
8						
9						
10						
11						
12						
13						
14						
15						
16						
17						
18						
19						
20						
21						
22						
23						
24						
25						
26						
27						
28						
29						
30						
31						
	TOTALS FOR MONTH					

INCOME LEDGER Month of _____

1	2	3	4	5	6	7
DATE	SALES PERIOD	TAXABLE SALES	SALES TAX	NON-TAXABLE SALES		TOTAL SALES
1						
2						
3						
4						
5						
6						
7						
8						
9						
10						
11						
12						
13						
14						
15						
16						
17						
18						
19						
20						
21						
22						
23						
24						
25						
26						
27						
28						
29						
30						
31						
	TOTALS FOR MONTH					

INCOME LEDGER Month of _____

1	2	3	4	5	6	7
DATE	SALES PERIOD	TAXABLE SALES	SALES TAX	NON-TAXABLE SALES		TOTAL SALES
1						
2						
3						
4						
5						
6						
7						
8						
9						
10						
11						
12						
13						
14						
15						
16						
17						
18						
19						
20						
21						
22						
23						
24						
25						
26						
27						
28						
29						
30						
31						
	TOTALS FOR MONTH					

INCOME LEDGER Month of _____

1 DATE	2 SALES PERIOD	3 TAXABLE SALES	4 SALES TAX	5 NON-TAXABLE SALES	6	7 TOTAL SALES
1						
2						
3						
4						
5						
6						
7						
8						
9						
10						
11						
12						
13						
14						
15						
16						
17						
18						
19						
20						
21						
22						
23						
24						
25						
26						
27						
28						
29						
30						
31						
	TOTALS FOR MONTH					

INCOME LEDGER Month of _____

1 DATE	2 SALES PERIOD	3 TAXABLE SALES	4 SALES TAX	5 — 6 NON-TAXABLE SALES		7 TOTAL SALES
1						
2						
3						
4						
5						
6						
7						
8						
9						
10						
11						
12						
13						
14						
15						
16						
17						
18						
19						
20						
21						
22						
23						
24						
25						
26						
27						
28						
29						
30						
31						
	TOTALS FOR MONTH					

INCOME LEDGER Month of _____

1	2	3	4	5	6	7
DATE	SALES PERIOD	TAXABLE SALES	SALES TAX	NON-TAXABLE SALES		TOTAL SALES
1						
2						
3						
4						
5						
6						
7						
8						
9						
10						
11						
12						
13						
14						
15						
16						
17						
18						
19						
20						
21						
22						
23						
24						
25						
26						
27						
28						
29						
30						
31						
	TOTALS FOR MONTH					

INCOME LEDGER Month of _____

1	2	3	4	5	6	7
DATE	SALES PERIOD	TAXABLE SALES	SALES TAX	NON-TAXABLE SALES		TOTAL SALES
1						
2						
3						
4						
5						
6						
7						
8						
9						
10						
11						
12						
13						
14						
15						
16						
17						
18						
19						
20						
21						
22						
23						
24						
25						
26						
27						
28						
29						
30						
31						
	TOTALS FOR MONTH					

INCOME LEDGER Month of ———————

1	2	3	4	5	6	7
DATE	SALES PERIOD	TAXABLE SALES	SALES TAX	NON-TAXABLE SALES		TOTAL SALES
1						
2						
3						
4						
5						
6						
7						
8						
9						
10						
11						
12						
13						
14						
15						
16						
17						
18						
19						
20						
21						
22						
23						
24						
25						
26						
27						
28						
29						
30						
31						
	TOTALS FOR MONTH					

INCOME LEDGER Month of _____

1	2	3	4	5	6	7
DATE	SALES PERIOD	TAXABLE SALES	SALES TAX	NON-TAXABLE SALES		TOTAL SALES
1						
2						
3						
4						
5						
6						
7						
8						
9						
10						
11						
12						
13						
14						
15						
16						
17						
18						
19						
20						
21						
22						
23						
24						
25						
26						
27						
28						
29						
30						
31						
	TOTALS FOR MONTH					

INCOLE LEDGER Month of _____

1	2	3	4	5	6	7
DATE	SALES PERIOD	TAXABLE SALES	SALES TAX	NON-TAXABLE SALES		TOTAL SALES
1						
2						
3						
4						
5						
6						
7						
8						
9						
10						
11						
12						
13						
14						
15						
16						
17						
18						
19						
20						
21						
22						
23						
24						
25						
26						
27						
28						
29						
30						
31						
	TOTALS FOR MONTH					

INCOME LEDGER — Year-End Summary

1	2	3	4	5	6	7
	TOTALS FOR MONTH OF	TAXABLE SALES	SALES TAX	NON-TAXABLE SALES		TOTAL SALES
	January					
	February					
	March					
	April					
	May					
	June					
	July					
	August					
	September					
	October					
	November					
	December					
	TOTAL FOR YEAR					

EXPENDITURE LEDGER

DATE	CHECK NO.	PAYEE	TOTAL	1 INVEN-TORY	2 SUPPLIES, POSTAGE, ETC.	3 LABOR NON-EMPL.

4	5	6	7	8	9	10	11
EMPLOYEE PAYROLL	ADVERTISING	RENT	UTILITIES	TAXES & LICENSES		MISC.	NON-DEDUCT.

EXPENDITURE LEDGER

DATE	CHECK NO.	PAYEE	TOTAL	1 INVEN-TORY	2 SUPPLIES, POSTAGE, ETC.	3 LABOR NON-EMPL.

4	5	6	7	8	9	10	11
EMPLOYEE PAYROLL	ADVERTISING	RENT	UTILITIES	TAXES & LICENSES		MISC.	NON-DEDUCT.

EXPENDITURE LEDGER

DATE	CHECK NO.	PAYEE	TOTAL	1 INVEN-TORY	2 SUPPLIES, POSTAGE, ETC.	3 LABOR NON-EMPL.

4	5	6	7	8	9	10	11
EMPLOYEE PAYROLL	ADVERTISING	RENT	UTILITIES	TAXES & LICENSES		MISC.	NON-DEDUCT.

EXPENDITURE LEDGER

DATE	CHECK NO.	PAYEE	TOTAL	1 INVEN-TORY	2 SUPPLIES, POSTAGE, ETC.	3 LABOR NON-EMPL.

4	5	6	7	8	9	10	11
EMPLOYEE PAYROLL	ADVERTISING	RENT	UTILITIES	TAXES & LICENSES		MISC.	NON-DEDUCT.

EXPENDITURE LEDGER

DATE	CHECK NO.	PAYEE	TOTAL	1 INVEN-TORY	2 SUPPLIES, POSTAGE, ETC.	3 LABOR NON-EMPL.

4	5	6	7	8	9	10	11
EMPLOYEE PAYROLL	ADVERTISING	RENT	UTILITIES	TAXES & LICENSES		MISC.	NON-DEDUCT.

EXPENDITURE LEDGER

DATE	CHECK NO.	PAYEE	TOTAL	1 INVEN-TORY	2 SUPPLIES, POSTAGE, ETC.	3 LABOR NON-EMPL.

4	5	6	7	8	9	10	11
EMPLOYEE PAYROLL	ADVERTISING	RENT	UTILITIES	TAXES & LICENSES		MISC.	NON-DEDUCT.

EXPENDITURE LEDGER

DATE	CHECK NO.	PAYEE	TOTAL	1 INVEN-TORY	2 SUPPLIES, POSTAGE, ETC.	3 LABOR NON-EMPL.

4	5	6	7	8	9	10	11
EMPLOYEE PAYROLL	ADVERTISING	RENT	UTILITIES	TAXES & LICENSES		MISC.	NON-DEDUCT.

EXPENDITURE LEDGER

DATE	CHECK NO.	PAYEE	TOTAL	1 INVEN-TORY	2 SUPPLIES, POSTAGE, ETC.	3 LABOR NON-EMPL.

4	5	6	7	8	9	10	11
EMPLOYEE PAYROLL	ADVERTISING	RENT	UTILITIES	TAXES & LICENSES		MISC.	NON-DEDUCT.

EXPENDITURE LEDGER

DATE	CHECK NO.	PAYEE	TOTAL	1 INVEN-TORY	2 SUPPLIES, POSTAGE, ETC.	3 LABOR NON-EMPL.

4	5	6	7	8	9	10	11
EMPLOYEE PAYROLL	ADVERTISING	RENT	UTILITIES	TAXES & LICENSES		MISC.	NON-DEDUCT.

EXPENDITURE LEDGER

DATE	CHECK NO.	PAYEE	TOTAL	1 INVEN- TORY	2 SUPPLIES, POSTAGE, ETC.	3 LABOR NON-EMPL.

4	5	6	7	8	9	10	11
EMPLOYEE PAYROLL	ADVERTISING	RENT	UTILITIES	TAXES & LICENSES		MISC.	NON-DEDUCT.

EXPENDITURE LEDGER

DATE	CHECK NO.	PAYEE	TOTAL	1 INVEN-TORY	2 SUPPLIES, POSTAGE, ETC.	3 LABOR NON-EMPL.

4	5	6	7	8	9	10	11
EMPLOYEE PAYROLL	ADVERTISING	RENT	UTILITIES	TAXES & LICENSES		MISC.	NON-DEDUCT.

EXPENDITURE LEDGER

DATE	CHECK NO.	PAYEE	TOTAL	1 INVEN-TORY	2 SUPPLIES, POSTAGE, ETC.	3 LABOR NON-EMPL.

4	5	6	7	8	9	10	11
EMPLOYEE PAYROLL	ADVERTISING	RENT	UTILITIES	TAXES & LICENSES		MISC.	NON-DEDUCT.

YEAR-END EXPENDITURE SUMMARY

			TOTAL	1 INVENTORY	2 SUPPLIES, POSTAGE, ETC.	3 LABOR NON-EMPL.
		January total				
		February total				
		March total				
		April total				
		May total				
		June total				
		July total				
		August total				
		September total				
		October total				
		November total				
		December total				
		Unpaid bills (Acct's. Payable):				
		TOTALS FOR YEAR				
		ADDITIONAL EXPENSES:				
		Return Checks (from your "Bad Debts" folder)				
		Uncollectible Accounts (from your "Bad Debts" folder)				
		Auto expense (if you take the standard mileage rate) Mileage for year ———				
		Depreciation (from Depreciation Worksheet—Col 11, 13, 15 or 17)				

4	5	6	7	8	9	10	11
EMPLOYEE PAYROLL	ADVERTISING	RENT	UTILITIES	TAXES & LICENSES		MISC.	NON-DEDUCT.

EQUIPMENT LEDGER AND DEPRECIATION WORKSHEETS

1	2	3	4	5	6	7	8	9
DATE	DESCRIPTION	METH.	WRITE OFF PERIOD	NEW OR USED	%	COST	REDUCTION FOR INV. CREDIT	WRITE OFF

10	11	12	13	14	15	16	17	18
BAL. TO BE DEPR.	DEPR. 19__	BAL. TO BE DEPR.	DEPR. 19___	BAL. TO BE DEPR.	DEPR. 19__	BAL. TO BE DEPR.	DEPR. 19__	BAL. TO BE DEPR.

PAYROLL LEDGER

Name _____

Address _____

Social Security _____

Pay Rate _____

1	2	3	4	5	6	7	8	9	10	11	12	13
			HOURS									
PAYCHECK DATE	CHECK NO.	PAY PERIOD	REG	O/T	GROSS	F.I.T.	SOCIAL SECURITY	MEDI-CARE	STATE INCOME	OTHER WITHHOLDING		NET PAY

PAYROLL LEDGER

Name _____

Address _____

Social Security _____

Pay Rate _____

1	2	3	4	5	6	7	8	9	10	11	12	13
			HOURS									
PAYCHECK DATE	CHECK NO.	PAY PERIOD	REG	O/T	GROSS	F.I.T.	SOCIAL SECURITY	MEDI-CARE	STATE INCOME	OTHER WITHHOLDING		NET PAY

PARTNERS CAPITAL LEDGER

1	2	3	4	5	6	7
DATE	DESCRIPTION	ACTIVITY	BALANCE	ACTIVITY	BALANCE	TOTAL BALANCE

PETTY CASH LEDGER

Period _____   Page _____ of _____

DATE	DESCRIPTION	AMT.	BAL.
	Beginning Balance		
	TOTAL		

Check Number _____   Posted to Ledger _____

INVENTORY RECORD

Item _____   Supplier _____

DATE ORDERED	QUANTITY ORDERED	DATE REC'D.	QUANTITY REC'D.	QUANTITY SOLD	BALANCE ON-HAND

CREDIT LEDGER

1	2	3	4	5	6
SALE DATE	CUSTOMER	INV. NO.	TOTAL SALE AMOUNT	DATE PAID	MEMO

INDEX

QUALITY SMALL BUSINESS BOOKS
from BELL SPRINGS PUBLISHING

Software
for the Small-Time Operator
Ready-to-run disk & instruction manual

by Bernard Kamoroff and Steve Steinke.

Painless Computer Power—complete and ready to run. A complete bookkeeping system, the exact same system that has won so much praise in *Small Time Operator*, has been set up for you on a ready-to-run disk. Easy to understand, simple to use. No programming, set-up or experimentation required. Just enter your numbers—it's that simple.

This is not a program. This is a complete, tested, error-free set of ledgers on computer disk. The disk contains 23 different ledgers, schedules, forms, worksheets, and files, including: income ledger, expenditure ledger, profit & loss statement, balance sheet, payroll, cash flow, net worth, petty cash, partners' capital ledger, credit ledger, inventory control, loan amortization schedule, invoice form, business plan, mail-order mailing list, and a telephone/address file.

Unlike most accounting programs, this system also gives you the flexibility to alter the ledgers, worksheets and schedules—to change the design around, and around again, until you have exactly what *you* want.

Included with the disk is a detailed 160-page instruction manual. It explains how to use the ledgers and how they may be expanded. The manual includes illustrations of all the applications and step-by-step descriptions of all the formulas used to create the disk. Should you ever wish to alter or experiment with the bookkeeping, the formulas will be invaluable to you.

To use this system *as is*, no programming or alterations required, **YOU MUST HAVE**: an IBM-PC computer, or a computer compatible with IBM-PC, or a Macintosh computer.

YOU MUST ALSO HAVE a Lotus 1-2-3 or Microsoft Excel Spreadsheet Program, or a different spreadsheet program that can read Lotus 1-2-3 or Excel instructions. (Our system is adaptable to spreadsheet programs other than Lotus 1-2-3 and Excel, but may require some alterations or experimentation).

Bell Springs Publishing backs this **Software** system, and guarantees it 100%. If you need help getting it to run or if you have any questions, call our customer service number, (707) 984-6746, and we will put you in contact with our computer experts, no charge. If you don't like the system for any reason, or if it will not operate on your particular spreadsheet program, you may return it for a full refund.

This **Software** system is designed to be used with *Small-Time Operator*, but it is a complete package by itself. It can be used in conjunction with other business books, school programs, or alone. It does not duplicate any information from *Small-Time Operator*.

When ordering, please specify what disk you need: IBM 5¼", IBM 3½", or Mac 3½". $29.95

We Own It:
Starting & Managing Cooperatives and Employee-Owned Businesses

by Bernard Kamoroff and Peter Honigsberg.

This clearly written book gives you the legal, tax and management information you need to start and successfully operate all types of consumer, producer and worker co-ops. It covers non-profit, for-profit and cooperative corporations, ESOP's, partnerships and all other forms of employee-owned businesses.

Includes detailed chapters on the different types of cooperatives and how each is structured. How co-ops can be legally organized—corporations, partnerships, associations, joint ventures, trusts, etc. How to incorporate. Financing. Insurance. Permits & licenses. Bookkeeping. Personnel—employees, volunteers, members, owners. Income taxes. State laws. And much more.

WE OWN IT is recommended by the National Consumer Coop Bank, Industrial Cooperative Association, NASCO, Co-op America, New Ways To Work Foundation, and many national and regional cooperatives.

"It's uncommon to find a how-to book written and published carefully and caringly about an area everyone involved knows well. *WE OWN IT* is such an exceptional book...Sure to become the bible of everyone interested in shared ownership."—*San Francisco Chronicle & Examiner*

160 pages, 8½"x11" $14.00

Marketing Without Advertising

Michael Phillips and Salli Rasberry

Thousands of small business open every year. Most of them struggle, many fail. How do you make your business one of the exceptions that prospers? The conventional answer is to advertise, and if that doesn't do the trick, advertise some more.

"Just plain wrong", according to *Marketing Without Advertising,* the most thought-provoking book we've ever seen on the confusing and often frustrating subject of advertising. The first chapters of this startling book argue convincingly, and with documented proof, that almost all advertising is totally ineffective and an utter waste of money; and that most business owners, including top executives of large corporations, have been successfully duped into believing advertising is both necessary and productive in spite of obvious evidence to the contrary.

Marketing Without Advertising is much more than an argument against advertising. Packed into this large book are more than a hundred tried-and-tested marketing secrets that have worked for all kinds of small businesses. You can successfully promote your business without spending money on advertising.

8½"x11", 200 pages $14.00

Free Help From Uncle Sam to Start Your Own Business

(Or Expand the One You Have)

William Alarid & Gustav Berle.

This little book is loaded with names, addresses, telephone numbers, and brief descriptions of over 100 government programs and agencies that purchase from small businesses and that offer services, publications, and financial assistance to small businesses. Includes government loan programs, grants and financial incentives; import and export assistance; census information and statistics; special programs for women, minorities and handicapped people; and a large variety of free small business information and counseling. The book also lists government agencies that purchase from small businesses and explains how to sell your goods and services to these agencies. Once you have this valuable book, for $1 a year, the author will send you his annual Update. So this book will be useful to you for years to come.

Now in its sixth printing, FREE HELP was selected as the "Best of the Best" by the Public Library Association. 200 pages, 5½" x8 ½" $13.95

Getting Into The Mail-Order Business

Julian L. Simon.

For years we recommended one and only one mail-order book, the best we've ever seen: Julian Simon's famous How to Start and Operate a Mail-Order Business, a $46 textbook published by McGraw Hill. At last, the most important information in this book—everything the beginner needs to know to be successful in mail-order—is now available as a trade paperback.

Getting Into The Mail-Order Business is especially valuable to newcomers, whether they are starting from scratch or looking to mail-order as a way to expand a well established business. This is an honest book, loaded with practical, valuable information on every page.

Learn about the kinds of products that naturally sell well in mail-order, and those that don't. How to locate and test your market. The least expensive and most effective ways to promote your products. How to enter the fast-growing field of catalogs. Ways not to compete with the large mail-order houses. How to create mail-order copy that will sell your products. How the current mail-order laws affect the business. And much more. "The wisest investment a mail-order hopeful could make."

291 pages, 6"x9" $14.95

How to Write a Business Plan

Mike McKeever

Unlike most books about business plans, this valuable manual has two different functions. It is actually two books in one. First, it explains business plans in detail, how to create them, how to change and adapt them to changing situations, how to make the best use of a plan to put your new or growing business on a successful course.

This book is also a guide to help you get bank loans. It contains detailed forms and instructions to help you prepare a well-organized professional loan package, and shows you how to use the loan package and business plan to convince potential lenders and investors that your business idea is sound.

Includes: cash flow and profit-and-loss forecasts; break-even analysis; debt vs. equity investments; main sources and secondary sources of financing; complete loan application instructions; developing marketing and personnel plans; risk analysis; and a wealth of other information and advice. 200 pages. 8½"x 11" $17.95

Negotiating the Purchase or Sale of a Business

James C. Comiskey.

This thorough book will help a prospective buyer determine if a business is worth buying, how much to expect to pay for the business, and—equally important—are buyer and business well matched? This book will help the seller determine a fair asking price, how to prepare for the sale, how to deal with prospective buyers.

The guidelines and worksheets in the book will enable you to determine the value of the business inventory and assets; how profitable the business presently is; prospects for the future; how good are the location and the lease; how tough is the competition; how easy or hard will it be for a new owner to take over; and a host of other very important, and too often overlooked considerations. You will learn about the terms "goodwill" and "blue sky," and the legal and tax aspects of a business sale.

More than any other buy-sell transaction, the price of a going business is tremendously negotiable. This book will assist both buyer and seller in this critical, and delicate, negotiation process. The final agreement, sales contract, and common financing arrangements are all covered. 137 pages, 40 worksheets, 8½"x11" $18.95

The Partnership Book

Dennis Clifford and Ralph Warner.

A thorough, comprehensive guide to small business partnerships. It covers *everything* there is to know about: Start-up requirements, accounting, taxation, budgeting, insurance, and the rights, responsibilities and legal obligations of partners. General and limited partnerships, joint ventures, real estate partnerships, and quasi-professional partnerships are all included.

Partnership agreements are explained in great detail, including a number of sample agreements you can actually use for your own business. The agreements include: purpose, goals and terms of the partnership; common rules and clauses found in most agreements; cash, property and skills to be contributed; salaries, withdrawals and distribution of profits; how to handle losses; valuation of partnership assets; management and financial responsibilities (which partner is responsible for which decisions?); admission of new partners; departure or death of a partner; handling disputes; terminating the business. Well organized, easy to read, and up to date. 220 pages, 8½"x 11" $18.95

Import/Export:
How to Get Started in International Trade

Dr. Carl A. Nelson

Anyone interested in importing or exporting must learn about an entire new world of U.S. and foreign government regulations and the ins and outs of international trade. Here is a book that covers it all: duties, tariffs, and getting through the customs maze; export licenses and Shippers Export Declarations; import quotas; special tax incentives; and all the government regulations, permits and licenses required of U.S. firms that want to import or export goods anywhere in the world. The book shows you how to get started in international trade, how to make contacts overseas, how to negotiate and close deals, how to prepare international contracts, how to make overseas payments, and how to make sure you'll get paid by overseas buyers. You will learn about the international business world—the export/import brokers, freight forwarders, international insurers, overseas bank services, buying agents and other international services—when you need and don't need these people, how to find and deal with them.

The book includes sample forms and licenses, names and addresses of government, customs and overseas agencies, and a mini-dictionary of all the unfamiliar international business terms you'll need to know just to be able to talk with and understand the people you'll be doing business with.

There aren't too many books that warrant the description "essential." But if you want to make a success at importing or exporting, this book is, unquestionably, essential. 200 pages, 6" x 9" $14.95

The Small-Time Operator Update Sheet

Bernard Kamoroff.

You can keep your copy of *Small-Time Operator* up to date, year after year. The *Update Sheet*, published every January, lists changes to federal and state tax laws, IRS rulings, social security and Medicare tax rates, self-employment taxes, federal requirements for employers, FTC rules, SBA loan information, excise taxes, and other government regulations—referenced to the corresponding pages in *Small Time Operator*.

For a copy of the *Update Sheet*, please send $1 and a self- addressed, stamped envelope (#10, business size), to: **Small Time Operator Update**, P.O. Box 640, Laytonville CA 95454.

SUPPORT YOUR LOCAL BOOKSTORE. Small-Time Operator is available in many bookstores across the country. If you are unable to locate it, or any of our other titles, please order directly from us. Our mail-order department will be happy to fill your order promptly.

OUR GUARANTEE: All Bell Springs books are fully guaranteed. If you are not satisfied for any reason, return the books within 30 days for a full cash refund, no questions asked.

TELEPHONE ORDERS

In a hurry? We accept Mastercard, VISA, and American Express. We are open 9am-5pm Pacific time, Monday-Friday.

(707) 984-6746

BELL SPRINGS PUBLISHING   43
Mail Order Sales Dept.
Box 640 Bell Springs Road
Laytonville, California 95454

Please send me:

_____ copies **SMALL TIME OPERATOR**	$14.95	_____
_____ copies **SOFTWARE**	$29.95	_____
Specify disk: MAC ☐ IBM 5¼″ ☐ IBM 3½″ ☐		
_____ copies **THE PARTNERSHIP BOOK**	$18.95	_____
_____ copies **WE OWN IT**	$14.00	_____
_____ copies **MARKETING WITHOUT ADVERTISING**	$14.00	_____
_____ copies **GETTING INTO MAIL ORDER**	$14.95	_____
_____ copies **NEGOTIATING PURCHASE OR SALE**	$18.95	_____
_____ copies **WRITE A BUSINESS PLAN**	$17.95	_____
_____ copies **FREE HELP FROM UNCLE SAM**	$13.95	_____
_____ copies **IMPORT/EXPORT**	$14.95	_____
Book Total	$	_____
Calif. residents please add sales tax		_____
Shipping		**2.00**
Enclosed is my check or money order for .... $		_____

NAME _____

ADDRESS _____

CITY _____ STATE _____ ZIP _____

Credit Card Orders: MasterCard _____   VISA _____   American Express _____

Card Number _____ Exp. date _____

Signature _____